THE KISS OF THE WHIP

Explorations in SM

Jim Prezwalski

Leyland Publications
San Francisco

1st edition 1995

ISBN 0-943595-51-7
Library of Congress Catalog Card # 94-76971

Leyland Publications
P.O. Box 410690
San Francisco, CA 94141

Complete catalogue of available books: $1 ppd.

Contents

Jim Prezwalski, an American gay rights activist for the past fifteen years, has been involved with education for several SM organizations. He is a past board member of The Gay and Lesbian Press Association and former producer of *The Lambda Report*, a statewide cable program for the Michigan Organization for Human Rights (MOHR). He has used his background in medical education to produce a number of videos on AIDS health issues. He currently resides in London, England, but views Chicago as his North American home.

Jeffery Beam (b. 1953) is the author of several books of poetry, among them *The Golden Legend* (Floating Island 1981), *Midwinter Fires* (French Broad 1990), and *The Fountain* (North Carolina Wesleyan College Press 1992). He has been widely published in magazines and anthologies, including *Gay Roots* Vol. 1 (Gay Sunshine Press 1991). He lives in rural North Carolina. He wrote the poems, excerpts from which appear at the head of most of the chapters in this book.

Preface

If you need hormonal stimulation, put this book down. This is not one-handed reading material. It is an attempt to provide a cohesive framework of thought for the SMer, concentrating more on the 'why' of SM instead of the 'how-to.' It's not meant to be a cookbook of techniques for novices, since nothing can substitute for first-hand learning from an experienced SM practitioner. This book is the outgrowth of my educational activities on behalf of several SM and fisting groups and so it aims to acquaint the beginner with the fore-thought and planning that good SM requires. For the more experienced, it attempts to map certain topics not often surveyed by SM writing.

The book is divided into two parts. The larger first deals with practical matters, the smaller second with more philosophic concerns. Scattered throughout the text are extended commentaries by SMers which expand or illustrate points within the text. Rather than using quotation marks extensively, I have eliminated them as much as possible.

SM embraces a wide range of people of different abilities and intellects. Read what you can and get out of this book what you are able. I have written hoping that this will promote intelligent discussion of SM. There's just too much hype and hysteria in current discussions.

Although the pressures to be PC are immense, I write as a gay male and therefore my choice of personal pronoun is masculine case. English lacks a flexible neutral pronoun. Readers remain free to substitute their own gender-preferred pronouns.

Immeasurable thanks to those SM men and women in the US and Europe who shared their stories and bits of wisdom. Sadly, the book took longer to prepare than some had left to live. Lastly a special thanks to the unsung heroes of our liberties, the librarians who daily battle the would-be censors of information. Their defense of freedom of information allowed me to research much of this book while living in Jesse Helms' bible-belt backyard.

—JIM PREZWALSKI

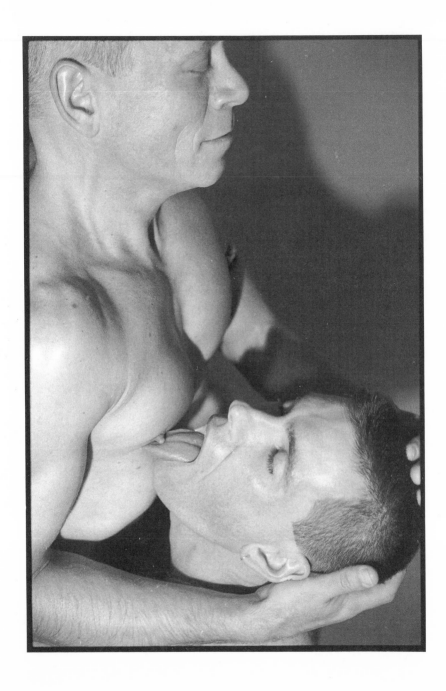

PART I

Chapter 1:
SM in the Late Second Millennium

There is a love that madmen know
howling in the night
like trees putting on new leaves
I will find it
from "The Well at the World's End"
—Jeffery Beam

WHAT IS SM?

Steve cleared his throat and announced the start of the discussion group. People grabbed chairs and arranged themselves around the kitchen table. Among those attending were men as well as women, several new to SM, some "just curious" and three experienced SMers.

"Well, shall we begin? As announced, the topic tonight is 'What is SM?' I'd like to start by going around the room and have each of you answer that question from your own understanding."

Uniformly, everyone shifted uncomfortably in the chair as each tried to define SM precisely. Explanations included: the eroticizing of a normally non-sexual object, the commission of specific practices and behaviors, power games of dominance and submission, sensuality and mutuality in a contract between two or more people. But what, someone asked, of the auto-erotic act of self-inflicted pain such as piercing your own penis while masturbating? One person said SM helped him transcend reality. Another disagreed saying that SM put him into excruciating contact with reality. Yet another claimed that SM permitted her to balance out her emotional pain with physical pain.

Matt, an experienced participant, refused to give a universal definition.

"I can only say what SM is for me and even then, I can only identify it when it happens. A lot of it depends on my perceptions and state of mind and those of my partner. An activity that's a heavy scene with one person becomes a piece of fluff if I attempt it with a different person. I try to put myself in situations that I hope will lead to SM, but I can't guarantee it will. I wish I could."

Todd nodded in agreement. Once, he had thought he knew what SM was, but the more he read, played and spoke with people, the more he

9

became convinced that SM didn't have a concise definition. Things have an exact meaning but SM isn't a thing. SM is simultaneously action and a state of being. Individuals create their own action based on their desires to reach certain needed emotional and physiological states. Power exchanges, role playing and reversals, pain and pleasure, tension and release are just some of the ways of achieving a wanted outcome. What makes it SM is their linkage to sex. Flagellation in religion is penance; the same in sex becomes sadomasochism. By the end of the evening's discussion, those who came looking for deft answers, left confused.

Books that speak of SM in a favorable light inevitably begin with the statement that it is misunderstood by people unfamiliar with it. I agree, but I would also include many people who practice SM. I've encountered some who validate nonsense as traditions, others who assert that only a certain knot is correct for rope bondage, still others who base their SM on the centerfold of the month and sundry others who adopt SM porn as revealed gospel. Well then, what is SM? Most proficient practitioners will admit difficulty in precisely defining it. Is it a practice, a philosophy, a balance of pain and pleasure, the erotic use of pain? Is ecstatic pleasure SM? Is a best selling book of SM photos by a pop star sadomasochism or just sales and marketing? If it's any comfort, the best minds in the history of psychoanalysis, Freud included, have floundered when they tried to clarify what sadomasochism is. And psychiatrists are the ones who coined the terms.

I believe that an indirect approach is needed if you're attempting to define SM. To most of us, the idea that something can be accurately described by not confronting it head-on seems a strange, rather curious thought, yet indirect observations often yield more information than do direct ones. The human eye provides a neat example. If you stare straight at a cluster of stars on a clear night, you'll see only the brightest points of light. If your vision is keen enough, you might be aware of other vague, dim and indistinct shapes. Squint as you might, they remain blurry smears. However, if you stare off to the side and observe them, not with your direct gaze but with your peripheral vision, a number of those fuzzy blurs will resolve themselves into distinct stars too faint for your acute vision to resolve. In much the same manner, SM has defied the direct approaches of those who have tried to classify it.

Despite recent commercialization and the slams of the fundamentalist right, SM retains its power to fascinate and influence. As a philosophy, it has shaped modern Western thought more than many realize or care to admit—even if only in the negative. After all, the most sanctimonious bible thumpers still must describe sinful practices to their followers in order to instill a proper loathing. Whenever they talk of "sins too grievous to be mentioned," they're obligated to list them in order to condemn them fully. Televangelists denounce SM yet titillate their viewers with shots of dykes on bikes, boys in dog collars and both sexes with pierced body parts. To condemn SM, they must inevitably publicize it. Among their adherents are those in whom the denouncements of SM instead cultivate its growth. Ironically, the commercialization of SM/leather, which generates significant friendly publicity, may harm SM more by reducing it to a marketable package and sales tool. [See chapter 13, *Threats to SM.*]

SM CULTURE

Black leather wasn't always the defining fetish for SM. Military uniforms and police regalia have long induced excitement with their connection to discipline and domination. Rubber and lycra have recently emerged as acceptable SM wear based on their sensuality. Although the precise fetish dress has changed over time, it seems to oscillate between authority and outlaw. The popular fetish scenes from the past have included Bedouins in flowing robes overpowering British officers, Czarinas in furs whipping their servants, cattle rustlers branding the sheriff, abbesses flagellating postulants and schoolmasters caning students. Riding paraphernalia—English with its riding crops and brown riding boots or Western with its chaps, spurs and ropes—sets up a great contrast of power and powerlessness with the implied relationship of human and animal. SM fetish dress is only a visual expression of power exchange, an addition rather than prerequisite to SM activity. A number of capable SMers don't bother with costumes. For the majority who do, the more popular attires are still the authority uniforms of the police and military ranged against the anti-authority black leathers of the motorcycle clubs.

TWO VIEWS OF SECOND SKIN
Sam, Detroit, Michigan:
Leather is not essential for SM but I do find that it's a real aphrodisiac. My leathers join me to everything that I consider the height of masculinity. Uniforms, although they are very butch, just don't convey that. They depend on the existence of an outside, often hostile authority and, face it, people in uniforms are taught not to think. Leather, on the other hand, requires that the wearer think and act independently. Its animal origins link it to a bestial independence and brute strength. When I put them on, I'm clothing myself in the macho essence of the outlaw as well as the hero and I have to choose between those two opposites. It's a way of saying here is a very masculine tough guy, someone with the courage to do what he wants without worrying about the consequences or what others think about him.

"That's one of the reasons that leather has become so popular. So many people, who are afraid to even jaywalk, try and tap into this by slapping on a piece of black cowhide. Leather used to indicate SM inclinations. That's no longer the case although you still have a better than average chance of getting that intense, rough masculine sex from a leather clad man than a pinstriped businessman.

▼

Kate, Chicago, Illinois:
Leather is sensual. It's my second skin and that means several things. The tanned hide of an animal hugs and moves and breathes with my body so that I feel I take on aspects of its primeval power. I own thick leathers for protection when I ride my motorcycle. In a way, they shield me against injury like the stiff leather armor that the Amazons wore into battle. I see leather allowing me to tap into that whole mythology of aggressive and independent femininity.

It has certain powerful associations for me. Dressed up and on the road, I feel very much in control and self-assured—important things for my self-respect. I feel very pagan when I'm dressed in animal skins as if they're binding me to primitive nature even though I've a machine roaring under me. I'm not trying to act like a man or be macho, though I know as a woman, whenever I wear leathers and ride, I'm genderfucking a powerful male image. Most people, especially straight families in their cars, respond by blankly staring but if I smile and wave, they usually break into big smiles like they've been told it's OK to share in some joke. My biggest problem comes from younger men who cannot stand to see a woman commandeer their macho image. It seems to be a real deep personal threat to them, as though I was trying to de-ball them. For that reason—for safety—I try not to ride alone.

I've been in the company of leathermen at some gatherings but I've found the hypocrisy of useless PC euphemisms too much. They feel obligated to speak as though they accept leatherwomen as equals, but I find their actions at times make it clear that they resent us "aping" them. I find it strange that men react so strongly. I mean, have you ever seen a group of women attack a drag queen for stealing their femininity? I happen to like wearing my leathers when I have sex, but it has nothing to do with masculinity or femininity. If it really did, then how can those boys feel a primitive masculinity coming from cowhide—a *female* animal's skin? Leather is just a sensual fetish and it happens to be one of mine.

▼

The current black motorcycle leather incarnation appeared in the late forties and early fifties as part of the drop-out culture of WW II vets and the beat generation. They simply withdrew from society rather than trying to change or cope. These were not protesters uniting to fight in-

12

justice, nor were they emotionally dead psychopaths concerned only with themselves. Instead, they were loners and misfits who couldn't adjust to the stifling conformity of the times. Newspaper accounts of the era referred to them as children of futility. They chucked the polite social games of courtesy, replacing them with blunt honesty and no tolerance for bullshit. United by a shared sense of rejection, they fashioned a strong sense of group loyalty, especially when confronted by a hostile world. A simple code of an eye for an eye existed. If you crossed one of them, vengeance tended to be rather unsportsmanlike. In 1947, a group ran amok in the town of Hollister, CA. Politicians and papers sensationalized it enough for Hollywood to glamorize it several years later. Its version, *The Wild One*, starred a very young Marlon Brando in black leather astride a motorcycle. The movie fixed the image in the public mind.

1954 saw the founding of the first gay motorcycle club, the Satyrs, with others soon following. SM was not a major focus of these clubs but their prevailing tolerance abetted its practice. For a generation stifled by McCarthyism, these were the few portents of a storm to come.

The sixties saw a movement of deliberate dropouts who looked for a form of protest against the gagging conformity. Excluded, down and out, they joined together to defy a world that had tossed them aside. They discovered strength in unity, power in the image and, most importantly, a feeling of family and purpose. Outrageous acts and contempt for authority connected them with the outlaw tradition of the old west, especially in California. Hell's Angels actively cultivated their image, declaring to the press their intent to be repugnant social outcasts and the ultimate outsiders against society. The popular press served-up sensational stories of towns terrorized by motorcycle gangs. The roar of a Harley unnerved many a motorist on the highway. The protective black leather and the worn, ragged Levis of the disenfranchised had become a symbol of power. Hunter S. Thompson's *Hell's Angels* is the best book on the reality versus the popular image. Interestingly, Hell's Angels complained about the numerous people, in particular the gays, who copied their image but who didn't understand what it was all about.

The open culture of the motorcycle clubs proved a haven for gays who looked for tolerance and acceptance. Excluded from society and forced into a position of alienation, they too saw social attitudes as their enemy and became more inclined to oppose them in the open guise of an outlaw. Rebelling against the effeminate stereotype, they adopted the motorcycle gang's look, attitude and, above all, its mystique. Phil Andros' *$tud*, published 1966, contains a barely fictionalized glimpse of this nascent SM/leather culture. The denim look, black leathers, motorcycles, boots, T-shirts, chains, tattoos, colors, runs, open sexuality and club loyalty began with the outsiders and outlaws.

When the police raided Stonewall, one of the drag queens who had been handcuffed ran to a leather bar where he knew keys could be had. Leather and lace took on the authorities and gay life took a new turn. The seventies saw radical leather sex really take off. SM play had been mostly a clandestine and very private scene. Chicago Hellfire Club's founding in 1971, with its Inferno gathering of SMers, marked a major departure. The opportunity for men from different regions to convene in one place meant that SM experiences, techniques and styles could be spread firsthand on a scale previously unknown. The gay urban culture of NYC, California and Chicago enthralled a generation with their proliferating leather bars and sex clubs like the Mine Shaft. Publications like *Drummer*, *Mach*, *Sandmutopia Guardian* and *Dungeon Master* allowed the vicarious experience of SM outside of urban areas.

But some nagging questions arose and still remained largely unanswered. Was leather validation or invalidation? Action or mere reaction? Were the ones responsible for the culture those whose intolerance created the ghettos or those who were forced to live there? John Preston *(Mr. Benson)* and John Rechy *(The Sexual Outlaw* and *Rushes)* took opposite views. Preston affirmed (some say defined) gay SM/leather identity while a surly Rechy grated raw nerves. Leather culture revisionists prefer to leave Rechy and his depressingly unorthodox views off the recommended SM reading lists. Historical truth rarely 'affirms' a particular outlook. My advice would be to read *$tud* by Phil Andros and *City of Night* by John Rechy, both of which were published in the early sixties. Make up your own mind.

The arrival of AIDS in the early eighties devastated the ranks of gay SMers. On the margins, they pushed further, played harder, died sooner. We know now that certain activities that involve penetration can spread AIDS. No one knew it then. Everything became suspected of being a vector of death. For a while, men feared to kiss even with lips closed. The sardonic irony is that, with simple precautions, SM is safe sex since much of SM play is non-penetrative.

This post-AIDS world of the approaching millennium is proving peculiar. The banding together of a few outcasts has, in forty years time, led to international SM organizations seeking social acceptance and political power. Yet simultaneously, police, under the guise of AIDS prevention, are again raiding leather bars and private parties both in the US and Europe. Visibility and intimidation are often lock-stepped.

But not all the negative peculiarities come from outside hostile forces. A German friend of mine complained about a party hosted by a club during one of the Mr. Cowhide contests. He likened the atmosphere to an amusement park where everyone waited in lines for a chance to play on the various benches, stocks and crosses. When a contest was announced for the best bondage, he decided that he'd had enough: "Why do you Americans reduce everything to a competition? OK, I know that people must have fun. For me though, tying someone up is something I should get excited about. It should be sex—not a contest like roping cattle in rodeos. It's like you are becoming afraid of the sexual."

In some leather clubs, that sexual edge has become so blunted among members that there's often a distinct lack of orgasmic activity, as though an orgasm, even of the vanilla kind, might reveal some hidden personal flaw. Or maybe SM's newly acquired and highly visible political power among mainline gay/lesbian organizations demands a toning down of overt sex. Perhaps the proliferation of seminars featuring antiseptic exhibitions of SM has fostered a cult of perfect technique that has sapped the intellectual and sexual energy. Instead of outsiders and outlaws pissing on formality, SM has itself become piss elegant. Good form has become a mania for the nineties.

England has a different history of SM behavior, centered on the English vices of caning, slippering and flogging. Slippering refers to the disciplining of a miscreant pupil in school by spanking his bottom with a shoe or slipper. Originally intended as a means for discipline and recollection, by the eighteenth century, caning, flagellation and birching had become erotic pursuits. Brothels and bawdy houses devoted exclusively to serving their customers' needs in these matters flourished throughout London—preceding the Marquis de Sade by several decades. Not until late Victorian times was the effort made to stamp out these specialty houses. Even today, the love of corporal punishment is still so ingrained among the guardians of English morality that in the very month they ruled illegal consensual SM which left marks, the same court upheld a father's right to whip his sons non-consensually with a leather belt so hard that bruises were visible a week afterward.

In England, SM has suffered from an official persecution that would surprise, frustrate and outrage US SMers. Subscriptions to US and EC magazines are routinely intercepted and confiscated by customs officials. I lived in North Carolina for four years and, sad to say, it offers more freedom for openly organized SM than does London. Clubs and organizations on the order or scale of those in the US are unknown. Motorcycle clubs are still mainly just that. No one dares be a member of an openly SM club. SM Gays of London purposely has no official membership that could possibly provide police with a witch-hunt list. Walking a tightrope of legality, it sponsors limited play parties that focus, out of necessity, on imagination, fantasy and fetish. Presentations can only be held on a limited number of topics; for everything else, talk must substitute for public demonstrations. Even then, they must be careful not to advocate too much for fear of becoming liable of conspiracy to commit grievous bodily harm. Yet SM flourishes even under this authoritarian threat. Private word of mouth parties substitute for club sponsored events. Fantasy fetish wear, close cropped-hair and hankies help individuals meet and negotiate SM encounters.

You'll undoubtedly hear talk of "leather traditions." Tradition is a word that depends on your historical sense. Having worked with historians and archivists to preserve gay and lesbian history, I get a bit uneasy around some of the leather traditionalists. A tradition is a custom that's been followed for generations, but the current manifestation of SM/leather is scarcely older than I am. I see things as merely being present practice. Besides, most of the so-called "leather traditions" are younger than the folks who cite them. Gay or straight, conservative or liberal, traditionalists yearn for a psychological anchor in a tempestuous world. That's fine, but it becomes dogma when they begin forcing compliance. You'll quickly find that SM dogmatics are dullards—unthinking and habit bound. SM is for the impertinent and outrageous. It is the journey of eccentrics and rebels who develop a personal approach to SM involving their own roots, sources and background. Private scenes, not public forums, remain its domain. Proficient and confident SMers still romp in their darkened rooms, ignoring a world hell-bent on establishing an orthodoxy of technique. Some things, fortunately, don't change.

SADOMASOCHISM

A SHARED EFFORT
Mike, Chicago, Illinois:
Sadomasochism is the ability to surrender to another. It's when sex becomes aggressive rather than complacent. It bothers me when people talk about SM and they tend to focus on the frightening aspect of giving up control to the top. But I think that the top has the more frightening role. He's supposed to be in charge. Yeah, I know that a lot of folks say that the bottom is really in charge of the action. The truth though is that if a scene crashes, most people blame the top. The bottom may ultimately control how far the action goes, but really most of them only take responsibility for pulling the emergency hand brake on a race car. The top, like it or not, bears the responsibility for success. He's the one often left to do the planning, steering and the strategy.

You know why there's so many bottoms out there? It's because people are more afraid of freedom than they are of losing control. This is an aspect that really isn't talked about in SM. It really terrifies them to be in control, making decisions and being in charge. They don't like facing the possibility of crashing in a big way. If someone is the passive in a scene that doesn't work, they don't experience a sense of responsibil-

16

ity or failure compared to what the person with the active role in the scene feels. It's very easy to be a passenger along for the ride and very easy to start criticizing the driver, but how's about a little sharing of the effort?

I spend a lot of time planning a scene because I want to come up with something new to do to him, to give him a different way to experience an orgasm. I enjoy the ingenuity and creativity of drawing out or delaying his sexual release. I find my own orgasm feeds on the response and the reaction of my partner. If I'm doing something to him that no one has ever done before, there's a real thrill of knowing that I'm etching this particular orgasm into that person's mind. I know that for the rest of his life he will always smirk when he remembers me and that particular orgasm. I'll have rewritten his orgasmic history. I know it's no big deal, nothing that changes the course of humanity like curing AIDS or cancer, but I will have left my mark on another human being. Considering the aggressive reputation of SM, it's really a nice and gentle way to be remembered, isn't it?

▼

Don't think that sadomasochism is wedded to a particular dress. Uniforms, leather, rubber or a host of other materials and costumes are just fetish wear. SM behavior itself is as old as the human race and spread throughout its cultures. Its sources reach back to Masoch, de Sade and beyond Rousseau to the mists of the ancient world. Mayan chieftains in the Yucatan pierced their genitals in a painful and publicly erotic religious ceremony. Hindi texts catalog sexual beatings and scourgings. Ancient Greek vases depict women slippering men while Roman writers chronicled the kinky, sometimes horrific escapades of their aristocrats. Late Medieval and much Renaissance art focused on the masochistic mortification of the flesh as suffered by Jesus and the saints. Much of it was fused with sex though not as eroticism but as theology. There are many paintings of the Crucifixion which depict Christ with a roaring hard-on underneath his loin cloth. The purpose was not to blaspheme but rather to emphasize his being fully man. Some of these shock even the most jaded. The *Flagellation of Christ* by Borrassa depicts soldiers scourging Christ with orgasmic expressions on their faces. They hold the phallic whip handles at their groins so that the spreading thongs appear as an ejaculation spilling over Him. (And Jesse Helms was upset with a crucifix in a little urine!) Flowing from these early sources, SM continues to filter into wider consciousness. As a philosophy, it has been formulated by some of the most original thinkers of the last two hundred years, providing for new language and approaches to ideas. Modern literature and art owes much to it. SM has reflected and foreshadowed changes that have been percolating beneath the surface of western culture over the last century.

A truly collective product without being designed, thus far, by corporate interests, SM is a point of intersection where deeper currents of irrational change first reach public consciousness. As part of a series of developing beliefs and values SM has generally been little understood and ill-defined. Many of its images are displaced from the familiar and become reflections of dreams and nightmares as it peels back the layers of submission and control. The white descendant of slave owners may become enslaved to a black descendant of slaves; Jews might become Nazi SS. Like nightmares and wet dreams, they do not readily conform to politically correct notions, embarrassing us as much as they excite and frighten us. In a world where no one, not even the US president, is really in charge, SM reveals that those in power are often subservient to those whom they would command. Dominants ultimately find themselves fulfilling the submissives' bidding. Icons of power fuse with erotic desire in a swirling ballet of submission, dominance and control. The dull doughnut-chomping policeman of the everyday world becomes a sexually-charged authoritarian Adonis. Nor is SM always direct. It pursues ends different from conventional sex play. Incoherent babbling often displaces dialogue as ritual theater replaces conjugal passion. Thus, the suspension of orgasm and not its release may be the goal as punishments, normally administered to discourage pleasure, themselves provoke pleasure.

SAFE, SANE AND CONSENSUAL

Current SM practice embraces three fundamental rules that establish a consensus for safe, sane and consensual play. These establish broad guidelines to insure that SM activity stays non-psychotic and non-life threatening.

▽ *Safe*

Commit no permanent mental, physical or emotional harm or injury. The exception to this is in specific cases of body modification such as scarification, piercing, branding or circumcision. To accomplish safe SM, you must know how to make any activity as accident-proof as possible so as not to endanger you or your partner. You need to understand enough anatomy and physiology, as well as something of medicine and hygiene, so that adequate precautions can be taken to prevent the spread of disease, especially AIDS. Lastly you must have empathy for your partner. If someone cannot envision the pain/pleasure that he produces in his partner, or if he cannot imagine himself in the other person's role, then he is incapable of playing in a psychologically safe manner.

▽ *Sane*

Make all decisions thoughtfully while sober. This applies to more than just chemicals. If you wouldn't play with someone fucked-up on drugs, don't play with someone suffering from testosterone poisoning. Some guys are out to prove just how 'masterful/masculine' they really are. Humility rather than arrogance, intimacy not aloofness are the marks of a proficient SMer. Attitudes of certain tops, who "know how to dish it out," and bottoms, who "want to prove they can take it," prevent them from operating under these guidelines. Know where the line between fantasy and reality is. Editors of leather magazines often publish reminders that their stories are meant to be fantasies, not a recipe for a scene, so keep your actions within reasonable bounds. Reasonable covers a broad area. For many people, blood sports, which involve cutting the skin, are too intense and beyond their definition of sane play.

When the activity is finished, no one's life or limb should have been endangered. All participants should want to *and* must be capable of reprising the scene. As death and dismemberment are neither reasonable nor repeatable events, they fall outside the domain of sane. Likewise, a slave, who wants to surrender so completely to his Master that he desires to be fucked without a condom thus risking AIDS, has stepped outside sane boundaries.

▽ *Consensual*

All parties must give their free, sober and full consent. Reluctant assent is not full consent. Being badgered into performing an activity is nothing more than being forced to comply with another's wishes. Consensual also means that the partners stay in communication with each other. If you're off in separate fantasies, that makes it unilateral, not mutual. A top doing a whipping must not suddenly go into a frenzy, mentally substituting his boss for his partner. Stay in touch with each other and let your partner know where your imagination is taking you.

The word *consensual* is also a pun that merges *consent* with *sensual*, implying something mutually erotic and agreed upon. Both partners should have their needs satisfied within safe and sane boundaries. If the play is mutually pleasurable, then a point will be reached when one or both is sated. A limit will have been reached. While it may be OK to try and push that limit, respect your partner's willingness, ability and comfort level. Remember, if it's mutually enjoyable, it'll be worth repeating and, as trust is built, the confidence to surrender or to control will increase.

▼

Before becoming involved in an SM scene, make certain that all three criteria of safe, sane and consensual will be met. As an extreme exam-

19

ple, someone might desire that I cut open their nutsac so that their balls hang out during the scene and then afterwards sew them back into the scrotum. With nearly a decade of Operating Room experience, I happen to have the training and skill to perform this act safely and sanely. But, although I understand someone's compulsion to undergo this scene, I lack the erotic desire to commit the act. My declining to participate has nothing to do with skill, knowledge or ability but everything to do with comfort levels. For me, it's simply not consensual. Similarly, although I delight in flogging others and can keep it within sane bounds, my eyesight has deteriorated to the point that I can't strike accurately unless I have bright light. Thus under low light conditions, I lack the ability to safely flog anyone. And I'd be a fool if I tried.

STAGED ANXIETY

Although SM may be therapeutic, it should never be therapy. If you need therapy, there are groups where you and others can work out your problems under the guidance of a trained therapist. SM does have a way of stripping the emotional and mental calluses off. But it should never be a substitute for the support of friends or the guidance of trained therapists who are SM friendly. It should be approached as self-validation, never as a way of invalidating you or your partner. Invalidation is a disastrous further reduction of fractured parts. You should never enter SM games because of low self esteem or as a way of debasing yourself to confirm feelings of inadequacy. Nor should SM result in the deliberate quashing of someone physically, emotionally or mentally. That's psychotic.

If your partner is unable to "feel" or imagine the pleasure and pain that he inflicts, then you may very well be dealing with a psychopath. Their common trait is their inability to identify emotionally with other people. They treat others as things or cardboard cutouts. Unfortunately the depth of their selfishness often goes unrecognized until the physical, emotional or mental damage has been done. Psychopaths are good at separating their contradictory personalities into different mental compartments. That charming hunk at the bar may have a hidden personality that would make Lucifer a dream date. Not all psychopaths are serial killers as the press and Hollywood would have you believe.

In the movie *The Addams Family*, little Wednesday explains her apparent lack of a Halloween costume as having disguised herself as a psychopath because they look just like you and me. Most manage to turn it into an asset and function in society as high achievers. To climb to the top in many professions requires a ruthlessness that comes natural to psychopaths. Corporate boardrooms abound with them since it's easier to swindle people if you have no feeling for them. Psychopaths, no matter how successful, are deeply dissatisfied with themselves with a deep-seated fear of being exposed as fakes. This frustration spills out as anger towards others and makes them envious and destructive of anyone else's pleasure or success. While not serial killers of the body, most psychopaths rack up a long list of mental and emotional victims.

SM should be more about becoming than being, exploring rather than retreating, ethics instead of expediency. SM must give delight to re-attract participants. The writer Sacher-Masoch, after whom masochism is named, described himself as a supersensual being who felt both pleasurable and painful things more intensely than the average person. This, he felt, compelled him to seek out intense situations in order to experience them. In SM, we also seek pain/pleasure settings precisely because they give us intense rewards. The kiss of the whip stings but gives such a delicious glow to the back. It exhilarates yet calms us.

SM accurately and sensitively mirrors the anxieties and preoccupations, the emotions and thinking of modern life. We live in an age of transition where medieval beliefs, scientific reasoning, Druidism, Eastern philosophy, eighteenth century rationalism and twentieth century barbarism swirl in a crazy mixture without clear separation. The certainties and comfortable assumptions of the past have been swept away like cheap childlike illusions. What's left is a sense of the senselessness of life and the inevitable reduction of traditional ideas, purity and purpose. Abandoned and confronted with the basic problems of existence, loneliness and the mystery of life and death, we are left pretty much on our own. SM reveals the inadequacy of the strictly Western conceptual approach by openly spurning rational thought. It can be seen as a search for the reality that lies behind mere reasoning in conceptual terms. In SM, instinct and intuition rather than conscious thought overcome and resolve dilemmas. It represents less of a proof than a presentation whose significance is reckoned after commission.

SM stages anxiety for pleasure. The playwright Adamov said that neurosis sharpens perceptions and enables the sufferer to look into depths not usually open to the ordinary mind. In real world politics, from which there is no escape, the manipulation of apprehension enforces social control. SM plays with these concepts of power, control and submission within a scene by fusing them to sex. This SM theater fashions experience into something significant. In a scene, you take your experiences and treat them as raw material, infusing them with your particular perceptions, insights and sensations, reshaping them into something that moves, disturbs, agitates and exhilarates you. As a representation of the outside world, staged anxiety is not meant to be real. (That uniformed soldier "torturing" you in your playroom nowhere approaches the real horror that occurs under third world dictatorships.) Staged anxiety

21

ought to be an extraordinary experience that sanctions the whole human spirit instead of the parts that our culture approves of and passes off as whole.

SM doesn't reflect despair or a retreat but expresses an attempt to come to terms with the world, to face up to the human condition and shake off the stupor induced by illusions and false promises. Tremendous forces in our world seek to inure us to the moral realities of uncertainty and ambiguity. Mass entertainment, organized religions, technocratic revelations, all promote self-oblivion by numbing the mind and spirit with their prepackaged solutions. Struggle, sex and death are increasingly hidden behind the euphemisms and emptiness of mass consumption. SM snaps you out of the electronic age's hypnotic lethargy by demanding you to face reality in all its senselessness, to accept it freely without fear or illusions and, most importantly, to learn to laugh at it.

SM INTEGRITY

SM takes courage to act on your choice. It is never without risk since activities cannot be 100% safe. Nothing in life is. Partners need to monitor the state of each other's emotional, physical and mental state, making sure that all these aspects are remaining in balance. A disaster can occur when any or all of these aspects crash. But courage is also needed to face public and private disapproval and pressure, particularly from your own mainline gay or lesbian acquaintances. You expect fear and ignorance from the homophobes, not from your friends.

Communication with a potential partner is vital in determining if you're attuned to each other. It's even more important during the scene. Janet Blevins once told me, "Communication means being responsive and sharing. I know I get terribly frustrated when some one just lays there. I need sound and visual stimulation. Dialogue and props are equally important for me. Dialogue is as important as the kiss of a whip. Quit worrying over correctness, just say what comes to mind even if it is just to moan a little. At least I know you're having a good time. I don't like structured talk or formal language. I prefer more of an improvisation. It has the edge of reality to it." Bottoms who dictate exactly how they want the scene to occur—either from something they've read or a scene that they experienced with someone else—are behaving like a spoiled movie mogul who demands that his storyboards be slavishly followed with no alterations allowed. Instead of a partnership, a dictatorship is established. No good top or bottom pretends that they know exactly how a scene will unfold. To hold someone to a hard and fast script or to profess to know just where the action will lead is pretentious.

A truly confident SMer can decide when a scene should conclude and stick to that decision in the face or butt of a partner writhing for more.

Judgment always calls for integrity and confidence. If you feel that either of you needs a break or has exceeded endurance or comfort levels, you stop. Period. This does not preclude experimentation with new techniques or practices. Most sMers are very eager to push limits and explore new horizons, but you gain far more respect by being frank about your capabilities than by pretending. sM trust is built on honesty, so be truthful about your abilities and your level of play. Don't pretend to be what you're not. Reputations are terribly hard to rehabilitate. The sM community is still comparatively small. Once you foul the nest, you have to live with the shit.

PAIN'S MEANING

As with sexuality, pain is not a thing but a complex relationship of individual and cultural interpretation. Most people have forgotten that as children they were taught how to react to pain. I grew up in a neighborhood of English, Italians, Poles and Irish. The Italians would wail and scream at the slightest injury with their mothers fussing over them. Being of Polish-Irish background, I knew that if I carried on like that, I would get a cuff on the ear for over-reacting. In my family, no matter how severe the injury, you stayed calm and showed that you could master the pain. Your reaction to an injury demonstrated your maturity and self-control and reflected your upbringing. The English kids found themselves in the middle ground. Their parents insisted that they keep a stiff upper lip but allowed them to cry if there was blood. Blood injuries put pain in a different category.

Our understanding of pain changes throughout time, place and culture. The old philosophy of "spare the rod and spoil the child" has now become grounds for arrest on charges of child abuse. Increasingly in the West, we speak of pain in the singular as if it were only a solitary thing that we must avoid. It's been reduced to a mere signal warning of injured body cells. Invariably, its complex nature is limited to a simplistic understanding of pain as a harmful evil and therefore a thing that must be defeated. Our culture has traded learning from pain for immunity from pain. Alternative models for pain perception have been abandoned.

CULTURAL CONDITIONING
James, Boston, Massachusetts:
When I was a kid growing up in the pre-Vatican Catholic Church, I was very drawn to the lives of the saints. Martyrdom held a special fascination for me, more than the usual child's interest in the morbid. I read every book from three different libraries on the mystic saints. I was also lucky to have had a close friend, now a priest, who shared my fascination. We'd talk for hours on the meaning of pain and suffering. Not just

the theological aspects of mysticism but the techniques employed by saints to obtain their beatific visions. We confided the details of our own "mortifications of the flesh" to each other. Of course this further fueled our penitential pursuits. Wool sweaters were the closest thing we had to hair shirts. Self-flagellation brought a wonderful calm to both of us. Strangely though, we never offered to whip each other. We did do mutual penance, walking together barefoot without flinching on gravel cinders while reciting prayers.

I began using straight pins stuck through the top layer of the skin on my legs, making neat rows of stainless steel that looked like the lines of barrel-buttons on the uniforms of the Austrian Cavalry. I have a needle phobia but somehow I could overcome it. Pain, where was it? In the mind mostly. I discovered that a slow and methodical application allowed me to enter a state of mind that permitted what I could not have tolerated if another had done it to me.

I was lucky to have grown up at the tail-end of a culture that still valued pain as a means of shaping a modest and unpretentious individual. That's a bizarre concept today but I had a culturally sanctioned way of embracing pain and using it to grow into adulthood. I never regarded my seeking-out pain as being sick or deviant. On the contrary. I was taught that these were holy, worthy and saintly pursuits. I don't understand all the fuss about those who explore pain. If people grasp the idea that not all pleasure is good, why can't they understand that not all pain is bad?

▼

Pain has often been used as means to insure recollection of an important event. Humans can remember having experienced pain, recalling the circumstances and the anxiety surrounding its infliction, but they cannot recreate or re-experience the sensation of pain in their minds. Writing in the early sixteenth century, Sir Thomas More recalled how the young boys in the bishop's household were summoned to witness legal agreements and occasions of state. They were soundly beaten before the ceremony so that they would remember the details of the event clearly. Afterward they were rewarded with gifts or a feast. Remnants of this practice still occur in the Roman Catholic ceremony of confirmation when the bishop gives a light slap on the cheek to the candidate to remind him of his pledge to the faith and willingness to suffer for it.

Achieving a peak experience has been described as the object of SM pain. The term comes from Abraham Maslow who defined a peak experience as a ritual transcendental, mystical experience that claims a metaphysical place of mystical union. (Got that?) I prefer to think of rituals as ways of achieving a transformation. Sociologist Alan Morinis defined ritual's purpose as "Any breach of ordinary consciousness induced by extreme experience from which individuals reach new realizations of themselves and so are forced to revise their relationship with the world [Morinis, Alan, *The Ritual Experience: Pain and the Transformation of Consciousness in Ordeals of Initiation. Ethos* vol. 13:2, 150–174.] The ritual experience uses pain to work a lasting change upon the mind which experiences real agony. The nature of change relies on the needs of that person and his society and upon the nature of the ritual. Rituals are most often intended to bring healing or mark initiation into a new phase of life and the leaving behind of the old.

For some, childhood meant pain inflicted by sadistic parents who also required that the sufferer repress any reaction to that pain. "If you don't stop crying, I'll hit you again," was the threat. For them, SM can heal by providing a ritualized way of reconciling themselves with their pain and of leaving it behind them.

THE BEAST
Ernesto, Toledo, Ohio:

The Beast within me is the legacy of a brutal father, an angry irrational midnight batterer of children. His footfall upon the stairs in the dark provoked terror. I still wake with my heart pounding in fear whenever I hear a stair creak at night. The repressed anger that rages within me is the Beast who destroys the normally calm me. It's a monster from the abyss which smashes at my veneer of civilization. When it bursts out, it views people not as my partners nor brothers nor equals but as objects to assail. It's a thing from which furious waves of wrath arise from nowhere to slam against others. It's as if I am turned inside out by a raw anger that roars from the depths of my guts and seeks release from its pain by lashing out at someone. It's an artesian well of emotion exploding out or a personality wrenched inside out.

I grew up with this secret feeling that no matter what I did or how well I did it, that someone, some power would attack me or punish me for something that I have done or failed to do. Whether I act or not, I am doomed. I am a rabbit caught in bright sunlight in the middle of a grass lawn. If I move, some predator with fang and claw will pounce down on me. So my muscles freeze and I do nothing. Paralyzation offers the only hope for escaping detection and punishment. Anxiety often disables me. Abuse and ridicule have gouged such deep wounds that fear disables ability. Confidence so often slapped and beaten and humiliated lies shattered so that only its jagged edges remain. Their myriad of remembered scalpel blades slit the scars open again. This is when the Beast bursts out of me and I'll suddenly undergo a complete change in attitude and action. It's so stunning to me that I snap out of my mental inertia and regain control over myself before things get out of hand. It frightens me. Some of my partners have been aghast at the naked anger that they've briefly glimpsed like a demon behind my eyes.

What hope exists for those transformed by brutish acts when retreat within and silence without have been forced upon a child as the way of survival? The saying goes, "What's learned can be unlearned." Overcome perhaps. But conquered? How do you unlearn an emotional response? As easily as learning not to blink or duck when a stone is thrown at your face.

Control of the Beast has come from ritualistic suffering. A therapist friend who is sm-friendly suggested that I bottom and concentrate on releasing my rigid control. She thought I had to confront the pain and denial that spawned the Beast. My running from it is what drove the Beast into the frenzy of the hunt like a dog on the scent of a rabbit. Avoidance had become a dance of death. I needed to grapple with the agony that I had been forced to simultaneously endure and deny when I was a kid. It took some time, but her hunch was right. I've learned to reconcile my controlled rational side with the satyr of oblivion. Reason meets rapture.

I'd always thought that ecstasy was just extreme pleasure, but it's pain too. I remember during one scene, after a really heavy work-out, floating off in ecstasy while getting fucked and drifting back to reality while laughing at the irreconcilability of it all. Of the freedom to get such pleasure from punishments that once hurt me. I remember staring at my grinning visage in the playroom mirror. It looked like someone else. I recognized it as my inarticulate self, the Beast, and it was calmed. For the first time, I felt I had a sense of balance. Several months after that, I visited some friends in NYC. On their wall was a painting of a devil or satyr with the same expression I had seen on my own face. When I asked about the painting, I was told that they had inherited it from an artist friend who had always referred to it as his alter ego. Although I never knew the artist, I felt as though I had discovered a long lost identical twin.

I feel as though I'm finally whole. There's still anger and pain, but I'm not afraid of losing control to the Beast. I still top occasionally but I'm no longer scared to let go and really get into it. I don't worry about getting carried away or transferring anger from some childhood event to my partner. I stay very much in touch with myself.

▼

SM ECSTASY

Ecstasy is a word that's been maligned in modern Western culture as the rationalists have debunked the extravagant claims of the spiritualists. The debate has obscured the simple fact that ecstasy is a very real, albeit special state of consciousness for humans. Humans have two types of consciousness to be reckoned with, the normal and the joy of ecstasy. In common with Eastern thought, Western religion still holds ecstasy to be a state of blissful union with God and therefore the ultimate reality. Medicine believes ecstasy to be a delusion and proclaims the everyday stupor of normalcy to be true existence. Taking note of modern man's efforts to stay level-headed and unimpassioned, Thoreau cynically commented that "most men live lives of quiet desperation."

Every culture has developed techniques to awaken man from his everyday lethargy. Today, Christianity espouses an approach that seeks to create religious ecstasy through deprivation, discipline and fasting. But in the past there were major Christian sects whose homo-erotic gospels advocated ecstatic pleasure to achieve union with God. The Roman Church inevitably declared these heretical and wiped out their adherents with a singular viciousness. Instead of repression, many Eastern religious philosophies, such as Tantric yoga, seek to channel and use feelings and sexual impulses to reach the clarity of mind necessary to approach divinity. Sex, in combination with awareness and consciousness, thus has meaning beyond basic procreation. One of the better books with this consciousness is *The Divine Androgyne* by Christopher Larkin writing under the name "Purusha." A former monk and film maker, he seeks to reconcile Eastern and Western ecstatic thought.

Ecstasy isn't always the heavens opening up with holy spirits showering you with bliss. You don't need to join an Eastern religion or Western monastery. Even if you're not mystically inclined, an ecstasy results when your physical, emotional and mental faculties are overwhelmed. This means that ecstasy can occur on a purely bodily, or emotional or psychic level. More commonly, it's a combination of these which can affect you profoundly. A really good orgasm is a minor physical ecstasy that rolls our eyes up, sets our mouths agape and makes us grunt in muffled cries. None of us presents a very pretty sight for polite society. And, from the descriptions of eye witnesses, neither did the saints who experienced religious ones. Read descriptions of St. Teresa of Avila's grunting, writhing transports of ecstasy while at church services and you'll understand why the Inquisition considered burning her. Any good ecstasy, including orgasms, can trigger complex emotions, sometimes joy, fear, weeping, laughing, sadness or terror for no apparent reason. After some really intense sm scenes, the bottom may find himself trembling with waves of conflicting emotions that seem to be without cause.

In general for a sustained experience of ecstasy, a rhythmic quality is needed for the change into the ecstatic trance. There are no rituals without regulated beats of dance or music or both. The combination leads to a more profound state precisely because it involves the body, the emotions and the mind. From the sacred chants of Christianity, to the dance of whirling dervishes, to the drumming of the Buddhist monks, to the tribal songs and dances of initiation ceremonies, the object is to leave this reality and enter into a transformed one.

What is reality to such an altered state of consciousness? Humans have grappled with that question. Beyond saying that reality exists, little more can be said. Discipline, whether of the religious, secular or SM bent, is a strategy of finding your way through reality. You can base it on intuition and feeling, or on fakir which is a working with the body to overcome its limitations, or on yoga which concentrates on the mind or on the Greek ideal of trying to achieve a balance among body, mind and emotions. However you enter into this altered consciousness, via the sling, the pew, through poetry or the whipping post, ecstasy is a valid and valued aim of SM.

SELF-FASHIONING

Levi, leather, rubber; FF, BD, CBT; black hankie, white hankie, lace? The choices confound the beginner. Often, speaking with experienced SMers only increases the confusion. Coded references to unfamiliar terms isolate the uncomprehending novice. But what should a beginner make of the more mystical inclined who spout transcendental jargon that would puzzle the Pope? Completely confounded, neophyte SMers easily fall into the trap of believing that only the purchase of certain items or the practice of particular behaviors will make them "real" members of the SM community. Thus many would-be SMers confuse image with imagination and deck themselves out in shiny new leathers with accoutrements hanging from their belts. But radical-leather sexuality is not a Chinese menu from which you pick a fetish from Column A, a perversion from Column B, with a choice of top or bottom. It's a conscious effort that essentially re-tools your identity through a process of self-fashioning—a process that our culture and society inevitably views as subversive behavior.

Sadly, in today's world, no one can be completely original or build in total isolation. Even in coming-out to the mainline gay/lesbian community, you picked from various roles and types. While less than completely independent, it nonetheless required much more than a simple assemblage of parts delivered in kit form. From thousands of possibilities, you seized upon a handful of arresting ones that embodied what you needed, that offered you intense reward, and that promised you greater awareness of yourself. Often, this meant settling upon a few role-models who seemed to exemplify those qualities and traits that you admired and aspired to.

Shaping your SM identity is similar and if it's to be successful, it must start with an honest introspection. Simply accepting an identity, for which someone else did the thinking, planning and imagining, is like trying to gain self-enlightenment from blueprints. You may look to others for support and reinforcement, but blind copying only subjugates you to another's invention and blocks the exercise of your own creative powers. Trust in yourself is essential. Even so, you can only refashion yourself by consciously choosing, interpreting and assimilating different patterns of behavior. Few SMers succeed in reaching the extremes of behavior such as peeling off flesh with knives heated by blowtorches. Few care to.

Forming your SM identity makes you keenly aware of how it perplexes society. For example, if you're confident enough to walk into your local gymnasium with a piercing, you'll find that it dramatically alters your interactions with others. Although everyone will politely pretend not to notice your glinting metal, from workout to locker room, people will act differently in your presence. Some will avoid you in the showers while others get visibly aroused.

More often though, America the melting pot acts as though it has not just the right but the duty to impose a common standard of decency to assure assimilation. Repressive laws and standards are aimed at the powerless minority. Rarely is a far reaching prohibition decreed lest the majority rebel. Regulation becomes control masquerading as a necessary protection to safeguard society from you—as well as the necessity of protecting you from yourself. Society will seek to saddle you with a sense of inferiority by branding you a troublemaker and warning society of your unreliability or dangerous nature. After all, only troublemakers resist the petty restrictions placed on small defenseless groups. The rules of authoritarian control are simple. Support social conditioning and you'll be rewarded or at least left alone. Subvert it by action or visibility and society will turn you into a moral lesson for others.

Free-choice, then, often means nothing more than the freedom to choose from the permissible possibilities. Society arrests development by invoking and evoking the fears of childhood where bigger all-powerful adults force compliance with their wishes. "Do this or else!" Family, friends, clubs—all exert pressure to conform to particular patterns, often producing a dreary sameness of people as if from an assembly line of set models and styles with limited options.

SM is not one of society's authorized forms of self-identity. The authoritarian forces recognize that the power to shape yourself confers the broader ability to transform others and therefore the means to alter society. Since institutions exist to guide and shape human behavior, SM becomes at best a sharing of this function and often a direct challenge.

Their hostility to perceived threats always results in a series of reactions to what you are able to do in theory and what in reality social institutions permit you to do. Any increased exercise of freewill sparks increased and relentless assaults upon the will by authority. The visibility of upstarts leads to attempts to wipe out any such visibility. Any increased awareness of alternative forms of social, sexual, religious and psychological behaviors leads to authority's renewed determination to impose control upon them and eventually to destroy them.

These points ought to be familiar; they're the main thrust of the reactionary agenda. But don't think that it's limited to the ultra-right. Dogma and intolerance raise their ugly heads in the sm world too. sm clubs, publications and individuals can also exert conformist pressure. Thus, one method, from a range of acceptable practices, may degenerate into the only permissible one. It runs along the lines of "unless you tie knots in this particular manner, you can't be a bondage expert."

If you thought that you were only indulging a fetish, guess again. sm *is* subversive behavior. Expect conformist pressures to range from snide comments to ostracism and brutality. To survive, form your sm identity to suit your needs first. Make choices without haste or intimidation, but rather with a confidence that your decisions are correct and true for you. Be so comfortable and honest with yourself that you never need to apologize. The Rt. Rev. Barbara Harris, first woman bishop for the Episcopal Church, said, "When you are sure of yourself and filled with righteousness, those who would do you evil sense it and get out of your way."

Chapter 2: Getting There

There's a storm in your eye.
I don't know who
put it there, or what,
but a lightning bolt
just shot through the
window. My mountain
trembles from its
rolled sound.

"Weather"
—Jeffery Beam

SM is not monolithic. It's been so hard to define precisely because its expression is so varied. These are six people who relate how they came-out to SM and its impact on them. These were chosen because they illustrate the different routes and odysseys that people make. As with most journeys of exploration, the final destination is not necessarily to where the traveler had intended. Consequently, the journeys are highly individualized and varied, sometimes running counter to the currents of political correctness.

PLEASED TO ENDURE IT
Kevin Drewery, Greensboro, North Carolina:
I came out to leather and SM separately. What I consider my first leather experience took place when my lover and I initially broke up. The night that he moved out, I headed to the bar for a drink and picked this guy up. Like me, he had been in the military and we got to talking. We had had similar training and been at the same service facilities. So it seemed very natural when the military context of our conversation carried over to our sex play. He wound up wearing my combat boots and dog tags while fucking me. That's something that turned out very nicely and that I had never done with my lover. I consider that my first leather sex experience because we were bringing props into a sexual situation. One major aspect of SM is that it entails the eroticizing of acts and objects which don't usually have a sexual context.

Leather attracted me because of its close ties with my uniform fetish. Most people into uniforms also indulge in leather. I've always had a thing for uniforms since I was a little kid, from high school ROTC to watching movies like *Patton* or even *Star Wars*. My experiences in the boy scouts, in ROTC and in the Army fed my uniform fetish. As a kid, I watched *Hogan's Heroes* just to see some class-A uniforms. The nicer

31

the uniform, the more I liked it and, usually, the bad guys had the best uniforms. I didn't care if the person wearing it was a shithead. Morals and politics aside, the Nazis always had the snappiest uniforms as did the evil empire in *Star Wars*. Why even the Klingons in the modern *Star Trek* series have better uniforms than the good guys. Butcher and better uniforms always appealed to me. When I was a teenager, the Village People were real popular, a group with formal and informal uniforms like the cop and the construction worker. They tied all of my uniform fetishes together in a nice hot package. And of course there was the Leatherman. His inclusion brought in the darker aspects associated with leather motorcycle outlaws and intrigued me with the shady elements of particular uniformed groups. That's why I adopted leather; why it drew me to itself. In the g/l communities, there's really no organized roles that mandate a certain type of clothing except for leather or drag. Otherwise, it's just another Izod or T-shirt night at the bar and I don't consider those assumable or well-defined roles. More importantly, I don't find them sexually stimulating. For me, a group in leather has a certain aura that's missing from a group of preppies. I equate the masculine element with authority and that authority is definitely connected with leather and uniforms. It's a visual cue that's missing from the madras plaid and Dockers crowd.

My lover and I reconciled but within a year had broken up again. At the same time there was the S. E. Conference for Gays and Lesbians in Raleigh, NC. They had a workshop—leather sex 101 or Everything-you-wanted-to-know-about-Leather-but-were-afraid-to-ask. I attended because I was curious. At the time, I did have a harness that I liked to wear but I didn't think of myself as being in the leather community. I asked if it was OK to be interested in leather but not in SM. I was interested in the fantasy and putting-on of roles but not in the pain. Of course, everyone assured me that it was alright. Ironically, later that evening, I had my first SM experience.

I realize now that I was in SM denial when I first came out to leather. I had always believed that SM involved a lot of heavy abuse where one person beat the shit out of another. But the psychological role play that went on as part of SM had never occurred to me. During the three hours that I spent with that person that evening, our dialogue triggered my awareness of SM's deeper meanings.

The person said, "Stand on one leg."

I stood on one leg.

And then he asked, "Why did you stand on one leg?"

I thought to myself, what is this, some kind of Zen SM? But I only shrugged and said, "Well, because you asked me to."

"So it pleased you to do what I wanted? You're willing to do as I command because you get pleasure from following my desires?"

That surprised me. I hadn't thought of it that way but it was true. So I said, "Yes."

That's a dynamic common to SM activities, doing something difficult or painful or taking something pleasurably and consensually from someone because it gratifies you to do so for that person. It's not co-dependent. I don't find SM a descent into self-invalidation. I work on my personal issues during therapy with a counselor—not during an SM scene. I thoroughly enjoy the experiences and the joys going on in a scene. The activities themselves are erotic turn-ons, pleasurable in themselves. Emotionally, I don't need to take it any further than understanding that SM, through its intense physical and emotional communication, helps me connect on an incredibly intimate level with my partner.

This realization was my personal coming out to SM. I had dealt with severe emotional pain all my life, both feeling it and causing it. In trying to conceal my homosexuality, I was torn by my feelings and what was expected of me by society. I had joined others in beating-up gays to cover-up my own homosexuality, hoping that I would appear straight. And the strain and irony of hiding who I was on a job I didn't even like tore me up inside and caused a lot of personal emotional pain—all negative pain. I wanted a positive channel for pain. That bit of Zen SM philosophy first showed me how subtle pain could be. Standing for a few moments on one leg was nothing, but standing that way for hours—to the point of painful shaking—because it pleased me to endure it, opened up a new way of seeing and experiencing. During my first really heavy scene, I experienced physical pain which was very stimulating and which gave me a positive psychological attachment to it that countered all my negative emotional pain—calming and very erotic. I had a complete feeling of gratification in an SM scene. I connected with the other person on a level of intimacy that I had never shared with anyone else. My non-SM scenes had never reached such intensity. There's honest communication from the start to the very end. You respond to him; he responds to you. You see his reactions and base your response on that. The intensity builds, bringing both of you closer to the goal which, for me, is a final release in orgasm. SM is a sexual thing. The intimacy from start to finish, its inner workings with different activities, and the highs and lows is something that I've not had in vanilla sex where you merely take dick A, insert in hole B, agitate and shoot. In SM, sex is an escalation of energy that comes from responding to each response. You share and help the person reach a certain point through your agreed upon activity. There's constant communication, verbal and physical. Intellectually, physically and emotionally, you bond with that other person. And that's my turn-on. It had become something very deep and profound for me. At that point, I started training, learning technical terms and bottoming in SM.

My public coming-out, being comfortable saying I did SM, occurred at a conference in Atlanta. At the time, I wore a GMSMA [Gay Male SM Association] patch on my vest, but didn't realize how public a statement that was. I had joined GMSMA because I liked their newsletter and educational resources. I was getting so much out of that organization that I wanted to be a member and help support it. I put the patch on my vest because I thought it was attractive. I was pretty ignorant of how different affiliation patches or how you display them can be such public and political statements. Of course now I take these things much more seriously than I did. At this conference I met someone who had seen my GMSMA patch and who was also a member. The next morning, I came out of the SM closet to anyone who could hear and have been out ever since.

It took me about nine months to become comfortable with SM. Part of me feared that this could be pathological behavior. "Is this as unhealthy as some of those traumatic events in my life?" It took time for me to see that I wasn't using SM to avoid issues or trading physical pain for emotional pain or even using it to shield myself from things. If you're dealing with emotional issues, you're still going to have to face them when the scene is done. For me, personal hassles had nothing to do with the scene. I have seen a therapist for a number of years and I work things out during our therapy sessions. My SM activities haven't interfered with me coping with issues, so it hasn't been unhealthy for me. SM has never been an avoidance or a diversion from confronting difficulties in my life.

Sometimes, SM can be therapeutic. My room-mate works through a lot of issues during a scene. I can't say that that's not SM. For me, SM is not therapy, but I can only speak for myself. For others, SM is what they make of it. I can't carve a definition in stone. I know that I have confronted issues while in a scene but those issues arose by themselves. I didn't decide, "Well hey, I think I need to resolve some personal issues, so won't you tie me up and flog me so I can work out a solution." It just doesn't work that way. I didn't plan it; it just happened. I was once mummified, swathed in plastic wrap and duct tape. Completely immobile and blindfolded, I was left isolated with nothing to focus on but what was whirling inside my twisted little head. Several things that I had been repressing popped out and sent me into a panic attack that my guide talked me through. He and I dealt with my personal crisis and then continued with the SM portion of the scene. I'm sure that some people latch onto SM as a way of bringing hidden issues into focus and confronting them. That's fine, but I like to keep SM strictly within the sexual confines of my nature and not get distracted from sharing with the person

I'm with. SM makes my dick hard. What more can I say? The activities, techniques and practices of SM are a sexual turn-on. And while SM sex may be therapeutic, it's not therapy.

I was lucky to have overcome the stereotypes that society saddled me with. And the hardest of those I had gotten from the movie *Cruising*. I saw it the year after I came out to the gay life and it shoved me deep into the leather closet for four years. The movie depicts leather people as a community of psychopathic killers. I had the misfortune of watching it with a group of friends who were already anti-SM. I had no positive role models or even a dissenting voice to question the movie's portrayal of leather. No one to speak up and say, "Hey, that's not the truth. This doesn't reflect the real leather world of safe, sane and consensual."

The only other SM I had encountered was in magazines. I've never been a fiction reader, even of erotica, so my main exposure to leather was through photos. The models, I now know, were really just street hustlers that the photographers dressed up. They weren't leather people, just punk chicken draped in cowhide and not at all what you find in the leather community. The models in the pictures had looks so chiseled-perfect that they frightened you. But leather people actually live in a not so pretty subculture. Most leather establishments host more beer-bellies in body harnesses than sleek Adonises in leather. Technique is of greater concern than looks. I would rather play with a competent bear whose looks are less than spectacular than with some smooth-chested pretty-boy who could maim me through ignorance. I won't lie and say that looks don't matter. There has to be some physical attraction for me even if the person has perfect technique. But given a choice between an SMer and a non-SMer, the SM player will win out. Technique and commitment are eminently more important than looks, especially if they've no concept of SM. But back then, I really had no access to positive SM materials. My resources were zilch. *Drummer* was unavailable in my town. *The Leather Journal* did not yet exist. Amazingly, I did run across *PFIQ*. But to someone just coming out, pictures of thirty genital piercings seemed mighty strange. Sick, like freaks at a carnival, I remember thinking. I was completely ignorant about the purpose, history, erotism and fetish of piercing. Now, I've five piercings of my own, want three more and would like to apprentice to a piercer.

I had started out as a bottom but I live in an area where there are far too few experienced tops. I'm a very pushy bottom and I often made novice tops too uncomfortable. As I had also acquired more technical knowledge and became their major source for information, many of them regarded me as too intimidating. Insecurity always makes communication difficult. Besides, there was so much that I was reading about and wanted to try but that they were not keen on learning or doing. I noticed that I had begun studying from a top's point of view. I stopped searching for a top I could trust to do these things properly to me and began to experiment on myself. But that's only fun for so long. It's also too difficult to stage direct while bottoming and not make your top nervously self-conscious. So, I began topping others. I never do anything to anyone without having first tried it out on myself. I couldn't read someone's reaction without knowing first hand how those experiences felt. I'm a firm believer in doing unto others what you'd have them do unto you.

sm has come far too naturally to me for it to be merely learned behavior. I think the inklings of it have been there all along. I've just seemed to have tapped into a well from which everything seems to flow so easily and comfortably. I don't recall any childhood experience or trauma that I could say made me this way. I grew up in a strict fundamentalist family, the holy-roller type. Both of my parents were in the military and practiced standard corporal punishment. Although we did cut switches from the tree for punishment, I can't point and say that this particular practice made me a sadomasochist. I think I was just born this way. After all, you can't learn anything unless there's a prior desire.

GETTING THERE
Jim Prezwalski, Chicago, Illinois:
I came out to leather over five years ago at a gay and lesbian campground near Saugutuck, Michigan called Camp-It. At that time I had been out of the closet for about six years and my initial rush of liberation was being replaced by a growing sense of confinement. I had discovered that the gay world I had come out to had well defined borders of acceptable behavior. Those limits were constantly marked and outlined in social interactions. At planning sessions for gay pride events, disparaging comments about "those freaks" in both the leather and the cross-dressing communities continually popped up. The rationale for this gay gay-bashing was that the press would focus undue attention on the weirdos while ignoring the normal members of the lesbian and gay community. I kept my mouth shut; after all, I wasn't one of those groups. I was just curious about leather. So I continued buying leather magazines on the sly and hiding them in the attic from my lover. All the while, I grew more restless, sensing that I had emerged from one small closet only to be trapped in a larger one.

I had been at the campground for five days when a red-bearded man from Chicago, named David, arrived for the weekend. Our eyes locked several times during the day and again around the evening's communal campfire. Something about him—his bearing, his close cropped beard, his soft spoken self-assurance—set off alarms deep inside of me, bells I hadn't had go off since first coming out. He drove me crazy, especially since I kept picturing him in leather. I tried to be casual and prayed he'd think my sweaty palms and flushed face were from the heat. But David saw. He knew.

After the campfire had died, everyone retreated to their tents. I lay sleepless in the humid night, naked on my sleeping bag. Outside my tent I heard a rustle and David's hushed voice as he fumbled at the zippered opening. Without a word, we dived at each other, mouthing salty pecs, touching skin, exploring flesh. Then, things changed. David began to wrestle, but not in the usual playful way. He had an attitude of insistence. His legs and knees locked mine against the ground. Struggling to remain on top, he pressed my wrists together over my head and pinned them to the floor. As he sat on my chest, I watched the outline of his figure bob up and down in rhythm to my heartbeat. It raced from more than just exertion. I could have thrown him. I had him beat by at least thirty pounds. But I didn't want to. Some barrier in my mind had at last been breached. I wanted to submit. He must have sensed the change in my muscles for he paused and spoke. "Trust me." It was a directive, not a question. I let him dominate me that night. Without words, without leather, without restraints—save his hands—David brought me out of the closet and into the SM world.

Within a month, I had my first piece of leather, a half harness. I slept in it for at least a week, marveling in the smell of its newness, the feel of its cold metal studs and the constriction of the straps across my torso. Materially, it symbolized my new sexuality. Two weeks after I had acquired the harness, I scheduled an interview with singer/performer Lynn Lavner who does a cabaret routine in full heavy leather. When I arrived and knocked on her door, she opened it as she was snapping her new harness over her T-shirt. I was floored. It was identical to mine. Lynn thought it a hoot and quipped that I ought to be flattered that I owned a harness butch enough for a leather dyke. The important thing, she stressed, was to look beyond the leather into a person's mind and soul. The outside often amounts to just theatrics.

I've found that coming-out to leather, or any other fetish, repeats the original coming-out process. First, you make a personal acknowledgement, accepting your orientation. Second, you confront the world with that self-acknowledgement, refusing to let anyone dictate terms of acceptance. Mercifully for most of us, the process of this second coming-out is far quicker than the first. What differs this time around is having to come-out to fellow gays and lesbians as well as the straights in your life. I have found that my straight friends have been more tolerant and accepting. Perhaps to them, since the gay and lesbian community already lies beyond their zone of control, nothing further surprises them. I had the distinct impression that many of them had actually anticipated or, more properly, had expected sm as a logical and normal progression of "deviant" behavior. But when I let my gay friends know of my entry into sm and leather, their hostility surprised me. One gay couple angrily demanded to know why I couldn't be "happy with normal sex," as though some pathological defect caused my orientation. They really had me stumped. I couldn't figure what they meant by "normal sex." Did they mean Vatican approved pro-creational hetero-sex, or was I un-aware of a socially sanctioned gay missionary position? Did normal in-clude lesbians? Did it encompass latex and plastic wrap? I needed some new definitions.

For me, sm is a state of mind and a continual exploration of myself. Although David and I had no leather and used no toys that summer night, we both were very much aware of the sm edge to our play and that I was crossing the border line out of that self-imposed ghetto of "nor-mal gay sex." We created our own sm space without the benefit of leather trappings. A piece of black leather is only an expression of who I am. I choose its design and have it tailored to me. The heat and sweat of my body molds it to my shape. My body chemistry interacts with it to make it distinctly mine. The leather does not make me. I create my leather persona according to who I am. Lynn and I may own an identi-cal style of harness, but we have altered them to match ourselves.

Leather and sm sexuality have radicalized my perceptions of sexual behavior. If a given behavior is safe, sane, consensual and fulfils your needs as a human being then it's normal behavior. All of us, straight, gay, lesbian, bi or fetishist create our own little ghettos and spend our time running from one refuge to another. We court danger by forget-ting that there are other worlds of which we know nothing. And often those worlds know nothing of us but lies and gross misrepresentations. By being open and comfortable about my gayness and my leather, I force others to at least acknowledge the existence of alternatives. It helps breach those ghetto walls.

BREAKING TABOOS
Janet Blevins, Greensboro, North Carolina:
I have never been quiet. According to my parents, I have always been on the fringe of society. I was supposed to be a good girl, get married, go to college. I did go to college but I soon realized, "Well, this is not for me—too structured." I hate being bored. That's why I've kept wan-dering off doing different things. I could never keep my mouth shut if I didn't like something. It got and still gets me into trouble. I always wore what I wanted whether or not it was appropriate for the event. Lit-

tle things like this soon give you a bad name in small Southern rural towns. But it was just meant to be that way. I break taboos without thinking about it. I know there are some people who will do anything just to be noticed or break any barriers they think they see, but I never did. I'm just a free spirit, just busy being me, like Idgie in *Fried Green Tomatoes*.

I came out to the lesbian world while I was briefly in college. I always knew I was gay but had never had the experience. Growing up in a rural town in the mountains of N. Carolina, I was surrounded by people who had shut their closet doors very tight. I was always so open about who I was that they didn't dare come near me for fear of being accused of being gay themselves. I was president of the student gay lesbian group and I met a girl. She was the co-chair of a group at another college. The sex was good but I kept wanting more from it. It was like I had this hunger, this intense hunger. She wasn't willing to do more than vanilla: "I do you; you do me; now roll over and go to sleep." I felt it was just a bit better than masturbation, having someone else present. But I really felt that something else could light-up the body, something with more rockets and fireworks so to speak.

Not too much later, in '84, I ran away from home with a carnival. I had just lost my best friend to suicide. We were the only two gay people that we knew in our town of Jefferson, way up in the mountains. To survive the pain, I just had to get out and see what was in the world. I knew that there had to be something different. I call it running away from home because I was leaving behind everything that I was supposed to hold as gospel, as Family Values. At the carnival, I worked as a leather vendor. I sold leather vests, jackets and brown tooled wallets and cigaret cases. I hawked them for this old toothless guy named Lester. Lester the Molester we called him. We would spend the week in one town and go the next to another town.

I'll never forget as we were setting up one Sunday, this girl walked across the parking lot with some other girl. When these two strolled by, I said, "Lester, those are two gay girls." And he said, "Well, how do you know?" "Well, I've got a kind of gay radar that can spot them. That's what's called Gaydar. Trust me, I just know." And he said, "Yeah, right." A few minutes later, both of them came up to the table and asked me if I wanted to party with them. Old Lester's jaw dropped. I said sure because the one had jet-black hair and deep, deep blue eyes that made me melt in my twat. No Problem! They came to pick me up later on motorcycles. I hopped on and we sped off and eventually got lost so to speak in things. She threw me on the hood of a car in a parking lot and had her way with me. It was very rough sex. The connection between SM and SEX occurred on the hood of that car. It was the whole forcefulness of it, sheer abandon yet I felt safe enough to let go and relinquish my sex to her. Yet I felt so secure. I know that it was also the leather. The smell was so intense. She had on all her leather and I had mine on. I hadn't really known what it meant to me and why I was attracted to it. I just sold leather and knew that it felt good to me. I hadn't thought of it as my second skin. I saw her everyday for the week I was there. Every year for the next three years, I hoped that I would see her when the carnival set up in the town of Fredricksburg—and I did. It was wonderful. I've been lost in SM ever since.

I came from a very child abusive background. My whole thing is my self-esteem. Through SM I deal with self-esteem. Part of SM to me is reclaiming myself. My mother's a Catholic and my father's a Southern Baptist, which made for a bad mix of things right there. Both of them had been in the military. My dad was at first a truck driver and then became the chief of police in a small town. So suddenly here our lives went public when I was growing up and I wasn't supposed to do anything wrong. SM gives me a nice combination of therapy and sex that I truly enjoy. It's positive for me because I feel the caring of these people. I mean there's so many lines of communication, so much before the scene and during the scene. They're always checking on my well being and it's building me up; it's not a degrading thing that says, "You're bad; you're ugly." It's more like, "Oh, you're doing well," or, "I like it when you do that." There's always so much positive and affirming talk during SM. There wasn't when I was growing up.

Things that I couldn't get out in therapy, I can deal with in SM. I find it comforting to undergo pain similar to that that I had suffered growing up. It makes me feel good. I know that this is probably hard for most to understand but I'm genuinely allowed to feel the pain and to experience it completely and it's ok. As a child I tried to be stoic and take it without complaint, hoping that my parents and others would get tired and give up. Now I'm allowed my feelings where before I had to shut them off. I never felt empowered to respond to something as basic as pain. My emotions were completely choked off. I think SM is bringing me closer to being a more sensual person. Without it I would probably not have sex very often because I didn't feel worthwhile enough.

I had long been attracted to tattoos and piercings. That's one of the things that set me aside from all the polite and PC lesbians. I wanted to do all of these things to my body. I got my first tattoo when I left town with the carnival and I kept adding on to my ear piercings. I had no idea that you could pierce and put jewelry into other parts of your body so I kept doing my ear till I went all the way around it. I was always sticking pins into my skin because it felt good. Now I've seen things at When Hell Freezes Over and at Powersurge where people had surgical needles stuck in rows on their bodies and I thought, "Wow, others do that too! Maybe I'm not so weird and strange."

In life you're always hemmed in by work and friends, always fenced in. SM is being able to go past those limits. In vanilla sex, you're only allowed to do so much. It's like someone has written a script and you're only permitted to say and do certain things. You can't ad-lib, make up your own lines or act out your own thoughts. In SM I can go past those restrictions. I like being scared. Being on the hood of that car, I was frightened, yet strangely I felt comfortable because it was so forceful. I'd never experienced that before. It shook away the sameness and I liked it. I wanted to do more and worse things. It felt comfortable to me, her arms around me, her body and all that leather. It was a blanket of protection with nothing else in the whole world. I didn't care if anyone else saw us. It was just her and me. Usually, I'm pee-shy. I won't do anything in front of anyone. Yet there I was on this car in an open parking lot, given over to a lovemaking with a bruising and a fisting aspect.

At first, all the experiences I had were with the motorcycle friends of the blue-eyed raven-haired girl, just like the drunkard-type biker gangs having fun in old movies. I really didn't learn much from her beyond the roughness, that it was ok to feel attracted to it and that I could feel safe playing that way. It wasn't until later on, when I went to the women's music festivals, that I learned the terms of things and about safety aspects when they held SM meetings. They didn't just talk. They had play parties where you could actually see people do things safely. A woman from San Jose took me under her wings. We had a good time at the festival and she visited me in the mountains. One year later, she flew me out to the West Coast where she introduced me to body piercing. We had a wonderful time together.

I became like a sponge. I wanted to know everything. I subscribed to *On Our Backs* and *Bad Attitude* and found every book and magazine I could. At first everything I knew I had learned from publications. Coming from a small, rural and extremely closeted town, I had no one who would talk about such taboo things. I started going to a regional g/l bookstore long before two of its male staff got into leather. I was known as "that leather person." I could tell whenever I special ordered books that someone had been reading them before I picked them up. I can't take responsibility for bringing out these two men, but it's funny to remember them in their preppie sweater phase before their boots, black leather and SM activism. For most people, you don't get to see what their lives were like before SM. It's nice having seen them on both sides of the fence.

Now that I've been into SM for a while, I've helped others explore their feelings just like the West Coast woman had helped me. One woman

41

had no idea what this was all about although she found the thought interesting. I gave her lots of stuff to read which was very explicit on certain subjects but also balanced and concerned with safe play. Then I showed her a few things about playing hard just to see if that was what she really wanted to do. It turned out that that wasn't what she wanted after all, but we had a great time exploring.

The mostly male Tarheel Leather Club that I joined and was eventually elected president of later allowed me to meet people from Atlanta and from clubs across the country. This was a new culture to me, I didn't know about these organizations. Talking with people who were very experienced and traveling to different events, I learned that some of the stuff I had read wasn't really true. It was only one person's opinion. With the Tarheels, I finally had a local group to share and talk with about these things.

Straight, feminist and lesbians strangely have the same idea about SM. It's a taboo. "Why do you want to hurt someone or be hurt? There must be something psychologically wrong with you." You feel as though you're pushed up against the wall. Even at the women's music festival, there's a small group of SM and the rest are clucking and disapproving, "How can you do that to your girl friend?" I honestly tell them, "Out of true love. I want it; she wants it. It's a mutual need. We talk about everything first. Nobody has anything happen to them that they don't desire." And they find that a hard concept. Usually it opens the door for more questions. Most times, we'll get into a nice discussion because many people are curious once they get beyond that barrier in their heads that tells them how they should react to SM in public. Slowly through small education exchanges, people are learning what SM really is.

Most of the straight males who find out that I'm in a mostly gay male SM leather club try to impose this fantasy idea of theirs that I'm the dominitrix of all these guys, that I can make them perform sexually whatever I want them to. They have this view of me cracking my whip like a lion tamer and these guys jumping through hoops. Straights just don't get it. I tell them, I'm a lesbian and a bottom. Most straights assume that if you wear leather, you must be the dominant one. I keep telling them, "No, no, I like it done to me—by women; it's so sensual." And a lot of lesbians who are just coming out mistake me as someone to dominate them. "I'm sorry, I don't do SM that way." I like being in a mostly male leather club because I have so many brothers who'll do anything for me. It's my family with all sorts of big and little brothers and a few sisters. They've stuck up for me when I've experienced trouble with some men who have difficulty relating to a woman in what they want to be an all-gay-male SM world. But on the other hand, I don't feel that I'm integrated with the all-female cliques.

Going to some of the women's sm events was different. I felt sometimes that I was over here in this corner and they were over there in that one. It's not all bad being out of that loop. They have their own power struggles and their own way of doing things. Some of it seems awfully screwy to me. "Don't sleep with her because she fucked so-and-so," as though political and sexual taste were identical. I once got a cutting done by a woman who I didn't know was on a lot of people's shit list. A short time later, I went to one event, where an entourage of people wanted to redesign the scar because they didn't like the woman who gave it to me. Very peculiar politics. But that's not limited to women. My deepest hurt has come from the fact that I've gotten friendship pins from clubs all over the country but for some reason, not one from any of my regional brother clubs. It's a very hard and disappointing thing. I wish I knew why people act in such small mean-hearted ways. [Friendship pins are small enameled pins of club colors—the logo of a particular club. Pins are often exchanged between members of different clubs as a token of camaraderie. Many place these on their bar vest with the result that some people have bullet proof vests from the numbers of pins.—*author*]

The sm image that most people have is a very scary Hell's Angel type, where there's killing and wild debauchery. Well, the debauchery can be fun at times, but the rules of safe, sane and consensual leave the real violence out of modern sm. During the planning for the March on Washington, I was delegate for the Mid-Atlantic Region for the National Steering Committee and the only sm/leather delegate from my region to attend. The first meeting that I went to dressed in my leathers, they were very stand-offish. "Well, we don't like this and that about you." It was clear that they were not using "you" to mean me, but the whole sm world. But by the end of the year, they learned that their fears were misguided and they've become much more tolerant. I think they were surprised at how well organized we are, that the sm contingent is really out there and has their shit together. I feel real good about that. It shows that we really are a community that can work together.

MULTIPLYING THE POSSIBILITIES
Mick, Ann Arbor, Michigan:
I came-out to sm in Chicago during a visit over a Memorial Day weekend. My lover of ten years had started exploring leather a few years earlier during a temporary separation due to job locations. I wasn't sure how to react. At first I thought, "Ok, this is just a phase he's going through and he'll soon get it out of his system and things will return to their familiar domestic harmonies." I convinced myself that this was just his way of avoiding intimate relations with others during our enforced

separation. Except that he didn't get it out of his system; he kept getting deeper into it.

Some things I just didn't understand. He'd tell me stories of play parties that he'd attended where he'd topped several people during the evening, yet he'd not had an orgasm. To appreciate the bizarreness of this, you've got to understand that the man telling me this normally needs to cum several times a day. I just couldn't comprehend how he could find SM satisfying if he wasn't having orgasms. That's when I really started to worry. What was SM giving him that I couldn't? I was terrified that our relationship was floundering. We'd been together so long and I felt we both had so much invested in it that I needed to explore SM a little. Perhaps I could get an insight as to what was going on with him. I just wasn't willing to watch helplessly as we drifted apart. I didn't want to experience SM, but I thought that if I could familiarize myself with it and meet some of his leather friends, I would feel more reassured. So I decided to accompany him when he went to visit friends of his in Chicago.

We attended a social hosted by Chicago Leather United, which is a social club of leather women and men. I found it pretty intimidating. After Ry introduced me to folks, we sat on some chairs on one side of the room, chatting. Suddenly, somebody he knew arrived and so he followed him into the kitchen to say hello. That left me alone nervously drinking my beer. A master sat on the couch opposite me with a collared slave at his feet. The slave had his tits and nose pierced with the master holding a chain connected to the nose ring. Whenever his master needed a drink, the slave would be freed to dutifully fetch one. That whole idea of a master/slave relationship intrigued me, but I was too insecure to say anything to them. Hell, I was too scared to look at them. I talked for a while with a young black fellow sitting beside me, but I was so fascinated by those two that I had to concentrate on not staring at them. It was extra difficult because the sunlight kept glinting off all their leather and metal, especially the slave's piercings. I gradually noticed that the two of them were staring at me intently. The slave looked at me, then turned and murmured something to his master who in his turn eyeballed me, then bent and muttered something to his slave who whispered something else back. Then, they both silently assessed me again, then whispered once more to each other. Gazing back at me, the master nodded in acknowledgement while the slave smiled and licked his lips. I mumbled hello, gulped my beer and fled into the kitchen where my lover was talking to some of his acquaintances. I was literally standing, clenching his arm. I remember he made some comment about me clinging to him like remora to a shark. I had to admit that I was excited, frightened, intimidated—and terribly aroused.

44

Later that evening, we met Ken, a topman whom Ry had played with several times. I found him an interesting, friendly fellow. We hit it off well. Somehow I didn't find him as intimidating as some of the other people I had met. When Ken proposed that the three of us get together the next night, I felt comfortable enough to agree.

Ry, Ann Arbor, Michigan:
What Mick didn't know was that I had already spoken to Ken about arranging an introductory SM session. I had planned on bottoming for Ken, figuring that Mick would feel less threatened if he could see what went on during SM play. I thought that at most he might assist Ken with restraints and the like. So after the three of us had kissed, sucked, caressed and done the requisite nipple tweaking, Ken grabbed the leather dog collar, but, instead of turning to me as planned, he faced my lover and held it open to him. To my surprise, Mick leaned forward and let the collar encircle his neck. As Ken buckled it shut, he glanced at me with a look of surprise and an eyebrow raised in question. I shook my head yes, this was OK, but signaled that we should proceed gently. I thought we'd just put tit clamps on him and maybe paddle his behind a little. Both of us were surprised at his capacity for bottoming. I clearly remember Ken's disbelieving face as he kept inquiring whether we should keep going. We bound him, buggy whipped his behind and reddened his back, applied clamps to his tits, dripped hot wax onto his torso, fucked him and almost got Ken's fist in him when he finally shot his load. Some people have a natural and incredible capacity for bottoming. I never suspected that my vanilla partner of ten years would have turned out to be one of them.

That was four years ago and our relationship is going stronger than ever. Mick is fond of saying that he'd never thought we could have become more intimate than we were. SM multiplied the possibilities for expressing that love between us.

Mick:
Most of our friends know about the SM part of our relationship. The most asked question is "How can you hurt someone you love?" It's difficult to answer because it shows that the person asking it believes that all pain is unpleasant. One friend, who was looking through an old magazine, saw a picture of someone at Inferno X whose back was striped from a whipping. He asked me, "You'd never let anyone scar-up your back like that, would you?" My lover knowingly smirked at me and gently explained that those were just welts—raised, red and angry but welts nonetheless. "Well, doesn't it hurt?" As I said, this is the hardest question to answer. Of course it does, but it feels great too. My lover

45

had already told him about slowly building-up the sensations so that the recipient has time to accustom himself to them, but our friend still didn't get it. I knew that he likes very hot curry so I made the analogy of getting used to hot spices. A dish too bland for him would burn the roof of my mouth off. However, I could push my pain tolerance limits and expand my pleasure for spicy foods in two separate but related ways. First, during a meal of progressively spicier dishes, I could work my way to one that would have been too spicy for me to have started with. And, second, if I kept eating spicy dishes for several months, I would eventually find pleasantly and exquisitely tasty the very dish of his that would have previously burned my mouth. So too, someone accustomed to flagellation may, rather quickly, want to accelerate to a full whipping, whereas a novice would take much longer just to achieve even a fraction of that level. In both the case of the spice and the whipping, the border between discomfort and pleasure has been moved for the more experienced person. So, while I still like my food bland, I prefer my sex to be very spicy.

IN SEARCH OF INTIMACY
Madoc Pope, San Diego, California:
Getting into sm was a long process and not as structured as I would have wished. I had no mentor to show me *the way*, no Mr. Benson. My first time in a leather bar was very brief. Within a month or two of my coming out, my boyfriend, Roger Powell, was amazed that I didn't own even a single pair of Levi 501s. (Imagine being a gay American without a pair of those?!) So he took me to the Leatherack store on the top of the D.C. Eagle, when it was on Seventh Street, to get a pair. The sales staff there apparently really knew how to fit 501s and the price was cheaper than anywhere else in town. I was rather apprehensive about going in a leather bar—even though it was during daylight hours on a Saturday! So I got to the front door, entered and marched double-time right through the bar, up the grand staircase and into the Leatherack without slowing down or acknowledging anyone. I left in much the same manner. For several years, that was the extent of my leather-sm experience, although I do remember getting incredibly turned-on when two guys opened their toy chest and fitted me with a leather cock-ring.

Today, I look back and laugh. I wasn't very afraid of the leather-sm crowd, I just hadn't much interest and so had little knowledge of them. As time passed, however, I became attracted to the mystique and the power that leathermen apparently had. I liked the turbulence they caused whenever they passed through. I also felt the need to submit and be taken by one stronger than me. By that, I don't just mean the physical; I also mean emotional and mental strength.

I entered SM through the periphery. I knew no experts who could teach me everything I wanted to know or thought I did, and the men that I met usually had little more knowledge than I. I'd try a little bit for a while and then back-off. I was fearful of becoming an SM freak, so consumed by the Scene that I no longer could have a normal life, afraid of losing my balance and becoming someone whom I could no longer respect. I had a lot of issues about that. I did a lot of introspection and was deeply troubled by my need to be so submissive.

I worried what that meant about me as a person. I was receiving all of society's messages about being strong, in control and aggressive and, while I acknowledged that they were society's hype, they still left their mark. Another unhelpful message that I got from some in the gay community was that those who liked to get fucked were somehow worth less than those who did the fucking. And I knew that I truly enjoyed getting fucked as a Bottom. I feared that if I did truly enter the SM Scene that I would somehow change into a sniveling, spineless, slave-freak like those I had seen at the bars or occasionally on the streets or at Pride rallies. It was an image that bothered me a lot.

It took a lot of time and advice from friends who were in the Scene for me to successfully deal with that issue. Basically, they told me to stop psychoanalyzing things to death and just have fun. A good friend from L.A. said that I would change no matter what and that I should just accept it. He said any worthwhile experience involves some sort of self-transformation, be that experience as profound as undertaking medical school, as light as having a perfect day of skiing or going truly deep in a scene. All of those things result in a changed person, in a transformation. I realized then that if I were to continue to grow and remain interesting as a person, then I would need to continue to change and transform in response to the world around me—including the world of SM. My fears, then, were invalid since I could not become something that I did not wish to be. If I were a strong, balanced person now, then I would remain one later no matter how deep or far I went into the Scene.

That thought helped me considerably, freeing me to explore this side of myself with greater ease and much more joy. It helped in my second coming-out which, in almost every way, was more difficult and involved more soul-searching than the first. When I had realized that I was more attracted to men than to women, I acted on that attraction and immediately accepted it. I was gay; I liked men; that was that—end of issue. No guilt, no pain, no regrets. I never understood why others had such a difficult and arduous time of that. Now I know. Friends of mine in the Scene couldn't understand my reticence. They were kinky; they liked SM; that was that—end of issue. No guilt, no pain, no regrets. I've learned from them.

A lot has changed, much has not. One of my first true teachers in this realm was a woman. I met her in an sm-Leather group in D.C., eventually becoming very involved with her and her husband. She taught me many things about the Scene, about sm and about dominant and submissive relationships—with ours being the first such for me. I grew tremendously, tearing down many of the walls that I had built-up in my life. I also became more comfortable with my sm side. The years have passed since then. I have met many others who are sm players, practitioners or "lifestylers." Most of these have been men, as have been most of my partners, and I have learned from them as well.

At IML a couple of years ago, I was invited to a party where the music was blasting and the drugs were a-snorting and there was quite a show to watch. Through the sea of beef, biceps, leather and tit rings, I saw this young, blond and blue-eyed innocent waif looking so out of place. We locked eyes and were soon deeply engrossed in each other. He was brand new to the Scene but his desire, curiosity and need out-weighed his timidity and inexperience. It didn't take me long to get inside his head and touch his soul. He inspired me to dominate where I normally submit. We backed off to another room that was quieter (slightly) and less crowded (somewhat) and I tightened my grip on his inner recesses. Eventually, I had him kneeling while I was straddling his torso, one leg on each side of his upper body, squeezing him with my thighs. It's a position that I first experienced with Guy Baldwin and one which I dearly love to be in. I discovered that night that it's also one I enjoy placing others in. It's very dominating to stand over a man that way, above him, over him and around him while being able to control him as your leg muscles are powerfully applied over the bulk of his body. Then too, his face is right at your sex giving him little choice but to see it and yield to it. At the same time, it's a very intimate and secure position. For the person doing the holding, it reinforces your roles as dominator and protector since no one else can get to him without going through you.

I don't think that he'd ever been in that position before. Its effect was telling. I didn't spank him, didn't whip him, didn't inflict any physical pain. Nor did we take any of our clothes off, nor did we break any of the sodomy or decency laws of the land. No sex occurred. To some, what we shared was vanilla compared to the seething action of the other party goers, yet it was deeply satisfying to the two of us. As I held him there and began running my fingers through his hair, he began trembling. His eyes grew wide with amazement and wonder as he looked up at me and asked what was happening to him; what were the sensations he was feeling. Within moments of my touching him, I had his soul in my hands and he was physically shaking, lost in it all. That is why I'm into sm. In those few minutes we had achieved something more "real" and intimate than most guys in that room, at that party, had ever achieved.

There was unfortunately no place for us to carry things further. It was near dawn; I was worn out and we were too intense. I ended it. I leaned over and ordered him to get up, put his coat on and leave—but without saying a word or making a sound. I gave him a minute to compose himself and then watched as he followed my commands and left. I went outside to the back stairs, watched the sunrise and cried. The wheel had turned another circle and I was crying with the joy of it.

I built myself to the level of actually attending Inferno where I had individual scenes in which I went deeper and further than at any other point of my life. For me, Inferno marked a very clear acceptance of my sm side. Yet, even while I was there, surrounded by some of the best male smers in the world (and that is no hyperbole), I was calling home each day to my partner, who is also my Mistress. I had introduced her to the Scene over a year ago and her natural dominance and intelligence allowed her to progress rapidly.

Even though I was surrounded by gay men—some of them very attractive at Inferno, I was yearning for her. I was getting the intense, high level sm that I craved but not that emotional intimacy that I needed. That is not very surprising for Inferno is not designed for deep, emotional, non-sm interchanges. Men go there explicitly for explicit sm. If they want the love as well then they come with their lover or they deal with it. I dealt with it. I had a great time but I missed her too.

For her part, she realized how close we had become and how much she needed me as well. So when I returned, we decided to do something about it. I needed a little time to accept this. I had always envisioned myself as settling down with a man, a strong, intelligent, loving, sexy, dominant man. Well, for over two years I've been seeking that perfect male partner who would fit my laundry list of desired traits and I've failed. Kim fit everything but the sex of that mythic partner. I guess that makes me officially Bi. She asked me recently if I consider myself gay. I told her "gay" because I'm oblivious to women but I notice all the men. The attraction to her is different.

Even though I am still very much interested in men, what she and I share is special; it is "supra-gender." What we have is above and beyond conventional sexuality. She is what I have been looking for in a dominant/submissive sm relationship (boy, is that a mouthful!). She is just what I need (at times), someone emotionally and mentally strong and who truly enjoys being in charge (at times). Together we are exploring this world and enjoying the journey itself as well as each other. I have been wearing her chain and padlock around my throat for many months. I even wore it home to my mother's over Christmas.

There are a lot of reasons why I am into SM. The power, the power-lessness, the freedom, the restraint, the intensity, the release, the bal-ance, the fun. On one level, I have learned that I need to give up control of my world once in a while in order to be balanced. I am under my own control in my "normal" life and I "balance" that by being under some-one else's control in the Scene. This provides me with a great deal of release and freedom. I no longer have to concern myself with the minutia of everyday life. I no longer have to be constantly thinking about what I'm going to do next. In the Scene, that is not my job; it's my Top's job. When I bottom in the Scene, I just have to be reactive—which is a drastic change from my normal routine where I am very pro-active.

Release and balance are not my only reasons. One thing about the Scene which has always attracted me is its explicit clarity and simplic-ity combined with its implicit intricacy and complexity. I enjoy puzzles of all sorts, and I admire the ironies of living paradoxes, and the Scene is definitely one. The surface image of the Top being in complete con-trol with the Bottom being viewed as nothing more than a slave dissi-pates in the face of the reality that the Bottom actually sets the limits within the Scene. Yet, upon further examination, if the Bottom is to achieve the true release he seeks, then he must give the Top his freedom and power and submit to him within those limits. I have found that type of balanced submission is very difficult to achieve, let alone maintain, yet, it is one of my principal attractions to the Scene.

There is also the intensity of the events. This relates to the release that I can achieve during a good Scene. I have found that when I am in an individual scene it can achieve a physical and/or emotional intensity which I have found in few other places. During a good Scene, time seems to dilate and emotions can become very pure, quick and basic. When things are right in a scene, I stop worrying about the rest of the world and focus on just what is going on within my personal world. Be it only as large as a candle dripping wax onto my nipples, as small as the cracker at the tip of a signal whip as it slices open a piece of my back or as deep as my Mistress's eyes as she applies one more clothespin to the already pained skin under my bound and outstretched arms. I en-joy that type of intense focus and find the clarity to be very relieving.

The emotional part of this is so wonderful. I have found that in order for a scene to truly work, nothing can be held back. I have to trust my partner completely—which also means that I have to respect him. This entails being very communicative before, during and after an individual scene occurs. When it all works, it tends to strip away the bullshit that normally crops up between people. Once I have had a successful scene with a person, I have found it so much easier to communicate with him outside of the Scene. Since we have opened ourselves to each other in a way that, in some respects, is more intimate than simply having sex, we now have that freedom to be very open with each other in other areas. Mind you, this is not all the time nor with every person. I'm not proclaiming SM as an EST therapy for the nineties that entitles you to speak your mind without a sense of tact or diplomacy. Nor am I saying that everybody into SM is angelic—far from it. I just mean that I feel closer to someone with whom I have only had a good scene than to someone with whom I've only had good sex.

The sense of illicitness is something that I like, the fact that I am actually doing something that most people only dare fantasize about. One of the stronger common bonds between SMers is the pleasure we take in doing something perverse in an otherwise vanilla—or normal—setting. Something as basic as using the urinal at work can give me an inner satisfaction because I have to take special care to position my cock properly and to direct the stream of urine so that it will not flow around my Prince Albert and soak my pants. (It has happened.) When I am in professional meetings, I also amuse myself with the thought that I am wearing that ring and none of them have a clue.

I also like to twist people's nerves, sometimes subtly, sometimes wrenchingly. Most people make all kinds of assumptions about me which I take great joy in dispelling one at a time or all at once. My bisexuality is one of those things and my practice of SM is another. As much as I enjoy the looks of confusion on my gay male friends when they find that my partner is a woman, I enjoy it even more when a "vanilla" friend (straight or gay) finds out that I am kinky. I think it relates to power issues. Knowledge of my SM attraction is a fact about myself that I like to control and ration-out. I like keeping people around me guessing for as long as possible so that just when they think they have me all figured out, I turn just a little bit and present a whole new face to them. I don't know; maybe I'm a sadist at heart.

INNOCENT DEFILEMENT
Robert Bemner, London, England:
I'm not at all sure I can say when I came-out to leather or SM because they're all sort of rolled together. I always did like the smell of leather. I associate it with the working men from my village in East Anglia. To protect himself, the blacksmith wore a leather apron which split when it came to the thighs. He had these huge, huge arms that I just loved and the sweat just poured off from him, completely soaking the leather apron. The workmen all used to wear these gaiters that came up to their knees and they would take them off and put them in the potting sheds behind the houses. I used to lie down among them and find the warm sweaty smell so reassuring. I liked to get fucked there by the farmhands

amid the smell of the sweat and the leather. It felt so comforting. Even then, I liked some roughness with sex. I often asked them to smack their belts against my bottom. I was so turned-on seeing their pants slip down so that the roots of their cocks were exposed.

The first time that I could say that I did something that could be described as a fetish was when I was about three or four in the late forties. England had rationing after the war so all the women were still wearing those plain sack-like dresses from the forties. Because material was so scarce, dresses actually tended to be quite tight. I had an aunt who was married to an American and she came to visit dressed in the latest style with a billowing dress gathered in pleats at the waist with a petticoat and a black patent leather handbag and matching stiletto heels. There was something that I found irresistible about her tiny leather shod feet poking out of all that flouncy material. I couldn't help myself. They were just so attractive that I got down on the floor beside her and started licking her shoes. She treated it as a game, enjoying it really, laughing and pushing me away but I was persistent. My poor mother was horrified and ordered me to stop but I wouldn't. She finally picked me up and put me outside just as she would the cat.

I didn't much think about these trends and tendencies as I grew older until this big man in full leathers on a motorcycle picked me up. It was in the early sixties and I was walking along the Thames when this guy pulled up on his bike, pointed to me and thundered, "You!" All the people around me just cringed. This was back in the days when motorcycles and leather were very much associated with violence. When I was younger, I had this very naive small schoolboy look, but with a gay edge to it. Everyone, including me, thought that he was going to bash me. Instead, he swung off his bike, grabbed me and said, "You're so innocent looking. I want to defile you completely," and then picked me off the pavement and kissed me. He took me home where he had this marvelous dungeon and did wonderfully nasty things to me. The roughness and the smell of leather brought back all those memories of when I was younger. This time they took hold.

As repressive as England tends to be, there still are areas which have a fair degree of toleration. Nottingham has had a reputation of permitting gay activities. There was a huge complex of a restaurant, hotel, dance floor and gymnasium that catered to gays from all over Europe. It was, at that time, the largest anywhere. The sixties were a time when massive urban renewal was being undertaken so that everything for blocks and blocks had been cleared and hidden behind barricades. Without even street signs, I was completely lost. I spotted a constable and asked him where this place was. He smiled and gave me directions just as though I had asked where the Post Office was.

Later that evening, my friend and I were on the dance floor when I felt a tap on my shoulder. When I turned around, there was the constable who had given me directions, still dressed in full uniform. He simply said, "You're coming home with me. I want to violate you."

I don't know why, but I followed him out. We went to his house where he handcuffed me to the bed, spanked me with his belt and used his truncheon in ways not sanctioned by official policy. After he came, he uncuffed me and told me to wait while he went out for a while. A short time later, he returned with six army recruits on weekend leave. The police know everyone's movements and, unless they're complete fools, they soon figure out people's sexual preferences. It wasn't difficult for him to find a half-dozen randy soldiers who weren't too concerned about what sex they were screwing. They abused me till dawn. It was absolutely wonderful. I never did make a conscious decision to come out to either leather or SM. They're things that just seemed to happen to me. Situations sought me out rather than me seeking them.

The one exception is when I decided that I wanted pierced tits. Well, in the early sixties, no one was doing it. I finally found someone who did ear piercings and was willing to try piercing my right nipple. Neither of us knew what we were doing. It was a surprise how tough nipples are and it did hurt. The first couple of tries were too crooked and so he'd pull it out and try again. He got it in straight at last. I really don't know how I stood the pain except that I really wanted a ring in there. When I finally decided to have the left one done, he'd had plenty of practice piercing other people so it was quite smooth compared with the first time. He tried to talk me into letting him do a number of other body piercings but the only one that I found interesting enough was the Prince Albert. You didn't see PAs back then. Times have certainly changed in thirty years.

Chapter 3: The Pretense of Senses

Every tree remembers his touch
and I hang from them
from "Apostrophe to Stanley"
—Jeffery Beam

The senses are receptors through which you perceive the world. Your eyes, nose, skin, tongue and ears provide your mind with details about your world. Through them, you discern the feel, taste, touch, sight, sound and orientation of your surroundings. But these organs aren't independent entities. They're biologic devices for intelligence gathering, nothing more than extensions of your brain that gather enough data for it to form a picture of the world. As with their electronic counterparts, they can be fooled, toyed with, given false information or even be overloaded. They provide the means for manipulating a person's reality.

Quite literally, people's perceptions are their realities. Alter, deny or sharpen those perceptions and you control their reality. Whether your play is directed toward physical sensation or psychological stimulation, the one body organ that you're aiming at is the brain. Learning to think of each sense independently will allow you to exploit each to the fullest. While you may not always take advantage of all during a session, be conscious of the possible nuances for greater creative play.

TASTE

Not often thought of during a scene, taste detects sweet, salt, sour and bitter. Scientists say that much of what we taste is actually what we're smelling. It's hard to discuss them separately since much of what can be said of one applies to both.

Everyone's body has a slightly different chemistry and metabolism. Your skin surface may taste saltier, oilier, or more acidic than others. This individuality means that your body will have a characteristic taste to someone else. The way in which your sweat interacts with your leather or rubber will leave a distinct taste on your skin for the discerning to discover.

Your body is equipped with special scent glands that produce sexual musk. Deodorant companies have convinced most people that sweat and bacteria will make you stink unless you use their products. If you don't wash for a week, your body oils will indeed turn rancid and, yes, you will be cheesy. But being gamy isn't a problem since generally Americans shower once if not twice a day. Mostly your spritzing is inhibiting or masking the natural "come hither" chemicals of the human species. These glands are in the armpits, crotch and nipples. You've hair under your arm and around your crotch to hold on to these odorous offerings. Their taste is a natural erotic stimulus. On occasions, some guys even secrete a bit of this musk from a tit that's really being sucked and nipped. If I'm lucky enough to get a taste of this musk, I'll deep kiss the guy. Most are surprised that male tits exude anything. Beyond that, the musk is a great turn-on, almost an aphrodisiac.

The taste of urine offers definite attractions for a lot of people. Some folks swallow every drop while others just taste it as it dribbles out of their mouth. Urine varies in strength. Your kidneys remove urea, a nitrogen based waste product, from your blood. They also take out any excess water. If it's a hot day and you've not drunk much, your kidneys will retain the water and produce a very concentrated yellow pee. That's just too strong for most people. Water sports typically requires a lot of very dilute pee and the most efficient method of achieving it is to drink beer. Beer produces a piss that's almost completely clear. Drink enough beer and you've both the quantity and the quality required for water sports.

The other way of diluting the urine is via an enema. Part of your colon's function is to absorb any liquid from feces before you crap it out. It's therefore very efficient in soaking up anything you put in there. That's why suppositories are an effective way of getting medicines into your system quickly. A wine enema is the quickest way to inebriate someone. (Don't use hard liquor because the higher alcohol will burn the lining!) An enema or a douching session will send your kidneys into double time working to remove the water that your bowel absorbed.

Urine is usually sterile but hepatitis and gonorrhea can contaminate it. As gonorrhea causes blindness if it gets in the eyes, never piss or splash urine in the eyes. The risk of HIV through water sports is very low but perhaps you might feel safer forgoing the taste and instead enjoy the sight, smell and feel of it flowing warmly over your body?

If you are planning on water sports, remember that mustards (broccoli, cauliflower), coffee and especially asparagus can scent and flavor the urine. They similarly affect vaginal and seminal secretions. In addition, what you eat affects what someone's tongue detects. Too much garlic will come through your sweat pores. The skin of meat eaters has a tang missing from vegetarians.

Foot fetishists and boot lickers are very often into the tastes that the objects of their desires can offer. Toe jam, smelly socks and sweaty feet can yield unexpected delight to the worshiper and the worshiped. I've known of a few foot fetishes that have begun with the taste of boot leather during a scene. The enforced licking of boots combines the psychological implications of submission with the taste of leather foot gear to form a powerful link in the submissive's mind. If you plan on having some foot adoration, don't dust anti-fungal powder or smear ointment over your feet. You would do well, in general, to avoid all deodorants, powders, lotions, ointments and colognes. A tongue coated with anti-perspirant or a mouthful of sun screen aren't exactly conducive to raw sex.

You can incorporate the taste of fluids and food into your play. Pass liquids, such as schnapps or beer, mouth to mouth when you deep kiss. Smear flavorings like vanilla over areas of your body that he'll be licking. Try rubbing a lime wedge over your dick head but take care not to burn sensitive areas like the testicles or anus with anything acidic or spicy. Syrups, peanut butter and honey can make for a very sticky mess in the playroom and are especially hard for even the hungriest of partners to lick completely off your body.

Taste is mostly perceived as a nurturing sense but it's an easy one to manipulate for reward, discipline or punishment. If you're served food or drink in a dog dish, you just can't help noticing that special SM flavor the food acquires. So what if it's really just a pulverized pattie from one of Ronald's hamburgers? The point is that you're on your hands and knees eating it like Fido or Fluffy. Think of it as SM nouvelle cuisine where presentation and appearance count more than the mere ingredients. Be inventive. Imagine the trip for both you and your bottom when you growl, "Pull that dog biscuit out of my ass crack, pig!"— especially if he happens to be a bank vice-president.

SMELL

Inter-related with taste, the sense of smell can distinguish among millions of scents. Most of the smells we associate with people fall into the categories of either natural or acquired.

Natural body odors are similar to those covered under taste. Sexual odors include the musk of the armpits and crotch as well as the protein-like smell of seminal (cum) and vaginal secretions. Raunchy smells encompass rancid body oils, urine, smegma, stinky feet, belches, farts and fecal matter. Even for folks who shy away from water sports, urine and cum stained underwear and jocks hold a special place in eroticism. The fetish for smelling soiled unmentionables is widespread, extending even to straights. Roth's *Portnoy's Complaint* created a stir in the sixties with its description of a young man masturbating with a pair of used panties pulled over his face. Raunch can be fun, but psychological conditioning might be more a cause for nausea than erotica. While I have friends who have attended scat parties, the slightest shitty smell makes me gag. I've changed too many diapers in my life to ever get past it, nor do I

56

really care to.

Acquired body smells often arise from something you've deliberately applied to the surface of your skin. Most sMers prefer natural body odors and find artificial scents a turn-off, therefore, only use them if specifically requested to do so. These include colognes, scented soaps and deodorants. Leave the perfumed scents to the disco culture, otherwise you may literally have people sniffing at your presence in the leather bar. Besides, as an asthmatic, I'm sometimes forced into a wheezy retreat by those wearing an excess of applied essence.

Acquired odors can also be exuded by your body from things you've ingested. (You are what you eat.) Better that all partners eat garlic rather than just one. And while alcohol produces keatones on the breath, beer does increase the amount and quality of urine produced for water sports. Certain foods will also cause you either to belch or fart. You may hide the noise, but where's that sauerkraut smell coming from?

Watch for sour mouth. Dairy products can cause a build-up of bacteria in your mouth. A little brushing and mouthwash is all that most need. Chronic bad breath is typically a sign of sinus infection and usually has little to do with oral hygiene. Some people are simply prone to reoccurring dragon breath. Physicians can prescribe antibiotics to help clear the infection. In some cases, corrective surgery to allow proper sinus drainage may be the solution.

Smells have such potent psychological associations that you can use Pavlovian conditioning on your bottom. Pavlov always rang a bell when he fed the dogs in his conditioning experiments. Eventually, the dogs associated the bell so strongly with eating that they drooled whenever a bell rang. The beauty of Pavlovian training is its subtlety. As long as an aroma is always and only present when you perform a specific activity with your partner, you can instill a conditioned response.

Imagine a top who only smokes a cheroot while doing a bondage scene with a particular partner. This same top always burns a particular incense during whippings with this partner. During tit torture, he heats up a bit of Tiger Balm with its fragrance filling the room. After enough times, his partner begins to connect each smell with a specific activity. Soon, the top can wordlessly direct his sexual thoughts. By merely smoking, he can cause his partner to think of bondage. By burning the incense, he elicits the contemplation of whips. The scent of fragrant balm leads to thoughts of tit torture. Thus prompted, but blissfully unaware of the manipulation, he may suggest the very activity that the top had decided on earlier.

Certain scents have long been used to establish proper moods. That's why religions burn incense as part of their ceremonies. Don't underestimate the power of association. One whiff of shoe polish transports former marines back to boot camp. Old Spice excites a daddy's favorite boy. Crisco's distinctive odor starts some fisters wiggling even before they're conscious of the smell. Poppers, grass, leather have scents that many associate with sex. Perhaps you can create an association of certain smells with specific activities. Be truly perverse and link the smell of new naugahide with his favorite activity.

With tobacco having fallen out of favor, individuals with cigars, pipes and cigarettes may find themselves re-evaluating their addiction. Although kissing a smoker may be like licking an ashtray, many others find it a definite turn-on. The cigar smoking Daddy is a common enough fetish that several cigar and pipe clubs exist. The smell of a cigar to them is like a hit of poppers. A former trainee of mine always got an erection at the sight and smell of a fine cigar.

TOUCH

Touch embraces the sensations of the inner and outer covering of the body that includes the skin and the mucous membranes of the mouth, throat, vagina, urethra and rectum. The sense of touch is able to perceive temperature changes (hot/cold), dry/wet, pressure/pulls, pricks, texture (hard/soft, rough/smooth), friction and hair movement. Not every piece of skin or membrane perceives all of these at the same level. The inside of your arm is more sensitive to hot water than your hands. Some parts of your body raise goose bumps when stroked. Know your body's erogenous zones. Understand that there are variations from one person to another such as unfeeling tits vs. live-wire tits. Sensations also change over the course of a scene as you accustom yourself to the feelings. Tit clamps can be gradually tightened; slaps and whippings increased in intensity. Some skin sensations are perceived identically by the body. Ointments such as Tiger Balm and Absorbine create feelings and pain similar to heat burns but without the tissue damage.

Fetish wear often focuses on a material's tactile nature. Leather is well known as being like a second skin. Lycra clothes are so thin that it's almost like being naked. Rubber and latex offer some interesting sensations. The elasticity of the fabric gives a firm constriction to movements as it hugs the skin. When someone strokes your rubber clad body, the garment spreads the touch in a rippling pattern that is eerily sensuous. (For the slightly out of shape, rubber wear is generally thick enough to hide the love handles, unlike lycra which tends to exaggerate pudginess.) Since rubber is water-proof, it does not breathe. Sweat cannot escape except by trickling out. Sometimes, pockets of sweat build up and then gush out in a warm stream. Many wear rubber boots that collect the rivulets of sweat so that they feel the squish of socks as they walk. Since a rubber clad body can't cool through evaporation, it increases sweat production to compensate. The water loss can be tremendous, so drink plenty of fluids.

HAIR REMOVAL

Hair figures prominently in a person's self-image. The absence of it radically changes the body's appearance and alters that self-image. One man, shaved for the first time, looked at himself in the mirror and observed that he looked like his great aunt's poodle after a clipping. Without his hair, he felt deprived of his masculinity and human status. At work, he felt exposed and embarrassed, conscious that he was so utterly naked beneath his clothes. With his suit and tie on, of course, no one could tell anything had happened. Business continued as usual but his own body sensations constantly reminded him. His pants caressed his denuded legs. His butt scraped against his boxers. His shirt sandpapered his chest and tits. A constant itch at his crotch kept reminding him of the encounter. He jacked-off in the lavatory stall several times the first day. He grew fascinated with his genitals. Without hair, his cock and balls seemed as if they belonged to another person, larger, more accessible and screaming for attention. He keeps things clean shaven now.

Body hairs concentrate most of our sense of touch to the area surrounding the hair root. Removal completely changes the sensations by effectively broadening the area of sensitivity. I first shaved in my twenties when I raced bicycles. I clearly recall the truly naked sensation it gave to my legs. One of my more sensuous memories is of wading into a lake and feeling the waves lap against my hairless skin. Shaving also scrapes off the top layer of dead skin cells anchored by the hair shafts which intensifies the perception of hot and cold.

Shaving occurs in many tribal rituals, especially those involving rites of transition since it makes people extremely conscious of their bodies. Among the Morsi of southern Ethiopia, young men shave their pubic regions completely to expose their genitals and to mark them as being temporarily different from the others of their community. Throughout the world, a number of other tribal groups include shaving of both body and head hair as a sign of passage into a new state of life.

Hair removal takes time and patience to do well. Stray and missed hairs, cuts, scrapes and an incomplete shave can be the results if you don't have necessary time. A decent pubic shave can take three quarters of an hour, while a full body shave will take the evening. It's a lot of work to achieve and takes constant upkeep. One friend shaved his partner over fifteen years ago, then ordered him to maintain it. Every morning since, he has dutifully shaved in the shower. Other than his head hair, I've never seen even a stubble on him in all these years.

Trimming the hair back with electric clippers greatly simplifies the task. Always use the comb attachment, otherwise the metal blades will chew folds of flesh, especially around the genitals. Have the person wash before you shave to clean and soften things. When you're ready to shave, keep a bowl of soapy warm water and some kind of shaving cream. Use disposable razors: they're cheap and safe. And better stock up. Leveling a forest of coarse pubic hair may require two or three. If you decide that straight razors are for you, practice shaving the fuzz off a peach or scraping shaving-cream from a balloon first. Then, practice on some delicate area of your own body. Straight razors also demand rigorous cleaning to keep them from spreading diseases from one person to another.

Cuts and razor burns allow for easier transmission of disease. Even the smoothest shave leaves nicks so don't cum or piss on someone who has been freshly shaven. Never use a razor on more than one person without sterilization. Disposables may lack the sex appeal of straight razors but you don't have to worry about spreading infections.

Take care when shaving the genitals. The dick is easier to shave if it's erect. If not, stretch it. The nut sac is very thin skinned and easily nicked. Try using a razor that's been dulled through use elsewhere but make sure it's not bent. When you shave the chest, put a finger on the nipple and shave away from it. Tit amputation isn't part of the scene. And lastly, leave the eyebrows alone. They direct sweat away from the eyes. Without brows, it dribbles right in and blinds the person. Supposedly, eyebrows take a very long time to regrow and people look weird without them.

One consequence of shaving is the itch of grow back. Not only do you suffer, but so will anyone with whom you care to cuddle. There's also the problem of ingrown hairs. To lessen these problems, get an abrasive sponge or rough cloth to vigorously rub the shaven areas. This helps the hair shafts poke through the skin and serves to dull the sandpaper feel just a bit. Routine shaving will gradually accustom your skin to the razor and the stubble.

Waxing is a means of hair removal that encases the hairs in a matrix of special adhesive. The effect lasts about two weeks and the new growth has downier hairs that avoids the six week joy of sharing your bed with a nuzzling porcupine. It's supplied as ready-to-use strips or in little tubs of wax which you heat and then spatula the sticky resin onto the skin. Waxing entails pain. As an SM scene, it definitely demands more from the bottom than being passively shaven. When the adhesive is pulled off, it rips the hair out by the root and avoids the sand-paper stubble of shaving. Follow the directions carefully. It's a slow process and care must be taken to avoid pulling skin off along with the hair.

Avoid cream hair removers. They're harsh chemicals that dissolve the hair shaft causing it to break off. They smell awful, cause allergic reactions in many people and can give nasty chemical burns to the genitals, nipples and anus.

When you're playing with a partner, learn to appreciate combinations of sensations. For example, if you stick your thumb in his mouth, he tastes your body salts and oils as well as any extraneous flavors and smells acquired by your thumb such as coffee, lemon juice or dog chow. He also experiences the psychological comfort of suckling. He feels the soft flesh, the hard nail, round fleshy tip, sharp-edge of the nail, the smooth nail surface, ridged finger print. You feel the rough texture of his tongue, the hard smoothness and sharp points of the teeth, the slimy lining of his mouth, the warmth and wetness of his orifice as it sucks your thumb. Now imagine that while you've done this to your partner, you've called attention to these details one by one. By guiding him through these individual sensations, you've sharpened the sensual experience. Which brings us to our next sense.

HEARING (SOUND)

Hearing is the most persistent of the senses. When you lose consciousness, hearing is the last to go and the first to return. (An important reason to always speak to anyone who appears to have lost consciousness.)

Humans have a strong sense of sound and of its extinction. What we hear is as important as what we see, so keep a balance between visual and aural elements. Although sound is always present, our perception of it is almost always subliminal. Sound helps us establish locality. The sound of the wind rustling leaves, waves on a beach or the roar of traffic conjures up specific images about your surroundings. If sound gives us no clue, tells us nothing about where we are or what time it is, then we're left with no point of reference. Cryptic sound frustrates our curiosity.

Sound also gives cues to the coming action. Moving things make noise; objects at rest are silent. These stops and silences create points of arrival and departure that set the pace of a scene. When you slap a paddle against the palm of your hand, you announce the coming of a new action in your play. Rattling the keys to his manacles can imply the end of bondage.

Manipulation of sound might also mean its removal from an encounter. I have two friends who are expert signers. They do a marvelous scene together as tops during which they talk to each other in sign language, leaving the blindfolded bottom "deaf" to their communication. Often the lack of sound is more noticed than sound itself. Its absence often arouses extreme anxiety. In nature, silence is a warning of danger being afoot. Sherlock Holmes once asked Watson to pay attention to the baying of the hounds. "But the hounds are silent." "Exactly!" The ces-

61

sation of noise is a cue for danger and causes anxiety—the proverbial calm before the storm. If all noise suddenly stops, you will unconsciously tense up. Isn't the quietest point in a movie when the monster attacks? If during a scene, everything suddenly falls silent and you've intended to make your partner uneasy, that's great. But if your tape simply ended and you stopped the action to flip it over or slide another CD in, you've disrupted the flow of the scene. Make certain that the music will be continuous. Murphy's Law guarantees the cessation of music will always take place at a crucial juncture and when your hands are otherwise occupied. Get an auto-repeat CD or tape-player. Don't rely on the radio. You haven't control over the music or the DJ's mouth.

Think of noise as a dramatic instrument. Understand the concept of a sound score as the integration and orchestration of noise with the activities of a scene. Define the action of the scene in terms of voice, music and other sounds. Is there a natural flow, say from warm openness to authoritarian control? How can you create this through sound alone? You may want to use soft comforting music and a gentle tone of voice to reassure and relax your bottom before you enter into heavy action where rough sounds will help promote the theme of domination and submission. Guide the subliminal aspect by planning the flow of the scene's music. Grasping the spirit of the scene with the right mix of voice, music and noise will ease your scene forward. A well thought out sequence of music and voice can tighten the otherwise episodic structure of a session and cue the submissive to the dominant's intent. A change in the music from fast-paced threatening chords to quiet tonal music may mark the transition from a furious spanking to reassuring caresses. It may also accelerate or slow the perception of time's passage. Sound can erase time or force the listener to be acutely aware of its passing depending on whether it's clean or dense noise. In other words, is it packed with lots of sound or simple and free of distractions?

Sometimes sound functions as "white noise." Its purpose is to hide other sounds. This masking works both ways: it blocks distracting sounds from the outside world but, equally, it covers up the noises you and your partner generate.

Many smers use music during their scenes. It sets the tone from comic to somber to threatening and oppressive. Vocals may be distracting especially if the piece is familiar to the bottom. This applies to Pop, Rap, Lite and Classical. But, it may enhance the scene if the bottom is riding the crests of the scene and the lyrics are appropriate. Then key phrases will stick in the mind and heighten the experience. For example, the rock soundtrack to the film *Metropolis* has a line that I first paid heed to when I was in bondage. "How does it feel to lose control? Feels like hell!"

Many sounds, especially music, are mimetic. This means that certain sounds or types of music are associated with particular situations, personalities or moods. A recording of the winter wind howling elicits an involuntary shudder from virtually everyone. Since music can imitate the feel of a sleigh ride, a flowing river or a cavalry charge, make certain that your selection conveys the correct mood. A light capering melody that conjures up visions of frolicking cartoon characters in your partner's mind while you're trying to capture the essence of Captain Bligh just isn't going to produce the intended effect.

Make certain that the music you choose is to your partner's taste. A friend of mine likes country and plays it during his scenes. I absolutely can't abide his taste. By the same token I know that I could select some great dungeon music from opera that would leave him writhing in agony. Try to find something that is acceptable or at least neutral to both parties.

Chants have always been popular. The controlled, repetitious nature of Gregorian chants helps reassure partners and promotes a meditative state. It was created by the early Church to free the mind from the cares of the world and allow it to focus on the actions and meaning of the ceremony. Although chants are good for a church-based fantasy, remember there are many recovering Catholics out there. Slavic and Greek Orthodox chants have both unfamiliar words and harmonics for most people. Their somber and ritualistic quality fit naturally with many scenes.

Percussion offers an elemental sound since its basis is the human heartbeat. Most people's hearts will mimic the rhythm of a drumbeat. It can be calming or provoking, subtle or pile-driving. The variety and artistry of Kodo Drumming can give an idea of the range and power of percussion.

From Andean flutes to Senegalese dance to Tibetan monks chanting, traditional folk music spans from tribal rites to religious meditation. The exotic nature of these recordings alone is worth a trip to your local library. The time taken to glean gems from among them will yield a payoff in the playroom.

Classical music remains high on many people's list. There's a great selection of many superb mood pieces but be careful when selecting the old familiar standbys. It's hard to imagine the "Hallelujah Chorus" being serious play music and "Night on Bald Mountain" may send your playmate into an unintended Disney fantasy. Go to a store that specializes in classical music and ask the staff, many of whom are music majors, for suggestions. You don't have to tell them what you're using it for but merely tell them that you are seeking a piece that conveys a particular mood. They'll be quite pleased to unveil little known works and composers that avoid the triteness of the popular masters. Investigate twentieth century ballet music. Dancers have a flair for drama and composers have obliged by creating works heavily laden with pathos. Many classical works have been rescored and updated for dance troupes.

The overall favorite seems to be New Age music, derogatorily referred to as crystal music. It provides a nice accompaniment for many SM scenes. Related to New Age is minimalist music. It revels in repetition and affords patterning from calm tracks that relax to menacing ones that intimidate. Philip Glass' works are the most famous. Jazz has also evolved along several lines, incorporating new harmonies and electronic instruments. Recent composers have created intriguing music that embraces some of the better New Age techniques. There are also special collections of music and natural sound that are intended for use during massage or stress reduction therapy. Depending on the nature of your scene, these may help relax a nervous partner.

Movie sound tracks on CD, tape or record usually offer cleaned up, abridged and overly polished performances but a great selection since this is music expressly written to evoke and enhance moods. A good classic music store will have soundtracks available from the old classic films, especially Hitchcock's. With the availability of hi-fi sound on videos, consider making your own compilation of music from video tape. Some silent movie scores are superb right off the video and may contain sound effects and longer, less dancey cuts. The rock version of Fritz Lang's *Metropolis* offers the best contrast between the CD soundtrack and that of the videotape. The sound direct from the tape contains nearly ninety minutes of music and industrial sound effects that offer tensions and contrasts which work amazingly well with SM scenes. Selections from porn tapes have the added advantage of "sound effects." Combined with the steady beat of the electronic music, it can really heat up your own action. I would advise transferring these cuts to audiotape for two reasons; not all the music is appropriate or current and the music is not always continuous.

Electronic sound effects are often thought of as just a cheap way of scoring B-movies. Yet, electronic noises can be highly unsettling and deeply disturbing because they mean nothing. Not danger, not safety. They are beyond human experience. They delay our foreboding, yet heighten our unease, making the scene starkly realistic and imposing. Electronic sounds are more suggestive than the conventional use of "dark" music with its predictable cues of foreboding chords.

Physical sounds other than music can be very effective. You create many of these as you play. A squeaking bed, clanking chains, creaking restraints, crack of the whip and slap of the paddle are sounds that can either be an annoyance or aphrodisiac. Collect wild sounds on a tape recorder by letting it record as you travel on the subway or sit in the park. When you play it back during a scene, you can create an instant bus terminal, subway, seashore, downtown office. It's a cheap way to fulfill a great location fantasy. Never underestimate the power of the natural noises that you produce while you move around your own playroom. Ordinary noises can become tantalizingly cryptic to a bound and blindfolded partner. The simple sound of a pitcher of ice cubes and water filling a glass can play havoc with his imagination. Knowing that something is being poured fills his head with possible scenarios. Is this sound a harbinger of an enema, or of ice being applied to his tits or of a water bath for melting wax? His imagination will create a host of images as he tries to identify sounds and then speculates on possible futures and situations.

Don't neglect your own voice. Sound obviously requires attention to the human voice to bring it into play imaginatively. Speech need not be talk ridden. It's a question of who does the talking and when. Use speech in close conjunction with sight and other sounds but guard against the tyranny of the human voice. Think of the purpose of your speaking—what is the meaning of a voice that conveys menace or hostility. Speech becomes a resource: when a voice is used to complement or contrast the action; with a special modulation or as a non-synched commentary (such as verbal abuse which may be divorced from any actual action); with alteration by varying pitch and timber, by changing speech patterns or through shifting dialogues (such as from rough interrogation to the reassurance of Daddy talk).

By changing your speech you can create different scenes. An interrogation scene acquires a stronger edge if you conduct the questioning and orders in a language incomprehensible to the submissive. (German, or mock-German, seems the overwhelming favorite.) During these scenes, the tone, pitch and timber of your voice convey the intent. It doesn't even have to make sense if the language is unknown to your partner. My neighbors once wondered why I kept demanding angrily in Polish how much eggs cost. Your voice, along with gestures, can strategically build or release tension. With-holding your voice when the action and visuals cry out for explanation can increase suspense. The dominant's speech can create a monologue that works as a psychic disguise to further set the tone, or to promote revelations (reluctant or planned). Speech may be a means of testing the other person's reaction to future scenes by describing what you'd like to do to him someday. You can use talk to recreate or re-experience some activity or to perform psychic masturbation. You can give erotic stimulation from dredging the storehouse of your personal relations. "Yeah, I like the way you do that. It reminds me of the time I had a hot young punk just like you and . . . "

Sometimes unwise acts attract us—acts which violate the guidelines of safe, sane and consensual. Talk can be the safe and sane way to act out otherwise reckless behavior such as a castration fantasy. This is where the fantasy of SM can help achieve a feeling of release from an irrational compulsion and keep the act within reasonable and repeatable bounds. Tom, who grew up on a farm in the Midwest, is obsessed with castration. One of his favorite scenes has him, blindfolded with xylocaine jelly smeared on his dick and balls, being led to the kitchen's self-standing butcher block. His nuts and dick are tied with a cord and painfully stretched over the wood, pulling him tight against the block's edge. His hands are bound behind him, his feet manacled. As the top talks about gelding him, he hears a metal knife scrape along a sharpening tool. Then, the broad edge of a meat cleaver skims the flesh of his torso and travels down his belly towards his crotch. He can feel the cold sharpness scratch his body hairs, so sharp, the voice tells him, that he won't even feel it slice through his swelling member. His genitals are now yanked so tightly that he feels as though they'll be torn out by the root. The cleaver suddenly thunks into the block as his stretched genitalia are instantly released. Startled and abruptly freed, he stumbles back. An arm encircles his shoulder as a hand stuffs something like a warm sausage into his mouth. A voice tells him to suck his severed dick.

Thanks to descriptive commentary, Tom has been able to experience "full castration" several times—safely, sanely and consensually.

SIGHT (VISION)

Vision is your major sense. More of your brain is used to process information from your eyes than any other part of your body. It's the sense that determines your perception of physical space. Think of how fun houses at carnivals make use of illusions to disrupt your sense of perspective. You've seen rooms painted and arranged to make a toddler look taller than her mother. Vision also greatly affects your emotional and rational reactions to environments and people. Blue rooms seem cold and oppressive while yellow ones seem warm and cheerful.

BODY IMAGE

Be conscious of the image and message that you're conveying. Pay attention to your physical appearance. Are your hair and beard neat or dishevelled? Are you striving for cleanliness or raunchiness? The state of your fingernails can tell a person much about you. If they're chewed, untrimmed, dirty, I'm not sure that I would venture far enough into a scene to see the feet. I don't insist upon a professional manicure but I prefer neatly clipped and filed nails. To me it's a sign of personal order and self-image. I remember being at one outdoor SM gathering when, from a distance, I saw the promising figure of a young man enter the compound. I worked my way towards him to check him out. He smiled and waved at a friend of his. The teeth were either missing or rotted. The hands and fingernails hadn't been near soap and his hair was so greasy his dandruff stuck to his head. I know that some cultivate this image and others seek it, but this guy had never learned basic hygiene.

Attitude and bearing convey a lot of information about you to others. Do your posture and demeanor convey self-control and assurance? Are you sober or so blitzed you're falling off the stool? Pay attention to your stance, gestures and other body language. You can meld into the corner, slouch in the shadows or stand self-confidently. Gum chewing, smoking habits and choice of drink can give others enough information to type you. One young fellow with a cigar fetish entered the bar puffing on an outrageously huge stogie, completely convinced that he looked like a tough customer. The whispered guffaws and gibes likened the cigar to his imagined prowess—ridiculously oversized.

ATTIRE

A Chicago leatherman claims that you can gauge the experience of a person by the style, age and condition of his foot gear. While his observation may reflect a personal bias towards feet, it does illustrate a general principle. My friend explains he never bothers with anyone who wears white athletic shoes to a leather bar. In his experience, they're often just tourists with overly vanilla tastes. Black athletic shoes at least indicate an attempt to mimic black boots and may suggest a desire to learn about leather. Brown boots, brand new black boots, fireman's boots, scuffed ones, well worn but polished boots—all tell him something about the wearer. It's not an infallible system, but it provides my friend with some indicators about people.

How you dress is as much a statement of individuality and preference as it is a comment upon how you regard other people. Dressing butch for a play session defines roles but can also signal to others that you care about their reaction. A uniform should be pressed and accurate (if police or military). Levi/western dress can be that of the urban cowboy, new and unstained, or of a real cowhand with grimy jeans and manure covered boots. If you're wearing leather, is it cleaned and shined down to the boots or old and smelly from rancid body oils? Each communicates something entirely different about you and your desires to others.

Know the hankie code and where to hang your keys, but don't overdo the advertising. Pick a color to flag; don't stuff five different ones in. Experienced SMers know that the color indicates a first choice, not an exclusive one. Rather than flying more flags than the UN, use conversation to fill in the details both for yourself and for a potential partner. Handcuffs, whips and cats have increasingly become sm design elements and conversation pieces, dangling from people's belts like lures on a fisherman's hat. The traditional view is that toys belong in the playroom but things change.

Anti-dress is becoming more common. While many smers consider leather *de rigueur*, some very experienced smers forgo the external trappings and deliberately avoid clichéd looks. Just because someone does not look or dress like a Tom of Finland drawing, does not negate his sm competency. Popular culture links sm behavior with leather fetish but the two are independent of one another. The growing popularity of leather has increased the numbers of poseurs of the Stand and Model school. A top notched smer might choose rubber, fur, cowboy, Argentinean gaucho or even Polo wear. So while leather may be the favorite garb, don't judge the book solely by its cover. Acquaint yourself with a few inside paragraphs before reaching a verdict.

Visual assessment reaches beyond the human body. The play space should also come under scrutiny. Look for safety factors. Its appearance should convey cleanliness both in terms of neatness and order. A glance around the playroom should immediately inform you that safety and precautionary measures are in place. Look for and inquire about condoms, nonoxynol lube, gloves and quick releases on bondage items. Is it a "play-friendly" environment with things near at hand or will someone always need to alter position or leave the area for something? It should be capable of sustaining the scene's fantasy. Can you really play POW Interrogation when tied to a colonial four poster bed that's festooned with pink satin and lace ruffles? Are toys concealed or revealed in the play space? Knowing that any of the variety of items hung on the wall could be used may add excitement for the bottom. Others may be frightened or panicked by such a display. A combination of displaying some things and keeping others hidden might be a good mix. Paddles, stretchers and weights may be hung out openly, but clothes pins, abrasion brushes and other toys kept from view. The bottom's uncertainty about the nature of a given item in use while blindfolded really adds much to the staged anxiety of a scene.

LIGHT

There are two schools of thought regarding lighting: one advocates close control; the other espouses a "Light is how you find it" philosophy. Since light can conceal as well as reveal, it can be used to delineate the perimeters of the play area. With a single light shining into his face while tied to a chair in an otherwise dark kitchen, the submissive becomes visually imprisoned to the small, bright area of light. Beyond that encircling wall of light may be an ordinary kitchen or perhaps the cold concrete of an interrogation room. Further, that single light shining into his eyes reveals him to the dominant yet simultaneously conceals the dominant from him. Light and dark are antithetical to one another, but not always as you would imagine. Dark is often charged with an ill-defined menace and may be isolating, yet its shadows can also be a comforting and enveloping womb. Light lets you spot danger, yet it raises your risk of detection and exposure to danger.

Light has various qualities. Different colors convey different moods and temperatures. Blues are perceived as cool and tend to heighten acuity, sharpening the sense of reality. Red light gives a warm feeling, yet is oddly both comforting and the cautionary color for danger.

Red light has some advantages in the playroom. It does not inhibit your night vision which is why it's used in military cockpits for nighttime flights. After about ten minutes in red light, things will appear noticeably brighter as the pupils fully open and the retina of the eye adapts for night vision. The open pupils add a devilish appearance to the participants. Violet wands have no apparent loss of light intensity under red light. This means that the electric flicker is as visible to the participants as it would be in total darkness. Red light is extremely flattering to human beings since it renders most blemishes invisible. The lack of other colors means that infected hair follicles and acne breakout appear to vanish. Most people appear to have perfect skin—very sexy. Red does not allow for sharp edge perception. The color softens edges of objects to the human eye and adds to a sense of semi-reality. It really does nullify the effects of acne scars and of aging lines. Red light does have some disadvantages. Welts and blood spottings are difficult if not impossible to see in red light, so have alternate lighting available for activities, such as floggings and canings, where this may be a concern. These spotlights may be track lights, clip-ons or goose neck lamps that can be pointed at the anatomical part under consideration.

Blue tends to chill mentally and physically, which may be a desired effect. It's considered the color of the moon when madness and things evil happen (werewolves and loonies). Blue light directly influences vision's acuity, making objects appear sharper and brighter to the human eye. It allows for easy detection of welts, bruises and blood since they seem to pop out under blue light. Unfortunately, every little skin imperfection and wrinkle also screams for attention. Because of its association with cold, blue light may provoke a psychosomatic case of the shivers.

Think also about lighting intensity. Brighter and harsher lighting implies a sharper reality. Dimmer and softer suggests fantasy and dreams. There's also the fact that the brighter the bulb the less the color saturation. A very bright red light becomes pinkish. You can increase the light without sacrificing the color saturation by placing a number of lamps with low wattage bulbs of the same color around the room. Four twenty watt red bulbs will give a bright but diffused deep red light, whereas a single red seventy-five watt bulb will render a harsh and hardly pink light.

Investigate different kinds of lighting. Other colors can be used for bizarre effects or disorientation (bug bulbs, strobes and psychedelic lights). Make sure you've asked about health problems before using strobes. The frequency pattern may induce epileptic seizures in individuals prone to them. Fluorescent is industrial but not at all flattering to skin. Veins, blotches and acne seem to be enhanced. True torture is making someone look in a mirror at their naked body under fluorescent light.

Direct or single point light creates sharp shadows with great contrast between bright and dark areas. Pinpoint is especially harsh, evoking an interrogation light. Shifting your position under direct lighting may require you to re-configure your lights in order to see what you are doing. Indirect lighting provides balanced illumination that can be dim but not dark. It has no sharp shadows and positions can be changed without having to re-aim light constantly.

BALANCE

Balance is a tricky concept. Often referred to as a minor sense, it's never considered equal to the five basic senses, although the phrase "sense of balance" is a familiar enough saying. Most people don't really give a thought to balance during a scene although many scenes have some form of disorientation, even if it's only the floating sensation of being blindfolded in a sling.

Humans have a simple mechanism specifically designed to determine which way is up. Located within the inner ear is sand-like grain floating in fluid. The position of this grain provides most of the information from which you determine your body's orientation in space. When you spin, this grain moves from its normal position and the result is a mild disorientation and slight dizziness. An injury to this area from a blow to the head can destroy this rather delicate mechanism. It results in complete disorientation producing vertigo with violent nausea and wild thrashing as the brain struggles to find its sense of balance. For this reason, never, *never* strike or cuff anyone on the side of the head. The injury may not show up immediately and if your partner happens to be driving a car when vertigo does hit, he may well lose control of the car with disastrous results. Even with medical care, the body and brain take weeks to reconfigure a sense of balance.

Balance is also determined by vision and by gravity's pull on the limbs. Blindfolding a person makes them prone to wobbling. Always steady them, especially when walking them to another point. Never leave them unattended, since they might keel over. Binding the arms and legs, as in a mummification, will increase the person's unsteadiness. It's not just the restricted movement that makes them want to topple. It's the loss of this part of their sense of balance which adds to their disorientation and contributes to flying sensation that some perceive. Have an extra person around to assist in moving a mummified person.

Chapter 4: Negotiating

He demands submission
As soon as their breathing hastens
he draws out

Red and swollen
        he finds
        that mouth again
        from "The Beautiful Tendons"
        —Jeffery Beam

First time encounters pose special problems. Unless you've the training of a social worker and skills of a professional arbitrator, negotiating is probably quite difficult for you. Dealing with your own shyness and embarrassment is hard enough, but often you're stuck with a lack of knowledge as to what exactly negotiation entails. Relax and don't be put off by its apparent complexity. Negotiation is one of those code words that everyone knows but few are really sure what it means. It's simply a meeting where each person expresses what they desire and want from the others and what they're willing to give in return. Most SM negotiations are on the level of a friendly chat. You just want to be sure that your partner understands what you expect to get out of a scene and you must learn his expectations. However you choose to communicate and discuss things, a successful negotiation should result in a mutually fulfilling agreement in which everyone is promised something worthwhile. After all, if the experience proves worthwhile, you'll find it worth repeating. Not every negotiated encounter is rigidly structured. It may be as formal as a slave signing a six month contract for training or as informal and non-verbal as when a daddy wearing blue hankie left meets a boy flagging blue right.

A bar is not the best place to meet people, let alone attempt negotiation. Many establishments play the music far too loud for decent conversation. The decibel level is not accidental; it's strategic. Unable to talk to one another, customers feel isolated and in their uncomfortableness they drink more than they would in less awkward circumstances. Adjourn to a quieter part of the bar or arrange to meet someplace where you're not forced to scream directly into a potential partner's ear.

If bars are your venue and you're the shy sort, try the non-approach. Don't go with the intention of meeting SM-man for a torrid scene. Instead, just drop in for a drink and some socializing. By purging the meat-market mentality from yourself, you'll be less on edge and more relaxed.

Set yourself the goal of talking with at least three people during the evening—even if it is only to comment on the weather. With even one person responding, you're still further ahead than if you stuck silently to the corner hoping for some dominating leatherman to pull you out of your shell. If others see you take the initiative, you'll be seen as gregarious instead of as a narcissistic stuck-up waiting to be worshiped.

THREE RULES

There are few hard and fast rules for negotiating. Mostly it's talk and compromise that eventually end in an agreement on activities and limits that are mutually satisfying. But before you can do that, you need to establish what you want, where you stand and what is and is not negotiable. The dictates of safe, sane and consensual express the mutuality of current SM practice. It requires that you be honest, informed and caring. You alone must choose what activities to investigate and decide how far to pursue them. SM does not mean Stand and Model nor Spray and Mousse. It's an informed interaction, so don't be afraid to speak up and ask questions. Don't badger someone into playing with you and never allow anyone to do it to you. Unless you feel that you have a rapport with a person mentally, emotionally and physically, the SM experience has no chance of really fulfilling anyone's needs.

▽ *Know Yourself*

This is the first principle. Before you enter into any sort of SM play, you must take time to reflect quietly and think clearly about your stance on a number of issues. Remember that your duty is to protect yourself at all times, so always err on the side of caution. Decide what you will and will not do. Most importantly, know what's not negotiable for you. It's crucial to consider what behaviors are too risky for you. Practices that you've decided are too dangerous for your physical, emotional or mental well-being become activities where the answer is "No"—end of discussion. Commonly, non-negotiable behaviors involve health and safety issues. If you've decided that rimming without a dental dam is too risky for you, you must be prepared, even under intense pressure from an insistent partner, to stick with that decision. Submission or dominance in SM should never justify negligence. You might need to prohibit any slaps to your face or verbal abuse because these remind you of an abusive parent. Even if you're the slave in a scene, your master should never infringe on areas that you've set aside as too risky. If he does, he's the one violating the mutual trust, not you.

Never let issues of personal safety become confused with issues of trust. Your insistence on following safe sex guidelines or of avoiding some activities altogether has nothing to do with how you judge your partner's character, ability or prowess. It does, however, have everything to do with protecting the well-being of both of you.

Any decision must be an informed one. Read, listen and learn. Become a sponge and absorb as much as you can. Make intelligent decisions based upon your needs, wants, and comfort levels rather than because of fear, peer pressure or an imposed guilt trip. No activity can ever be absolutely safe, so you must decide what risks are acceptable for you. You do this every day of your life without thinking about it. Despite the appalling auto statistics, you have probably decided that the risks are low enough for you to drive safely. You can't guarantee that you won't be involved in a fatal car crash, but common sense and skill diminish the likelihood to acceptable levels. Accidents will happen, but foolhardiness causes far more grief. Exercise responsibility for your own protection and remember, to trust someone else is literally to put your life in his hands. Just as you wouldn't ride with a reckless driver, you shouldn't play with a reckless partner.

Communicate your desires, fantasies and interests with confidence. Believe especially in your right to say "yes" or "no" without feeling fear, guilt or obligation. You have a right to your own fetish without someone belittling or condemning you. Don't let someone mock or shame you into abandoning your choice. It's your journey, not theirs, so be forthright about your interests and abilities. No one should ever pressure you into activities with which you are uncomfortable or whose safeness is a concern for you. A good partner will help give you the courage to push your limits—if that's your choice. Good sмers will not play with someone who is ambivalent or wishy-washy about certain scenes. They know that reluctant consent is not true consent. It must always be freely and completely given. Being forced, cajoled or hounded into a scene is only a variation of date-rape.

▽ *Know the Other Person*

This is the second principle. Find out if he's someone who can be trusted to respect you. Feel comfortable with him. Your safest way of meeting someone competent and caring is to contact a local club, organization or discussion group. Organized groups often establish standards that insure that their members possess a minimum level of ability and stability. Both *Drummer* and *The Leather Journal* carry periodic listings of organized groups along with mailing addresses and an indication of their interests or social leanings. If you live near a large city, check regional publications for these alternatives to the bar scene. They meet in quieter and less threatening environments. While the number of people present may not rival the crowd at the bar, you're virtually guaranteed to speak with more people who share your fetish than you would during a bar night. Many clubs and organizations have education committees whose members will be delighted to answer your questions. They may invite you to some of their activities or meetings. Many also sponsor seminars and talks that cover specific topics and often demonstrate various specialties and techniques.

Discussion groups tend to be just that; most don't throw play parties. Their purpose is to allow people to talk in a relaxed and supportive environment about the nature of their desires and ways of exploring and pursuing them. They may schedule special interest lectures and the occasional demonstration but many operate along looser lines with open discussion. The group's composition may be gay, lesbian, bi, straight or mixed. There's a lot that can be learned from these different groups, so don't turn your nose up because the sexual make-up doesn't match your taste.

Not everyone lives where these opportunities are available. Small communities and rural areas require greater effort. The personals have a jaded reputation but they can be effective tools for connecting with like-minded individuals in your region. Rule #1 is: never give out your address or telephone number in the ad. Papers and magazines offer a coded reference number that allows you to screen the responses. For the sake of your privacy and sanity, use it. Instead of meeting your ideal partner, you might end up procuring an unlisted phone number to rid yourself of a drunken pest who habitually calls you at 4 A.M. Rule #2 is: tell the truth about yourself. Don't describe yourself as a hot, young, hunky stud when you're an average fifty-ish chunky couch potato.

Computer Bulletin Boards are the most recent way of connecting with like-minded people locally, regionally and nationally. Generally, you pay a monthly fee for the computer service. Some just act as message boards; others let you pass messages back and forth; still others function as computer dating services. You do need a personal computer and a modem which allows your computer to access your phone line. However, you don't need a state of the art computer with expensive functions and megabytes of memory. You just need something that can send and receive a message over the phone lines. Even decade-old computers, which can be bought quite cheaply at garage sales, will work well.

If you're successful and you decide to follow-up on an interesting ad or response, arrange to meet in a neutral spot such as a restaurant, park or a quiet bar. Don't go with the intention of getting your rocks off. Try learning something about the person besides what he's "into doing." Small talk helps to establish a rapport and lets you gauge the individual's personality. Above all, be yourself. Save the role-playing for a future scene when you both can distinguish fanciful from truthful identities. Pretending to be what you're not will only destroy the trust crucial for

SM play.

If you meet someone in a bar, find someone who knows something about that person. Ask the bartender, members of local clubs who may be present or the bar regulars. If not, wait until a later time to play after you have gotten to know this individual. Negotiation may be spread out over weeks, months, or years. Prolonged desire will intensify a scene and if you feel secure with a person, you'll relax and enjoy it all the more.

A fear common among many beginners is that one may become a victim instead of a partner. Thankfully, true psychos are exceedingly rare. (The bigger danger comes from SM incompetents.) The first time you plan to play with someone, insure your physical and psychological safety in advance. Is this someone you have met before in the bar or at an outside function? If not, is he a member of a club or do club members in the bar know him or is he known by someone you know well? In short, who can vouch for him? Let someone know with whom you'll be playing and where. Not only is this wise, but it's your psychological trump card. You've insured that if the nightmare pick-up has happened to you, you've left an identifiable trail which may be your way out of a nasty situation. Tell the bartender, club member or friend and give him that person's name and number. If you follow the person in your car, copy down the license number of his vehicle and leave it in your glove box. But really, why play this paranoid game? If you've any doubts about a potential partner, don't take a risk. Wait until you're comfortable and knowledgeable about that individual. Actually, the commoner problem is meeting someone who promises more than they are willing or able to deliver. SM poseurs are quite abundant. Regional and national differences can cause some confusion in communication. As a rule, you're more likely to be underwhelmed than overwhelmed by that macho looking leather slut.

WET NOODLES
D.B., London, England:
During the early seventies, I had an opportunity to travel throughout the States for several weeks. Coming from England, I really wasn't sure what to expect. When I landed in New Orleans, I found first a gay bar, and then a leather bar. The best looking man in the place was a wonderful, older Tom of Finland man in full leathers who bought me a drink. I'd always liked older men and there was sexual electricity between us.

Then, all these people started coming up to me saying, "Oh, you're English! Look, I don't think you understand the situation. You really don't want to go with him. He's a pretty heavy top and he'll do all these nasty things to you." Well, I appreciated everyone's concern, but I *was* looking for a heavy scene. And I thought that everything they were warning me that he would do to me actually sounded pretty good.

I remember as we left for his home, those Southern leather belles stood and wagged their heads. You'd have thought that I was a lamb being led off to the sacrifice. We hadn't really discussed what we were going to do but based on what people in the bar had said, I had quite high expectations. When we arrived at his flat, the encounter failed to equal the billing. He wasn't a very convincing master when he ordered me about. More of a whiner, really. He didn't seem to know how to make his verbal fantasies really happen. It wasn't vanilla sex exactly since he bent me over his knee and spanked me. But it was hardly enough to redden my bum. I've had decent canings that leave welts, so I was quite disappointed. It's my fault, I suppose, because I didn't spell out to the fellow what I wanted. I had formed my idea of what would happen from what people had said. I do think that they really believed he was a heavy top. From their view, I'm sure he was.

As I became more familiar with the United States, I learned that the various areas of the States have different attitudes about SM. Being English, I'm used to people being very much reserved. I had a difficult time with the aggressiveness of people in New York who would suggest a scene before a proper introduction. On the other hand, I found Californians much more relaxed about sex but extremely odd. I had one person come up to me and say, "You've an amazingly orange aura today. It complements mine so wonderfully that we really must play together." I never quite understood all that.

While I can be assured that a black hankie means serious business in the Midwest, I've learned that, in the South, very often black means no more than a whipping with a wet, overdone noodle. It's what people are used to. As they say, these things are relative.

▼

Talking with someone also lets you evaluate their sobriety. If someone has drunk too much or is strung out on drugs, don't even entertain the idea of playing with them. Alcohol and other chemical substances impair judgment and ability as well as altering personalities. An impaired partner, especially a top, is a very risky choice. Not only is there the worry of him passing out, but he's liable to be forgetful. What's the use in negotiating with someone to have them forget your wants, desires, as well as your forbidden areas?

Try not to begin by asking the other person what he's "into" or what things interest him. That's too impersonal of an approach and puts the person on the defensive. He's more likely to dodge the question, or be vague or alter his response to fit what he thinks you want to hear. Instead, describe a hot scene of yours to him or ask him to describe the hottest scene that he's ever experienced or his most sensual masturba-

77

tory fantasy. You might want to point out someone in the bar and describe what you'd like to do with that person. (Pick someone neutral, like the bartender, who won't make the person feel undesired.) Ask him to do the same. Keep your talk on a personal level. "What really makes sex hot for you?" "Why?" "What do you get out of it?" "What erotic scenes would you like to try but haven't?"

Listen to the other person's desires, fantasies and interests, but respect his confidence. Never belittle him because of any mentioned interests. So you may find his enema fetish distasteful; he may think your foot fetish is weird. Offer ways that you can work together to achieve and realize these fantasies. Be brutally honest with yourself and him about your ability to fulfill his desires. Let him know your technical expertise, comfort level and interest in any prospective activity. Learn the same from him. Perhaps you have something new to teach him or he may have something to introduce you to. If you decide that you'd like to play, ask about any health problems, safety concerns and past surgeries. This gives you needed information and communicates to him that you care and can be trusted.

SM RAPPORT
W.M., Chicago, Illinois:
Of course, I prefer when one of my friends introduces me to someone. Having a third person who knows the preferences of the other two is certainly handy. We need more SM yentas to do match-making. I belong to a couple of clubs and I have a network of SM oriented friends, so I've regular outlets for SM. Still, I like to meet new people. Since Chicago is a major stopping point for a lot of businessmen, it's not unusual to meet a sadomasochist in town for a convention who's given the slip to his straight associates. In those cases, eye contact and a subjective assessment of the person—not just how he looks, but how he stands and conducts himself in the place—can tell me if this guy is experienced or someone wanting to explore SM or just a tourist. If he seems interesting, I'll introduce myself and ask him where he's from. I'll try to keep the conversation focused on him; people do enjoy talking about themselves.

Now and again though, things happen that seem like they're right out of a porn story. I was sporting red hankie-left one night at Deeks, when a handsome younger man wearing red-right simply knelt in front of me and started worshipping my hands with his tongue. Audacious introductions still do have their place.

I frequent two bars in Chicago. Little Jim's is a small neighborhood bar and Deeks is a leather bar. I actually like the non-leather bar better because it attracts a real cross-section of types from the gay community. It's also smaller, quieter and overall more conducive to getting to know someone. Both bars show homoerotic videos which provide a ready-made topic for small talk. I find that if I comment on the "actors" or their activities, it usually opens the door for some kind of sexual response. I try to guide the talk so that he tells me his favorite SM videos. From there, it's natural to ask if he's ever tried anything similar to his favorite scene in an SM flick.

If we establish a good rapport, the way is open for a more detailed discussion of SM abilities and interests. At this point, I'd say it's assumed that both of us have decided that the other is a potential partner for a scene. Before things go much further, I inform him that I won't do anything that could spread AIDS. The vast majority have no problem with playing safe and most agree that everyone should act as if all their partners are infected with the virus. This is when I spring the big one. I'm positive for HIV but I won't do anything that might pass this virus on to anyone else. Any virus that's in me is at a dead end. I won't let people suck me off and I won't screw anyone—not even with a condom because I got the virus when a condom slipped off during vanilla sex. My HIV status doesn't seem to intimidate most people, but a few are clearly upset by it. If I notice the slightest bit of uptightness, I leave the door wide open for them to walk away. If someone doesn't trust me enough not to infect him, then there's no way we could ever have a successful scene.

If we decide that we're going to get together, then we talk so that we both understand what the other expects and wants. I like to suggest clear-cut action so that we can decide who will be assuming what roles or if a turn-around is expected. I also ask if he has any problems or things that are off-limits. I've got a little list of my own. I had back surgery so I can't bend over or stand for very long. I also don't like anyone to touch my face because an accident ground glass shards into my face. It took lots of surgery to fix it.

My bedroom is equipped to double as a playroom, so often we'll head to my apartment. Sometimes, that's just too scary for newcomers to SM. So we'll just swing by my place to pick up a few items and continue to their place. That's OK because the location isn't that important to me. It's the SM space that you create in your head that determines how the scene will go.

▼

Be sure to agree on a plan for your scene. A scene begins by envisioning the ending or the goal. Without it, the scene won't have a direction and may founder. This ending will be continually modified as the scene's action progresses towards it. Since you are constantly altering your imagined ending, the final form may not be what you had originally envisioned. The important point is to have an idea of where you're heading. When you negotiate a scene with someone, don't plan it out in too much detail. Merely set down a proposed outline and leave the action vague enough to be flexible.

Think about who will be the author of the encounter. Is the effort of staging this session shared or is it falling on one person's shoulders? It really does help to think of it as theater; after all, why do you think it's called a scene? Just as in theater, actions and situations are significant, so visualize their unfolding. See it in your head. Describe it to your partner. Consider how you will create conflict, sustain suspense and achieve a resolution. Plan a line of action, establish interdependent activities and set the tone. Will it be satiric, serious, ironic or dictatorial? Decide what you'd like as the intended outcome emotionally, physically, psychologically. Orgasms may not necessarily be the ultimate goal of an involvement.

SM affects people deeply. Its disturbance at the core of your being has repercussions in your habits, responses and thoughts. Things, repressed or hidden, often surface in the space SM has opened. A particular emotion felt by you or your partner during a scene may not be deliberately elicited nor directly tied to the action. You instead may link the present action to another event whose remembrance triggers the rush of emotions. With a minimum of planning, your scene can put it in a context that makes it accessible for later reflection, discussion and understanding. In SM, insight may occur on either the conceptual or the gut level.

There is a very real danger of pursuing fantasy to the point beyond one's power to control it. Scenes are only a representation of human experience; they are not recreations of life. It's easy to fall into the mistake of blurring assumed roles with genuine feelings and states. If you ever acted in a high school play, you probably noticed how the male and female leads had a tendency to actually become sweethearts by the end of the production. Theater's powers are very seductive. Representation should never be confused with reality.

Just because you've agreed to play doesn't mean that your negotiation is at an end. You still need to iron out the fine print of an agreement. Unless you follow through, many of the things you had thought were non-negotiable may be disregarded and swept away as unimportant by your partner. I was invited to a fisting party where I found basic safety rules were not being followed. Gloves were not worn by tops and hands were not being washed after insertion—merely wiped on grease soaked towels. Cans of lube were being shared and some of the participants so drugged that they were barely aware of things. The situation deteriorated so that although I wanted to play safe, I couldn't. When someone tried to stick his ungloved, unwashed hand gobbed with someone else's lube into my butt, I left. The pity was that I got along great with all of them, but an unsafe situation had become decidedly dangerous. Don't be afraid to remove yourself from any scene that makes you feel uncomfortable or threatens your well-being. It's not worth it no matter how much you desire the other persons.

At the scene, do a fast survey of the play area. First Aid supplies, including a blanket, should be readily available. (If he's hemorrhaging from an accident, you don't want to waste precious time searching for bandages.) Check for minimal safety standards on the equipment, such as quick release devices on restraints. No burrs should be on the chains and no sharp edges on any metal. If there are wooden devices, edges should be rounded and well sanded. Digging slivers of plywood from tender and unreachable areas of your body is not generally a desired outcome of a play session. Ropes should look clean and unfrayed. The pulley should be the proper size for hoisting your weight. Clearly hazardous or perilous devices, such as naked wires that plug directly into the wall outlet, indicate an unsafe partner.

Look for signs of general cleanliness and order within the play space. Both are excellent indicators on how structured or chaotic your session will be. People who are otherwise disinterested housekeepers tend to be fastidious about their playrooms. If cleanliness of the equipment is a problem, you have a right to insist that devices and toys be properly cleansed. Tit clamps with dried matter on them or previously used latex dildos present a potential health hazard. Your duty is to protect your own health regardless of the situation. Walk away from potentially infectious encounters. If anal play is going to occur, better ask about lube, condoms and gloves now, before you're bound and gagged. Even after all the deaths, some folks are still using common cans of lube and others still try to stick their unsheathed dicks where they oughtn't.

You or your partner have the right at anytime to call an end to the scene. Please respect that prerogative. It's much harder than you might think. The ultimate frustration must be having a potential playmate change his mind shortly after arriving in your home, especially if the bar has closed. Try to be understanding and supportive. It's not easy when you're horny and your instincts are telling you to trash the indecisive little shit.

Pick your method of signaling both a halt and a modification to the scene's action, be it words, grunts or gestures. The signal for halt should be a word, sound or gesture so out of context that it will break the mood. If either of you becomes uncomfortable or panicked, call an immediate halt. Halt means just that. Stop all activity. All parties to the scene should honor the request immediately, discover the reason for the halt and correct it. If necessary, reassure or talk the person down from any panic. Failure to do any of these is one mark of an incompetent. A modification signals a change in the action. It too may be a word,

81

gesture or sound that indicates either an easing or increasing of a particular activity. A low, long moan might mean, "I love this. More, please sir!" A short sharp gasp could be saying, "Ease up a bit, sir." Make sure that you're communicating in common terms. It sounds stupid but if the bottom is really getting into a flogging and cries out with painful obscenities, should the top interpret this as a request to stop or as a verbalization of ecstasy?

Always adjust the level of play to suit the least experienced partner, whether top or bottom. Never set up a situation where someone will feel compelled to play beyond their ability to control the activities mentally, physically or emotionally. It's fine to push someone's limits; just don't dump them in unfamiliar territory and expect them to perform to your expectations. Instead of expanding someone's boundaries, you might elicit a panic attack.

Make an effort to communicate. Don't retreat behind closed-eyes. Private internal fantasies should be saved for solo masturbation sessions. Remember your partner! SM ought to be sensual and mutual. Share your ecstasy with him. If something is pleasurable, indicate it by writhing or moaning. If it's causing damage or becomes intolerable, speak up. You have a mouth; use it! Give your partner something to act on. If you're trying something new to your partner, concentrate on reading his reaction. Respond accordingly. This not only applies to tops but to bottoms who may be training a top. You might even expand your commentary to include a sounding-out of your partner's interest in other areas.

▽ *Set the Mood*
This is the third principle. The mood hinges on your skill in handling the elements that make up the scene. An SM scene is a paced sensory experience sustained by the participants in an agreed upon play area under controlled conditions. Manipulation of time, mastery of the activities and control over the location are important.

You can enter a scene in several different ways. In a tightly structured one, the dominant might issue a set of rigid instructions to the submissive detailing precise conduct, attitude and dialogue. A required regimen, garb or preparation (shaving, uniform or clean-out) may be stipulated. A specific situation or relationship (captor/POW, master/slave) might also be mandated. Alternately, a scene might have an extremely casual beginning. Two individuals might agree on activities with no formal conduct expected other than domination and submission.

You should discuss and arrange the location for your SM play. The physical location of play space may be public or private, indoors or out, urban or rural, formal or informal. It helps to somehow delineate your play space. Setting actual boundaries for the play area states that, for a time, this place is different than the rest of the world. This marking-off may be done physically through structures like an ordinary bed, a cage, dungeon, sling or a special "play" mat or rug on the floor. Outdoors, it may be within a group of trees or on one specific rock. It can occur through an apparent modification which may be tangible or illusory. You might rely on hanging fabric, laying out toys, using special lights or candles, burning incense or playing appropriate music. Recognize the contradictory nature of spatial perception. There is the theatrical paradox of limiting and defining a physical space in order to expand and redefine mental and emotional ones. By depriving a person of his senses, you can create the illusion of a different environment. A closet might just as well be an auditorium to a sound and sight deprived person. Any kitchen chair transforms itself into an interrogation chair when you're tied to it with a bright light shining in your eyes.

Assure a comfortable temperature in the play area. Adjust the temperature for the comfort of the person who will be the least active and wearing the minimal amount of clothing. A case of the shivers is destructive to a scene unless you're keen on creating an SM version of Nanook of the North. Always have blankets and towels handy. If your room is drafty, spend the money for a decent space heater.

The pacing of the action is important. Think of your activities as music. Very few scores are played at one monotonously set speed. Have a variation of quick then slow, intense then gentle actions that guide the mood toward the climax. Instead of minutes and seconds, time in SM play is measured in the scene's tension and contrasts. The judicious pacing of events lets you expand or compress time. Create the impression that much more time (or less) has elapsed. You can alter the perception of time by swift or slow movement from one event to another or by varying the level of intensity. Half an hour can easily seem like four, or four hours can pass by like half an hour. Remember as a child waiting for the arrival of a major holiday? In a wonderful agony of deferred delight, time seemed to creep by. Five days seemed like eons and a month was an eternity. By constantly focusing your attention on the approaching event, the preparations guided your anticipation. Time crawled, yet you loved it. Ultimately, the suspension of pleasure became pleasurable in itself. For myself, looking through the Christmas catalogue was an exceptionally exquisite exercise of enjoyable frustration. I remember becoming aware that the joy and fantasy of anticipation had become strangely more pleasurable than the actual arrival of Christmas could ever have been. Likewise, SM involves tantalizing delays and postponement of pleasure—in this case the pleasure of sexual release. His sense of time is highly vulnerable to your influence, so be highly conscious of it and pace his anticipation accordingly.

Set a length for the scene by selecting a start and an approximate end time. The exact time required by the partners varies from scene to scene and cannot be dictated in advance. But don't push yourself or your playmate beyond reasonable fatigue. Tiredness diminishes the impact of the play but, more importantly, it increases the chance of an accident. Keep in mind the adage that less is more. The painter Gauguin warned, "Do not finish your work too much." To ignore the proper time for stopping is to add irrelevancies that diminish the experience. The cessation point should be dictated by the nature of the scene and the partners' limitations.

At the end, never leave your partner alone. SM scenes tend to be ritualistic and profoundly emotional, so observe some sort of a "welcoming back." It may be a formalized ceremony or nothing more than an embrace or a drink of juice at the finish. In any event, it functions as a return to normalcy for you as well as your partner.

More experienced SM practitioners appear to bypass this entire negotiation process but many have known one another for a long time. The SM community is smaller than you would think. (I have met SMers in Europe whom I later discovered knew friends of mine back in the States.) Time and practice have given them a storehouse of ideas and experiences that make improvisation during a scene seem natural. Most have some specific activity in mind when they begin playing. They know how to go with the flow of a scene because they've learned to read their partners. All this stuff of negotiation needn't be so forced or formal. Eyes still lock across a room, energy flows, clothes are stripped, restraints snap and a jungle fuck is on. But serendipity in SM isn't solely a matter of luck. Experience, discipline and preparedness will allow you to extract the most when opportunity arises.

RAPE AND HARASSMENT

Don't think that sexual negotiating is always a gentlemanly process. In the leather world, cretins and predators exist who have embraced the idea that SM involves forcing yourself on someone. Sometimes, they're overbearing pests who won't take no for an answer. Other times they're sweet considerate fellows who make a habit of raping their "acquaintances." I'm over six foot and played football yet I've been sexually harassed several times, once to the point that I gave in. Worn down, I felt cornered. It was reluctant consent given less from a desire to say "yes" than from a lack of an excuse to say "no." It was a terrible mistake. I wasn't raped, but I felt used. When I tried to talk about it afterward, my male friends brushed it off. A big boy like me should have known better. My female friends offered me unequivocal and empathetic support. They identified immediately with the situation. They understood the circumstances of caving-in to someone's sexual advances and helped me recognize the conflicting emotional undercurrents that tore at me. They recounted their own clashing feelings and their ways of dealing with them. They helped me through a rough time that my male friends seemed not to comprehend.

Sexual harassment and rape are two fantasy themes that frequently appear in male SM publications. There's a degree of schizophrenia involved when SMers proclaim virtues of safe, sane and consensual activities while SM porn eroticizes rape and harassment. Many SM scenes also revolve around a staged "rape" in which the partners are actually engaged in a consensual fantasy that's only a representation of real rape. Some individuals cannot tell the difference between the fantasy of overpowering someone and the traumatic reality. Rape remains the violent opposite of consensual, safe, sane behavior. Badgering someone into sexual consent or fondling his body without permission is harassment. Reluctant consent is not the same as self-determination.

I don't know of any male SM club that offers help for victims of nonconsensual acts nor have I been at a run or gathering that held a seminar on the subject. As much as the dicta of safe, sane and consensual are touted, the SM community seems to pussyfoot around the issues of rape and harassment. As it is, only vague informal word of mouth warnings —gossip really—serve to identify culprits.

You will at some point be the unwilling recipient of some unwelcome attention. Disbelief that it's happening to you can result in a paralysis of action. We grow up in a patriarchal culture that doesn't teach males how to react to unwanted advances. Until recently, no one talked about the rape of men except sarcastically. Society gives us the message that a real man is capable of fending off an attack. Wimps and queens get sexually harassed and raped, not butch leather men. You've been taught to be polite and don't know how to tell some jerk to quit pestering you. In addition, when you're out cruising it does sound contradictory to demand that someone leave you alone. The rapist and the harasser play on this. They count on your own feelings and self-doubts to feed into it.

Don't be bullied or worn down. Politely, but loudly and clearly, tell him that you do not want him touching, groping or fondling you. A loud complaint puts him on warning and makes others aware of the situation. Think of it as turning a spotlight on him. Some will mumble an apology and slink into the shadows. Most will throw the accusation back on you, trying to portray you as the instigator. You asked for it by dressing provocatively or somehow soliciting their advances. You shouldn't be in a cruise bar if you're not looking for action. You're a cocktease with a problem. You're so wrapped up in yourself that you're just imagining that people are fondling you. As long as he leaves, ignore him.

Most folks in the bar are smart enough to figure out who the slimeball is. Sometimes though, the harasser will persist.

If he continues to bother you verbally or physically, don't resort to tossing your drink in his face or slugging him or yelling obscenities. Most of the patrons will have been oblivious to the previous activity. You'll be seen as the troublemaker and perhaps kicked-out of the bar. Instead, swallow your macho pride and complain calmly and accurately to the bartender or bouncer. It's not the way that Hollywood or SM porn writers resolve these confrontations, but it works. Establishments are very eager to maintain their reputations as safe and friendly places. The bar will either warn him or escort him off the premises. The odds are that the person will duck out of the bar when he sees you lodging a complaint. Depending on the situation, you might want to arrange for a friend to see you safely to your car.

If you're in the middle of a scene and your partner begins to overstep boundaries, leave quickly if you can. If you are bound, try and free yourself. If you can't, then you have to rely on your words and actions. As cooly as possible, inform him that he's gone beyond reasonableness. The key is to try to stay outside of his rape scenario and to snap him out of his derangement, if that's possible. Any visible panic or hysteria may feed his excitement of nonconsensual domination. If he's evidently turned on by your thrashing and struggling, go limp. If your loud protestations excite him, recite the Gettysburg Address or the Queen's Christmas message. In as level a voice as possible, let him know that he has overstepped consensual boundaries. Unfortunately, safe words, threats and reasoning mean little to the rapist. Many attempt to justify their assault by claiming that they were only fulfilling your secret fantasy and that you "really wanted it." It's the same tactic that all rapists use: they blame the victim for having encouraged or provoked the attack.

If you have been raped, assaulted or beaten, file a complaint. Rapists count on their victims remaining silent. Contrary to popular male belief, these people are usually acquainted with the victim and rarely strangers. If you can identify your assailant, your prosecution can stop him from harming others. Although men are the victims of about 10% of reported rapes, the police aren't the most sympathetic, especially when gay SM is involved. I would recommend that you go immediately to an emergency room. The police are less likely to scoff at you under the watchful eyes of an ER staff that has documented the evidence and provided medical treatment. Additionally, every major ER has social workers and counselors who can assist you with the emotional and psychological trauma.

If your assailant has penetrated you without a condom, you've the added worry of sexually transmitted diseases, including AIDS. Try to expel the semen onto a hankie or tissue and put it into a sandwich bag to bring to the ER for evidence. Don't douche! It only increases your chance of catching something. The hospital can give you a dose of antibiotic to ward off the common infections. They may also recommend shots to prevent hepatitis. You may need an HIV test in six months to check for infection. Sorry, but there's nothing preventive the ER staff can do for possible HIV exposure.

Lastly, get counseling. The trite way others regard the incident can lead to anger and frustration. The feelings of having been violated can be devastating. Rape Trauma Syndrome shatters many lives with symptoms of depression, fear of leaving the house and feelings of isolation, guilt, shame and self-loathing. Don't sink into blaming yourself. You are not the one with the problem, your assailant is.

INCOMPETENCE

No one enjoys labeling another as incompetent. Unfortunately, the world of radical sexuality has its share of unqualified practitioners in full measure. They range from the nervous bumbler to the affable self-confident schmuck. Incompetents can be identified by their attempts to perform beyond their capabilities, by their masquerading to be what they aren't, by their lack of standards and, most of all, by their lack of concern for their partners. Their dearth of knowledge, training and sensitivity makes them great dangers in the SM community.

The thing about incompetents is that they never seem to learn. They don't really care about the people they play with. They're only concerned about themselves. For them, SM is narcissism. In their hands, it's just a tool for self-aggrandizement. Attendance at SM workshops, demonstrations and seminars never changes the nature of their egocentric play. Incompetents aren't just people who lack experience. They're often people who have done a lot of playing, but who have never mastered anything, not even safety. Their self-centeredness gives them an air of confidence that can be very misleading. Most incompetents aspire to be the epitome of the concocted image of what a leatherman does. They've never learned to separate fantasy from reality and can't tell the difference between exploration and exploitation. If you are a beginner, don't try to hide your inexperience by bluffing. It's OK to be ignorant of something. Admit it and learn. If, however, you pretend to know what you don't, you've made a decision to remain ignorant, and that's stupidity. As the philosopher Nietzsche observed, "Against stupidity, the gods themselves contend in vain."

Incompetence arising from a lack of communication can be a real problem. Assumptions and unspoken expectations head the list. Somehow, many bottoms just assume that a top should be able to read their minds and deliver the fantasy experience of a lifetime. When things don't develop, they'll blame the top, claiming that a real top would have had the cosmic insight to send them to Nirvana. To hold someone accountable for a half-formed idea that wasn't shared beforehand is grossly unfair. Yet it happens frequently. Without exception, these folks know what they don't want, but haven't a solid notion as to what they do desire. They've also a tendency to treat tops as machines whose sole function is to service the bottom. Face it, when many submit to a dominant, they want to be totally passive. The top is left to plan, stage and carry out the evening's events. Topping is tough work. The bottom may be the one who is ultimately the one in charge, but how about making sure that he's treated as a partner rather than a slave, servant or machine? If you're bottoming, reciprocate. SM should be consensual which means mutually sensual. Inquire about his fantasies and do what you can to fulfil them. How about something as simple as a massage for his aching muscles after he's strained them while whipping you?

SM MIND READER
C.L.M., Raleigh, North Carolina:
I was invited to a play session by these two guys that I had met at a run in Atlanta. They were really keen to play but didn't seem to have anything particular in mind. I suggested abrasion as a way of searching out possibilities. They hadn't heard of it, so I explained it and how it could lead to different things like CBT or whipping or a number of other things. The one thought it sounded interesting so we went into their playroom. Hardly five minutes into it, he pulled off the blindfold and stomped out, clearly mad but without explanation. He refused to talk about it for several minutes, then suddenly began screaming that he didn't "have an itch that needed to be scraped all night." (He evidently didn't listen when I explained what I was going to do.) What kind of SM did I think that was? His real fantasy was to be dominated by an abusive cop and he wanted it NOW. But I was a lousy top because I didn't know that verbal abuse and uniforms were the only *real* ways to top! I stormed out angry and bewildered. If I hadn't been into SM for such a long time, this guy would have destroyed my confidence. I have to say though, I was shaken up for a while. I'm still trying to figure out what went wrong. If he knew what he wanted, why couldn't he say so?
▼

Also under "lack of communication" is the lack of response. When discussing activities, don't shrug your shoulders and acquiesce halfheartedly. That makes your partner feel as though he's on par with a TV program that you watch only because there's nothing better. Decide and choose. When you are in a scene and someone works you over, respond by moaning, writhing or wriggling a little. Give your partner some feedback. I've had people, whom I thought were bored with what I was doing, tell me afterward that they wished I had continued a given activity or intensified it. They couldn't understand why I had stopped so soon.

Both tops and bottoms can be incompetent. Being drugged-out or drunk dulls feelings, affects judgment and can lead to a partner passing-out or becoming sick. Incompetents can also be overly pushy, berating a novice to exceed his skill and comfort level. Bottoms can sin grievously by not trusting the top so that the bottom is constantly calling out stage directions. Dogmatism may cause incompetence by holding your partner accountable to your particular way of doing things, your private SM canon. This denies your partner his own style. If he wants to tie you up using granny knots or hang mismatched weights from your balls, what's the harm except to your tyrannical sense of aesthetics?

One of Ben Franklin's rules for a balanced life was sex not to the excess. Keep this as your motto and know when to call a halt. Trying to continue when one shouldn't remains a major SM transgression. A top was plugging a large dildo up an insatiable bottom when he noticed a spotting of blood. The top called an end to the scene, but the bottom forced the huge dildo back in by sitting on it. By morning, he had a slight fever but refused to go to the Emergency Room. Peritonitis set in (that's an infection within the abdominal cavity that occurs when shit leaks from the bowel). The man died in agony. He was a U.S. District Attorney for a major city. Common sense and education do not always go hand in hand.

Pretending to be more experienced than one actually is violates a basic tenet of SM. Honesty is the foundation of the trust necessary for one person to commit his well-being to your hands. The potential for a serious disaster or irreparable harm is always present. Often, injuries due to improper use of whips and restraining devices yield simple bruising, but a slight injury to the brachial nerve near the armpit can permanently paralyze an arm.

An experienced friend of mine related a horror story that had occurred when he was an SM beginner. A top had asked if he wanted to play with electricity. He assumed that this top knew what he was doing. Had he asked questions, he would have discovered that he was about to become guinea pig to a person who hadn't learned the basics of playing safely with electricity. This top produced a train transformer and hooked both leads onto my friend's silver tit ring. When the top turned on the juice, my friend felt nothing. So the top cranked the voltage up. Still nothing. They were mystified. They double checked it on the train and, sure enough, it worked fine. They hooked it back up to the ring and again nothing. They gave up. What saved him from cardiac arrest was electricity's propensity to take the shortest route which, since the alligator clamps were almost touching, happened to be through the part of the nipple ring outside his body. He was also lucky that his tit ring was silver. It has a low resistance to electrical current and so did not heat up. A stainless steel ring would have barbecued his nipple.

Time and experience alone do not guarantee someone's competence. Attendance at clubs, runs and sponsored parties does not automatically certify the competency of everyone present. At a well respected SM run, a self-styled top did a ball inflation (that's where a hospital IV of sterile saline is placed directly into the ball sac causing it to enlarge like a water balloon; the body absorbs the fluid within a week or so). The top grew bored with the amount of time that the technique takes and asked a bystander to watch the bottom while he ran an errand. He never returned and the bystander, inexperienced with IVs, had to remove it when the saline solution ran out.

Another person presents himself as an expert piercer but most of his piercings are crooked with a high infection rate. He did a demonstration in the basement of an old bar undergoing renovation. Besides the dust raining down and asbestos falling from rusty pipes, there was a lack of sterile technique. He soaked the ring and washed the penis with betadine. But then handled everything without gloves. The needle was steam autoclaved but handled in a way that compromised the sterility of the implement. Finally, he did the piercing from the inside of the urethra—into a raw potato placed against the penis! It's impossible to sterilize a raw tuber of all spores, bacteria and paramecium. The recipient was extremely fortunate; his Prince Albert healed without complication. However, what might the asbestos cause ten or twenty years from now?

At a well known SM club, a beginner listened as experienced SMers trotted out their horror stories of incompetents. One told of a fisting demo in another city where the bottom, normally capable of taking two hands, was forced by pain to grab the top's arm to stop his brutal fisting after requests to ease up went unheeded. Not more than fifteen minutes later, this particular incompetent waltzed into the clubhouse. Throughout the evening, this "experienced top" verified his reputation. He had no build-ups to scenes. Now, while some bottoms desire this, the recipient that night was a neophyte. A whipping started at full intensity. He didn't demonstrate concern for his bottom's needs or expectations—a perfect example of a masturbatory top.

I spoke with the bottom in the above case and asked why he didn't call a halt or request a modification of the whipping scene. His reply surprised me, although it shouldn't have. He's new to SM and the mystique of the club overwhelmed him. He feared being labeled a wimp and felt obligated to suffer any abuse in order to live up to the expectations of those present. In his mind, speaking-up would have demonstrated weakness. So, he "manfully" suffered the excesses. He admitted that the adulation wasn't worth the agony. Reluctantly consenting to activities simply to impress others is sham SM. It has to rely on honesty and trust, but it also has to be mutually enjoyable or it's simply not worthwhile.

A partner who constantly asks, "How'd I do?" is either suffering from a performance mentality or is too insecure. You should only gauge the success of the scene in terms of whether both partners are satisfied emotionally, physically and mentally. A good SM session will give a sense of repose, of being at peace. If you worry about whether you've lived up to someone else's expectations, I'd say you missed the point of SM.

I've focused on physical harm arising from incompetence but the damage can also be mental and emotional. Humans can be very fragile creatures. SM play strips the protective layers away from the psyche. Trauma, more damaging than any physical pain, can occur. Violation of the bottom's trust by a top with an attitude remains lamentably common. SM requires an acute sensitivity by the top towards the bottom. An inappropriate word such as "mercy" may have an unintended psychological wallop that reduces a person to tears and fright. A spanking with a belt can be reminiscent of an abusive parent. Regrettably, actions sometimes revive forgotten emotional hurts. If you cannot comfort your partner, cannot offer the consolation and support to stabilize a troubled companion, then you should not be in SM.

THE DARK PLACES OF THE SOUL
Mike, Chicago, Illinois:
I really don't get into formal role playing, master/slave, daddy/boy, though each certainly puts its stamp on a scene. I'd rather put aside or minimize the acting and concentrate on activities. Playing with the senses is the main purpose of an SM scene to me. It's the amplification of sensations in a very special sexual encounter. I feel my energy is better spent in developing real skills rather than acting abilities. Playing with someone on multiple levels of consciousness, emotionality and sensuality requires real expertise and a lot of sensitivity to the other person.

A lot of guys are just like their heterosexual counterparts. They're overly focused on one activity, say flogging and many of them will do that particular thing quite well. But it's the only thing that they do. And many times there isn't a caring development, an interplay of personalities and a building of intensity that assures that the bottom is moving to where he wants to be emotionally, mentally and physically. I've watched tops who display consummate skill and technique but whose focus isn't on the receiving individual. They might just as well be working over a store mannequin. That's not a dialogue; it's a masturbatory monologue by someone interested in demonstrating a particular prowess. And really that's just the same problem that heterosexual men display when they're out to prove their masculinity.

I try to alternate behavior so that for every rough thing I do, I offer compensatory actions. If I paddle someone's butt red, I might mist it with cool water. I did that after whipping this guy who's been a really heavy bottom for years and he jumped. He was startled both from the contrasting feelings and from the fact that no one had ever done that before. I may start out by ordering someone to lick my boots but compliment them on the fine job they're doing. Or if I direct them to do something in a certain specific way, they get the message early in the scene that I'm accepting control and that they can begin the process of ceding that control to me. I guess I tend to be more like a daddy that way. I make them work, but I give reassurance and encouragement.

Most people think of discipline as something rough, and it certainly can be. But often it's just a demonstration of your being in charge. Something as simple as telling your bottom to control his breathing during a clothes pinning, or affording that person a respite by ordering them to kneel as they grasp your legs and embrace your chaps. It's simultaneously taking charge and showing concern for your partner. It builds an incredible confidence between top and bottom.

Topping or bottoming, you want to help your partner let go of inhibitions and guide them to where they haven't been. There are a lot of complex emotional issues that we think that we've resolved, but really all we've done is bury them beneath the weight of the intervening years. The intensity of physical feelings can trigger unexpected reactions. The power of the scene may affect the emotional state of the person so profoundly that he may weep or be angry or feel overwhelming guilt. And it's all the more perplexing because the individual may not have a conscious focus for these feelings and quite honestly does not know why he's experiencing them. You need to be understanding and self-confident when these irrational feelings come to the fore. Don't leave the person. He needs the reassurance of your physical presence that sometimes entails talking him down and hugging him, and other times means just being nearby and respectful of the silence he requires to compose himself.

Don't ever impose pop psychology on a person. Cheap answers belittle what you've helped the person achieve. At the end of a scene, you're there to listen. They've experienced a catharsis and may need time to absorb the shock of that transformation of feelings. SM begins a pilgrimage into the dark places of the soul—the moral underworld that we dare to enter. It's a journey that takes courage, commitment and lots of communication with your fellow travelers.

Chapter 5: Putting It Together

SURETY AND IMPROVISATION

The moon is full and the bar has been packed all night. The smell of leather and sweat surrounds you. You glance up across the crowded bar and your eyes lock with another's. You smile; so does he. Your gaze drifts down his leather-clad body. He flags a hankie of the same color as yours but both it and his keys are worn on the side opposite yours. Swigging your beer, you decide to submit to him and follow wherever he leads. You saunter through the crowd toward him. Suddenly the lights dim, the bar patrons clear from around you to watch admiringly from the edges of the room. As you fall into his arms, he sweeps you effortlessly up and begins dancing to the orchestral strains that float from the jukebox. Swept away by pulsing hormones, you both improvise steps, gliding and dipping across the floor. With a pirouette, he swings you onto the bar, jumps up to join you and waltzes you down its length as customers raise their beers in salute as your booted feet spin past. Then, with a twirl, he leaps with you to the brink of the stairs that lead to the basement dungeon down which you and he tap dance in ecstasy and where the magic continues, happily ever after. Or so goes the fantasy. It makes for great cinema and pleasant wanks, but reality, Ginger, just doesn't work that way.

No one really believes that old Hollywood trope of two total strangers with no dance experience being so transported that passion magically inspires their feet—and in synch no less! Even professional dancers with years of training need to discuss, plan and decide what they're going to do and who's going to lead even in the most spontaneous of dances. Yet somehow, the myth of being swept away by "Mr. S-or-M" persists. Slapping on black leather or purchasing colored hankies doesn't imbue one with SM competency. Having simply watched videos, perused books or seen demonstrations won't do the trick either.

The necessary knowledge, skill and rapport for good SM doesn't come easy. You can certainly learn it through a long tedious process of trial and error, but the school of hard knocks is a rough one. Most people prefer learning from an experienced SMer or by a combination of reading and tutelage. This last is the best and quickest way. You can learn more in one year from the combination of books and a good teacher than from experience alone in ten. It's also much safer. Trial and error SM often leaves you more miserable than wise. Long wanderings will eventually teach you the short cut, but isn't it easier to ask directions or use a map?

Master and mastery are words often used more for their promotional value than for a true description of someone's ability. The hallmark of someone who has achieved mastery is his ability to create something wonderful seemingly without effort. Sprezzatura is the term for this knack of making a difficult task seem easy. Often, the artistry is so fluid and lucid that the untrained mistake it for simplicity and assume that they could do as well or better. It's actually quite difficult to maintain a sense of balance in combination with a smooth presentation that gives the impression of effortless creation.

Bob Buckley delighted in recounting a wonderful story of sprezzatura. Arriving in Los Angeles to demonstrate an abrasion scene, he discovered that his luggage with all of his implements was still in his native Australia. Forced to improvise, he stopped at a supermarket where he purchased toothpicks, cuticle sticks and a nylon nail brush. Pricking, tickling and tracing with these few tools, he managed to give the best demonstration of his SM career. The most impressive aspect of the story was his ability to control his nervousness. The distraction of an edgy, uptight partner often results in a scene being still-born. That he overcame his panic and succeeded in creating new techniques is the sign of artistic mastery.

Improvisation rests on the mastery of a medium, the disciplined use of materials and a knowledge of the steps necessary to achieve an excellent outcome. Proficiency and discipline mark competence in SM. Spontaneity does not mean artlessness. A true artist has mastered technical skills to such an extent that he need not apply them with conscious effort. His invention springs from depths of profoundly experienced emotions, mirroring the real obsessions, dreams and images from the subconscious.

COPING WITH THE MYSTIQUE
J.B., South Bend, Indiana:
When I was still new to SM, I had a friend who invited me to one of Hellfire's club nights. Now this club has this international reputation of sponsoring Inferno, the number one gathering for serious sadomasochists. Needless to say, I was more than just a bit nervous. As the time for the party drew near, I considered backing out, but I didn't. When we walked in, I had more butterflies in my stomach than I'd ever had before a football game. Coping with the mystique of Hellfire took a lot of confidence, especially when it became even more unsettling as members and guests watched as I started to play with another fellow. At first, I had a feeling of panic and a loss of focus. I kept thinking, "Do I measure up to their standards?"

Now, the clubhouse's play space is wide open and full of distractions from other people playing nearby as well as people talking and socializing in the area. I was also using someone else's bag of magic tricks. When you're not familiar with the particular toys, there's a tendency to start fumbling about as you look for something to use. I had to concentrate and really keep my mind on what I was doing. I began to do something intricate to absorb my attention and keep my focus on my partner. I did an involved cock and ball bondage with straps and expanded into full bondage. I finally relaxed and got over the feeling that everyone was watching and grading me. In the end, I had a good time and so did my partner. I just had to become confident and comfortable with where I was as far as my SM knowledge and abilities were concerned. Once I did that, everything was fine.

▼

Depth and unity of vision in SM is recognizable and beyond chicanery. You can have a great and satisfying scene without elaborate equipment but you can never be sloppy or indifferent and expect results. If you throw out any old thing, then you'll soon find your reputation tossed aside. Eventually, every SMer runs into the "smorgasbord" top who serves up a sampling of every SM practice known to them. He lacks the skill to combine and sustain the reality and truth that SM activities embody. Anyone who simply does what comes to mind finds that the supposed flights of spontaneous invention crash without take-off. Mere combinations of incongruities produce mere banality. In place of a compelling experience, the incoherent fragments never quite fuse into an imaginative whole that makes sense in its own right.

The expectations of SM fantasy are grounded in past experiences that reflect the habits of everyday life. A good SM scene taps into this past, reworks this realm and reveals a new world beyond expectancy. Don't be caught up in the routine and pre-set patterns or you risk turning into a robotic top in whose hands SM becomes no more than a computer program that inflexibly whirls along. Mindless and insensitive, Robo-top follows a predetermined course of action heedless of the situation or the needs of his partners. Like a technically proficient automaton, he's incapable of invention or flights of fanciful improvisation. How often can you be tied up and spanked without variation before monotony sets in? You have to keep your imagination well-oiled. The more that we expose ourselves to other people and experiences, the more that we have within ourselves from books, music, film, theater, the greater the storehouse of ideas that we can draw from. I worry about people who straightjacket themselves into one perfect activity as their personal signature. Life is too multifaceted to make a fetish of only one aspect. You should develop and explore. Above all, you must keep inventing.

95

UNCHAINING SM
Mike, Chicago, Illinois:

As time goes on, I find myself really getting turned-on by the fantasy aspects and the possibilities offered by role-playing in a scene. In SM, I don't merely want to reproduce what either my partner or I have previously experienced. I'm not interested in slavishly re-creating past scenes or repeating in agonizing detail the same experiences endlessly. That's like watching one video over and over. After a while, what's to be gotten out of it? I mean, isn't SM supposed to have that edge of the unknown, to be unpredictable? I'd prefer that my remembered experiences serve as a guide that leads me to produce something new that's really worth experiencing. Sure, some really hot scenes bear repeating but not in every little specific part. I've been with some people who think that that's the job of their partner, to provide them with a re-run of some incredible scene they've had or, more likely, that they've imagined they had. I want to keep scenes from slipping into routine or coyness. It takes an effort to isolate and free them from repetitiveness and the hectic pace of the world. SM takes time and thought. If it becomes just a habit or an obligation, it's reduced to something along the lines of left-overs or prepared food for the sexual appetite. That's a hell of a thing to communicate to your partner—that you can't be bothered with a well thought out SM partnership.

HUMOR AND IRONY

The projected image of SM is rather dour. Walk into any leather bar and count the number of stern, serious-looking macho men who stand around and pretend not to be desperate for companionship. What good does an image do if it results in going home alone at closing time to jack-off in frustration?

Humor affects us on all levels emotionally, physically and mentally. The father of masochism, the writer Sacher-Masoch, would incorporate ludicrous situations in his stories that marked turning-points for his characters. Humor has really been neglected as an SM topic. The fantasy shows staged at many runs and contests still largely feature stoic machoism, but it's refreshing to see spoofs arise from time to time. At one fantasy leather show, a participant pranced about stage as a mincing buccaneer-top administering a flogging to a butch sailor-bottom to the pizzicato strains of the classic Delibés' ballet *Sylvia*. It was a memorable counter-point to the dull seriousness of the SM weekend. Humor gives a sense of fun that relieves the long, dull stretches of seriousness that often are the only feature of the SM world. It provides for a varied landscape, a topology of ups and downs.

I've had some sessions with friends that have had a humorous mood from the start. Sometimes the pull of the moon and the phase of Venus seem to conspire to add a touch of lunacy in the dungeon. Once during a party, several of us had restrained one fellow in a sling and began to use a violet wand which produces a static electric discharge. Instead of gasps of discomfort, gales of laughter burst from the playroom as he found the wand tickled him even as it shocked him. As he bucked away from the wand, the sling would gently swing him back for another shock to his butt hole or a peppering of his genitals with little blue sparks. I simply held the wand in place. We all began laughing at the absurdity of the situation where his attempts to escape merely returned him for yet another eye-popping zap and another fit of giggles. Within a few moments, everyone at the party had poured into the dungeon to see what was provoking such funny business. No one present doubted that this was an SM scene. The bottom was in restraints and feeling the electrical stings. He, and everyone else, just found great humor in his predicament. It was seriously funny SM.

Humor isn't just frivolous. It can have several functions in a scene. First, it crumples false egos by whacking them with the truth. Humor often provokes a hollow ring when it raps against a false facade. People unsure of themselves are less able to tolerate a quip that strikes too near their inflated identities. Remember the adage: Fuck them if they can't take a joke. A well-balanced, secure person is more likely to appreciate quick-witted people than a neurotic concerned with protecting his image. Second, humor serves as a counter-point to the seriousness of the scene. It gives a needed pause that discharges some of the energy and apprehensions building between the participants and allows them to achieve an even higher level of intensity in their activities. In mellowing out the participants, a joke, a quip, a bit of lightheartedness reduces tension. A laugh really does produce physical changes that relieve anxiety and diminishes the stress of the flight-or-fight syndrome. By putting anxieties and fears into perspective, humor can restore a sense of control to an uneasy bottom. Third, it humanizes the participants and increases the level of trust. A little self-deprecating humor by a top can restore a sense of perspective to an overwhelmed partner. It works to reaffirm his decision to entrust his care to you and helps him flow with the energy of a scene. Increased confidence will help you both expand your limits.

Don't use humor off-handedly. It must be relevant to the situation and participants. Using humor out of context rapidly destroys the mood of a scene. Suddenly launching into an unrelated comedy routine or telling a joke you heard at the bar when it has nothing to do with the scene at hand will only add awkwardness to an already tense situation. Instead of relaxing him, you may cause him to question your mental health.

Appropriately used, humor can be a more powerful means of manipulation than the heavy-handed approach. As part of a farewell party for a club member, a tit-piercing ritual had been planned. The person to be pierced had paled, the piercer's hands had begun to shake, the attenders were chattering nervously. One club member had already yelled at everyone to shut-up and show the proper decorum. While he did succeed in gaining silence, the tension in the room leapt higher. Taking stock of the situation, Janet scurried from the room and then moments later, with a nurse's cap folded from white paper-towels perched ludicrously on her head, she paraded haughtily back in. With the solemnity of a surgical nurse, she requested one of the members to ink a black cross onto the cap, then turned and assisted "Dr. Piercer" with his preparations. Patting the piercee's hand, she pressed and rolled his head between her breasts in an exaggerated act of comfort. With this simple, yet appropriate bit of tomfoolery, she calmed and discharged the anxieties of over a dozen people within seconds, simultaneously relaxing the witnesses, the piercer and the piercee. The piercing proceeded with all of the participants correctly focused on the ritual aspect. That's an incredible display of control and mastery through adroit use of inspired nonsense.

CREATIVE PLAY

Boredom should never be part of sm play. It may be a form of torture, but your partner probably will not have freely consented to it. smers are usually quick-witted and highly inventive people. A visit to a hardware store to them is like being let loose in a sex shop with a shopping cart. A lycra lesbian, with a fondness for chains and padlocks, once pointed out her local hardware store to me. "That's where I buy all my clothes." Thinking creatively about play will bring a better sense of satisfaction. The following includes just a few suggestions. It's meant, as is most of this book, as a point of departure for you. Other variations will suggest themselves to you or someone may delight you by introducing a new one to you. You would do well to keep Drewery's rule. Never do anything to a person that you first haven't done to yourself or had done to you.

CONCEAL/REVEAL

Place your instruments on display. A playroom might have everything hanging from chains or peg boards. During the course of the scene the bottom might wonder which of those paddles is slapping his ass now. On the other hand, you might simply point out a closed cabinet and say that it contains devices of various kinds and numbers hidden in its drawers. Will you merely select a few items from it for tonight's session or will you keep going till all the toys have been used?

Use progressive disclosure. With the bottom blindfolded, take a pair of tit clamps. Rattle the chain and snap the jaws. Drag the cold metal chain across the chest or mislead him by drawing it over the genitals. Draw the chain over the lips and let him taste the metal. Use their jaws to nibble and gnaw at his tit before clamping. As you toy with each of his senses you reveal more detail about what you hold in your perverted hands.

MIRRORS

Hang mirrors strategically to give a real visual thrill to most people. Mirrors bring out the voyeur. Some activities like rope bondage are intensified by the bottom's ability to watch himself straining against his bonds. Others like to treat their reflection as a third person involved in the scene. They can also be a way of gauging progress. "How deep is that dildo? Well , just look over there." Blindfolding someone before you begin a clothes-pinning or a mummification or a shaving scene, then removing the blindfold at the appropriate moment lets them revel in their changed appearance. I've known very few who didn't enjoy mirrors. Only one has ever said that the infinity effect always made him dizzy.

PARALLEL PLAY

This is also known as "mirroring" or "monkey see, monkey do." Set up a scene where there are two submissives and possibly two dominants. Try mirroring restraints, toys and action with the bottoms facing each other. For example, you might want to place matching dog collars on them and chain them together with tit clamps. Perhaps you'd like to make one lick the other's armpits and then, reverse it.

If both are blindfolded, use sound effectively. Bluffing with sound is possible. A whack between them will be interpreted by both bottoms as having landed on his opposite. Exercise psychological control. What's done to one bottom is anticipated as a sign that the same will be done to the other. You might toy with their expectations by slapping one with a belt, then striking the other with a feather duster. A spanking with an established pattern can also be deliberately and randomly broken.

The adventures of *Alice through the Looking Glass* began when she entered the mirror and discovered an intriguing place. Parallel play is an excellent way to give a novice the courage and the desire to mirror the activities of a more experienced bottom.

THROUGH THE LOOKING GLASS
Frank, Milwaukee, Wisconsin:
Joe is a tall, middle-aged man with a bushy moustache. His rugged olive skinned face is impassive and stern yet deep-set eyes belie his gentle

nature. Joe is new to the SM scene. He has difficulty saying what he desires in his fantasies. A lot of play with him is still spent on trying to allay his fears and to coax his masochistic nature along. Yet, already he's become one of those bottoms who are sensory blackholes, the sort who suck up attention and from whom little comes back. Since he rarely moans or speaks when being worked on, I took to calling him "Old Stone Face" after Buster Keaton whose face never changed expression no matter what happened.

Joe and I bottomed one night with two experienced tops. Our separate activities eventually converged to where Joe wanted to mirror my actions. He became swept away by the momentum of events, saying "yes, sir" and "thank you, sir" without prompting. When my top began whipping me, Joe got really turned on. He even begged to get scourged and later was successfully fisted as he and I knelt facing each other and passing the poppers back and forth. Scourged and fisted! Two firsts in one night! Previously, he'd only experienced some light bondage and mild abrasion. Still, I could tell that he was a bit embarrassed by things. A tradition is that the first person to fist you presents you with a red hankie. Joe reverted to being too embarrassed to accept it. But hey, he pushed his limits beyond what I had thought he ever would. And all because he started copying me.

SHOW AND TELL

Two bottoms enter a mutualistic piggy heaven, each one simultaneously topping the other (or is it bottoming for the other?). The basic example is the classic 69 but it can range from double dildos to mutual canings. It can turn into a game where one person tries to go one further than the other. "You've thirty clothespins on your chest. Take them off you one by one and place them on me. Then add two more. I think I can take 32."

ROLE REVERSAL

Top and bottom reverse roles. Sometimes, it's part of a scene wherein the bottom "rebels" and turns the tables on his top. A lot of prison and teacher/student fantasies revolve around this theme of the oppressor becoming the oppressed. The nature of the power reversal is not always violent. It could also be part of a mutual turn around. "Well now, Daddy's taken care of his boy and now it's Daddy's turn to have his butt hole serviced. . . . "

TEASE

Do the unexpected to keep the person off-guard. Stroke the skin around the nipples with a clothespin as though you're going to clamp the tit. Suddenly fasten it on the lip of his belly button instead. After poking someone with a toothpick, stroke him with a feather. If done just so, he'll jump. I was blindfolded during one scene where I heard a click every time something pricked me. I thought my partner was poking me with one of those adjustable mechanical needle jabbers that diabetics use to prick blood samples from their fingers. Finally, after a slight pause, I heard the click and jumped reflexively but instead of a needle, a feather brushed my skin. Because I associated the sound with the skin prick, he was able to deceive me. Nor would he ever tell me what clicked as it jabbed me. About six months later, I found a toy pistol, a box of toothpicks and the feather in a drawer of his playroom's toy chest.

OUTDOORS

Stripped down play in the great outdoors has truly naked feeling that gives a near sensory overload. All your skin is exposed to the elements and everything seems extremely tactile. Sun, air, water and rain (very erotic with the sensations from the temperature, the pelting and wetness), all become very erotic. The noise of the outdoors is very subtle, yet quite marked. Real sounds have a dimension to them that the human ear can detect. Microphones lack the ears' capacity for handling unlimited variations in sound intensity. Natural outdoor sounds are often soft edged so that the wind seems to generate a dance rhythm in the leaves, not a march.

Playing outside in a country environment is decidedly different from an urban. The city has hard edged noises, is artificial and more stressful than the country. Both contain an element of danger and discovery. Nosey neighbors who call the police or hunters illegally invading private property may be cause for concern. Plan an escape route if one may be needed.

One of my more erotic sessions took place on the narrow balcony of a house overlooking the bay in San Francisco. A fortuitous planting of trees completely hid the balcony from either neighbors or passers-by. Stepping out to play on the balcony with the vista, the smell of settling dew and the rustle of the leaves was quite sensual and erotic. Below us spread the night lights of the city and bridge. It was the perfect fusion of city and country.

SUMMER CAMP
Gary, Birmingham, Alabama:
I really like to bring special partners to my eight acres by a small lake. It's secluded with a number of trees and bushes hiding most of the property from the road. There's a clearing which has several trees close together that lets me do outdoor bondage scenes. I've even worked out

a way of hanging a sling from the branches. I bought the property as an investment, but to be honest, I think a major reason was the psychological wish to fulfill a fantasy.

I'd had my first sexual encounters at the summer camp in eastern Michigan that my parents used to send me to. The staff kept a close watch on the girls but let the boys have a lot of freedom. We were allowed to pitch tents on our own—probably because they were glad to have us out of their hair. Some of those nights around the campfire turned into grand circle-jerks with the other boys. A very hot scene with the light from the dancing flames flickering over those tanned naked bodies with their incredibly pale butts.

What I think as my first SM experience occurred during my last summer there. This one kid and I had become buddies the previous year. He was a bit aggressive, not mean but kind of hyper and very physical. I remember that it was one of those really sticky, hot nights when there just wasn't any air moving. We snuck off to the lake for a mid-night swim to cool off. We couldn't use the camp's beach because the staff kept everyone off it after dark, but we all knew of a path that went right along the lake, so we went skinny-dipping there.

Of course, he started horsing around, dunking me under water and such. Pretty soon we were wrestling on the bank with each of us trying to pin the other. I was fifteen and a half and I think he was a year older than me, but I was much bigger. I kept him underneath me for much of the time. It felt wonderful with our bodies in intimate contact like that, especially with our cocks rubbing against each other's muck covered bodies. He kept wiggling so much that I couldn't pin him and he wouldn't say uncle, so somehow I started spanking him while holding onto his dick and nuts to keep him from pulling away. After several good hits, he settled down and quit trying to pull free. Instead he began bucking as he fucked my hand and shook his butt at me. He shot his load in my fist, then turned around and jacked me off. We laid there for a while, holding each other and listening to the waves and the night birds. The memory of that became a stock jack-off fantasy for me.

Nude wrestling outdoors remains my favorite activity. Often it leads to other things like corporal punishment. I like to assume military roles, pretending that we're out on maneuvers or that my partner is an enemy spy. I did one scene where I hung this guy from the tree with a parachute harness and did an interrogation scene with him dangling. I shredded and ripped his fatigues off and then did CB&T torture while he spun round in the harness like a mobile. I had also cut a switch from a sapling and struck his ass and backside each time they floated past me. The sound of the trees rustling through the leaves and the feel of the sun made the whole thing a real turn on. I really like playing outside when

102

it's warm and the wind is really gusty. The approach of a really good thunderstorm adds an incredible rush. It's a sound and fury that indoor play just can't have.

▼

There are a few cautions if you play in the outdoors: Make sure that you have a first aid kit. If you're going to play in the woods and fields, you should know your plants! Poison ivy, sumac and oak can ruin a scene. Watch out for sunburn, dehydration and know how to recognize and prevent both hyper- and hypothermia. Heat stroke and freezing are not part of a sane or safe scene. Have sunscreen, blankets, towels and liquids handy. Be aware of allergies and bugs such as bees, wasps and fire ants. Tick searches can be a fun way to conclude your play session. Mosquitoes, too, are a nuisance in many parts of North America and although a roll in the meadow sounds inviting, chiggers may be lurking on the grass. These are tiny mite-like creatures that burrow under the skin where they cause a pimple-like reaction that itches and weeps. They can't survive in humans, so they promptly die. Unfortunately, it takes a couple of weeks for your body to dissolve their bodies. In the meantime, you've got acute itching. Chiggers are mostly a problem in the southern regions of the U.S., but occasionally summer weather favors outbreaks in the north as well.

CLUBS, ORGANIZATIONS AND GDIs

Clubs and organizations exist for a basic social reason, to provide a framework in which you can interact with others of similar interests. Their small membership allows everyone to know their fellows personally, something that society as a whole is just too big for. Clubs and organizations provide a way of reclaiming the affirmation once provided by the smaller, more manageable societies of the past.

Most people join clubs to meet like-minded individuals and to feel connected with a community that welcomes them. They find identity in clubs, discover an outlet for their talents and receive recognition for their contributions, often rising to a position of authority and respect. Clubs offer people a chance to prove themselves at tasks for which they would never otherwise have the opportunity. A truck driver can write an article for the newsletter and be taken seriously. An auto worker can excel as head of an education committee. They also allow different levels of society to mix without the cultural stratification that separates blue collar from white collar. SM groups have often been at the forefront of fundraising and civil rights work for the larger gay/lesbian community. SM/leather clubs and organizations function as local social units that often tap into various regional and world-wide affiliations and support networks. While memberships have increased over the last decade, the community is still small. Interactions between different clubs are frequent and numerous. The monthly list of events, runs and seminars is astounding. The companionship, advice and news shared at these events help individuals living in even remote areas of the country feel connected to a larger group. (Runs are a vestige from the days that leather clubs were synonymous with motorcycle clubs. A run was a getting together to ride and socialize with other bikers. These days, few members of most clubs have ever been on a motorcycle, much less owned one.)

By joining or associating with an organized group you also open the road for an accelerated learning process as the experiences and resources of the group become available to you. Most clubs promote sm education by supporting meetings and discussion groups and by offering demonstrations of techniques by knowledgeable sm practitioners. The educational opportunities extend beyond the mere how-to. Contact with others opens the possibility of learning about sm philosophy, its history and getting involved in the struggle for equal rights. Reading groups, runs, parties and invitation-only affairs will help integrate you into the cohesive group.

Don't join a club simply to tap into a pool of possible dating material or just because you've the hots for a particular member's member. Nor should you think that joining a certain group will make you instantly popular. Clubs are social organizations with their own pecking orders and cliques. It takes time to establish your identity within the group.

A down-side exists to all organized groups whether straight, mainline g/l or sm/leather. Petty political agendas have a way of screwing up many fine organizations. Clubs are like all bureaucracies. They begin as tools to accomplish certain tasks or reach particular goals, but gradually they can become focused on their own existence with their membership more concerned with who should be allowed in and who excluded. Many clubs can get bogged down in arguments over minute points of order with political rivalries and conformist dogmas leading to a lack of focus and a breakdown in the group's cohesion. You're also guaranteed to meet egomaniacs who believe that only they have the messianic vision to lead others. Listening to them, you'd think that the fate of the four inner planets hung in the balance. This tunnel vision of limited views can seep through an entire club or region when people forget that their organization is just one small social unit that fits into the larger world.

Sadly, gay and lesbian organizations seem particularly vulnerable to group psychosis. When the wrong mix of people assembles in a room, they seem determined to rip themselves apart. The viciousness that we can unleash against each other is truly terrifying. One woman explained it as the anger of an oppressed group feeding in frustration on itself. Unable to pummel the real enemy, it transfers its rage to available targets. Like trapped animals under stress, we maim ourselves.

Integrity is a word that comes from Latin and means whole or intact. It's often bandied about in the SM speech. One cynic remarked that whenever he hears someone invoking it, he checks on the whereabouts of his valuables. Whether you're an independent or a member of a club or organization, integrity begins with you. You, not the group, are the guardian of truth as you see it, especially of unpleasant truths that rouse the ire of your "brothers and sisters." Uncomfortable, politically incorrect truths may place you briefly in the "enemy's camp." In any organization, yours must be the voice of an individual, not the mouthpiece of a clique, dogma or faction. To be an SMer requires patience and the courage to stand alone for what you perceive as truth without either intimidating or being intimidated. In the short run, you may feel the brunt of unpopularity, but here's the paradox. People need to know that someone has the integrity to articulate what they themselves really feel and think, rather than saying what's expected or most comfortable or favorable to the group. It takes time but what begins as the voice of one, often becomes that of many.

SM integrity requires the fierce independence of the individual's unique vision. The group may be needed for protection, nurturing and a sense of community, but it has no right to stifle the individual's voice. Groups often settle into complacency, finding it less demanding, less troublesome to bless and support mediocrity. The rally cry too often becomes, "Dare to be adequate; strive for mediocrity." Satisfied with the status quo, such groups have already begun to waste away. Without the infusion of fresh ideas, they are doomed.

To avoid a traumatic mistake, attend several meetings of a club before you petition to join. Get to know some of the members on a social basis. Keep your ears open and your mouth shut. Evaluate the group carefully to determine if you will fit in. If you won't get as much from it as you put in, you'll quickly sour on the group. Is it one whose members show more interest in throwing an orgy when you're hoping for a protest march to City Hall? Or are you dying for a whipping but the club members only want to sing Broadway melodies while posing on a white piano in their shiny black leather? Are the rules for membership ones that you might have difficulty fulfilling? Participation may entail an excessive amount of time. If you live a hundred miles away and attendance at business meetings is mandatory, be realistic about your chances of fulfilling your obligations. Once you fall out of favor with a group, you rarely get back in.

Reckon too on dues and levies. Clubs and organizations require some sort of annual fee. In addition, most sponsor special events or runs and may exact a special levy to cover expenses. Money is a perennial source of contention. In any gay/lesbian organization, next to politics, club coffers generate the greatest conflicts and scandals. From outside the club come promoters, worthy causes and a hundred different charities with hat in hand. From within, honorable members with good intentions and sticky fingers combine with improper accounting, deficit spending and territorial imperative to spell the ruination of finances. Bankruptcy through sheer stupidity and over-commitment has been the fate of many otherwise noteworthy clubs and organizations. Like safe sex, an insistence on sound financial practices, proper accounting and open books has nothing to do with whether you trust someone or not. It is after all your money. Be certain that some mechanism is in place to guarantee that the dicta of safe, sane and consensual apply to the governing of club finances.

So think carefully before you sign up. Weigh the options of joining or affiliating with a club or organization. You might consider some sort of connection other than full membership. Some folks prefer to avoid formal affiliations and are referred to as GDIs (God Damned Independents). Many GDIs interact frequently with those who had joined associations. Don't regard being a GDI as something undesirable. As a competent and honest SMer, you needn't worry about being isolated. I was associated with one organization for years before I officially joined. Its members always seemed to let me know of events and I shared their friendship as well as their parties. You can still informally associate with clubs and work with them on various projects if you choose. You won't get club colors, or the right to vote, but then you've no dues, no vested interest and no politics that you need become mired in.

CLUB COURTESY

> *"Things once allowed are now reproved."*
> —Coxton's Book of Courtesyes, 16th century

Whether you choose to join a club, organization or remain a GDI, you'll learn that SM has its own set of rules known as courtesy. It's not just the etiquette of social niceties and knowing whether you use the whip on the outside or the inside first. Courtesy encompasses a wider purpose of social interaction. Its main function is to grease the social wheels and preserve order by minimizing conflicts. Instead of slugging your way through a crowd, you politely ask to pass and excuse yourself if you step on someone's toes as a way of preventing him from stomping on yours. Courtesy even extends to the dungeon. If you attend an SM party, the standard rule is you never intrude on anyone else's scene unless you've been asked to join in.

Courtesy also differentiates social groups into the savvy and the ignorant. The entire system of colored hankies and their placement on the left or right side is an example of coded communication that makes cryptic anything that needs to be kept from outsiders. A black hankie is just a snot rag to your mother but it tells that hot number in the leather bar something about you. Moreover, it serves to coalesce SMers into a cohesive and knowledgeable clique separate from those ignorant of the code. Courtesy also establishes a pecking order. Club colors on the back of a bar vest distinguish the full member from the pledge. But these things are far from hard and fast. They change and sometimes fade from use. Wearing brown leather once indicated the wearer was exploring an interest in leather. Few of the younger leathermen are even aware of this former dictum.

Finally courtesy ritualizes or codifies behavior patterns necessary for the well-being of a particular social group. The kosher food requirements of Mosaic Law were a ritualized way of preventing parasites and food poisoning among the ancient Hebrews without the need for extensive explanations and rationalizations. Likewise, fisters have adopted Mid-America Fists In Action (MAFIA) rules for safe fisting. You don't need a degree in Public Health to play safe; just follow these rules religiously and you will be protected.

It's human nature to invent formal ceremonies as well as social situations where prestige and correctness come into play. Many runs feature a parade of colors that may range from a casual display of club patches to a pseudo-military precision drill complete with band and the singing of the Star Spangled Banner. It's not usually conscious but rather the result of our own hidden insecurities about group status coming to the fore. The SM world has its own yearning for legitimacy and so we create rites and traditions. It's not a bad thing. Certain clubs have attained an international reputation by carefully cultivating their image and making sure that there's sufficient substance behind it. Their name and colors bestow an aura of SM sophistication to their members.

If you do join a club or organization, listen to fellow members and be tolerant of different views. If some desired proposal of yours gets shot down by the group, don't sulk and blame the defeat on this faction or that person. We have enough real enemies without transmogrifying our allies into our adversaries.

Learn the fine art of compromise. A natural tendency is to crush the opposition. Yet, despite the political legacy of recent years, the true American tradition is to hear everyone's opinions and incorporate as much as possible into any decision. Compromising serves two purposes. First, it covers all the angles since no one can think of every aspect surrounding any issue. Someone will always see a point that's been overlooked. Second, it allows everyone to feel that they've contributed.

Participation binds an individual to a group. And that's better than the hostility generated from feeling shut-out and excluded.

Make a special effort to be sensitive to the plight of others and try to relieve it. The Reagans had lots of sympathy and empathy for their friend Rock Hudson as he lay dying of AIDS. We know this because they told us many times how saddened they were. But their emotions never went beyond vaguely feeling sorry. Compassion compels action. Feeling something in your heart means nothing if it doesn't improve your behavior. Before you speak, put yourself in the other person's boots. How would you feel? Alter your behavior so that, at the least, you do no harm to others. Often, it's as simple as making sure your brain is in gear before your mouth is engaged.

Don't immerse yourself in suspicions and grudges. Sometimes, people actually do things without having hidden agendas. (Lord knows it's the quickest way to drive crazy those who look for hidden motives.) Don't brow-beat your fellows. Be gracious in allowing for human failings and show a bigness of heart. Be generous in forgiving and overlooking faults or failures. If you demand humiliation for everyone who disagrees with you, then you'd best prepare yourself for your own public feeding from the dog dish. When you must complain about a given situation, give thought to a possible solution and leave a gracious way out for the other person. Otherwise, you're just bitching.

AIDS and the New Intolerance have changed the world for all gays and lesbians, especially in the SM community. We are besieged and cannot afford attacks on one another. But, none of us can stand idle and claim neutrality. In Shakespeare's *Romeo and Juliet*, the two warring families are both punished by the deaths of the lovers. But the play has another moral. At the end, the Prince of Verona, who did nothing *decisive* to end the quarreling, has himself also lost two relatives in the fighting. Heaven judged his guilt and dealt his punishment as equal to that of the feuding factions. By non-involvement, by withdrawal from debate, by not holding our leaders, officers, members and one another to proper account, we in the SM community risk a similar fate where "All are punished."

Chapter 6: Risk Reduction

Risk cannot be separated from SM. Common sense, preparedness and safety precautions serve to keep it at acceptable levels. Risk reduction is essential for safe, sane and consensual play. While a few might get a thrill from sprinting through a mine field, fewer yet would care to follow them. You have an obligation to learn how to spot dangerous behavior and respond accordingly. Your first duty remains to protect yourself at all times. Your second is to safeguard others. Much is common sense along with knowledge and experience. This chapter is divided into two broad areas. The first deals with accident prevention, the second deals with drug use and abuse.

ACCIDENTS

Prevention is the key. SM involves a certain measure of risk-taking but never recklessness. It requires attentiveness and preparation to keep it safe and sane. Whether you top or bottom, the responsibility begins with you. Learn how to do SM as safely as possible by reading about SM and by training with someone. Attend demonstrations to learn safe techniques. I'd also recommend that you take a First Aid course and learn CPR. Keep a First Aid Kit handy and post emergency numbers prominently.

SOME SIMPLE SM SAFETY RULES:
—Never tie blindfolds too tightly. Too much pressure on the eyes will damage the optic nerve and may cause permanent loss of vision. Blindfolds should also be free of any material or fuzz that you can easily pinch off. Loose fibers will get into the eye.
—When using headphones, keep it at a reasonable level. Don't create hearing-loss by pumping up the volume.
—Never stretch, tape or bind the neck! You could all too easily constrict someone's windpipe, cut off the brain's blood supply or pop a cervical disc. Death, paralyzation and vegetable states are not part of the safe, sane and consensual trichotomy.
—Never obstruct both the nose and mouth. Play with one or the other. Whenever restricting or regulating breathing, you must monitor your partner *constantly*. If you gag the mouth, better guard that his nose doesn't stuff up during your scene.
—Never bind the chest too tightly. Have your partner take a deep breath, then wrap or bind him. This will prevent unintended restriction of breathing.
—Provide padding during prolonged bondage. Place some foam between bony joints. Otherwise, you may create instant bedsores.

—Know of any medical quirks your partner may have. Asthma, heart problems, allergies, diabetes and bad backs are things to know about ahead of time. Poppers can trigger heart attacks in susceptible people.

—Ask about drug use, both legal and illegal. Any drug reaction is always an urgent matter.

Accidents can happen to either the top or the bottom in a scene. If an accident occurs, your priority is to stay calm. Get emergency help but, if possible, stay with the person while someone else calls. Your injured partner needs your physical and emotional aid. Remember your *ABCs* which stand for *Airway, Breathing, Check the heart.* Make certain the *Airway* is open and unobstructed. Be sure the person is *Breathing.* Check for a heartbeat or pulse and, if necessary, begin CPR. Stop any bleeding. Make the person as comfortable as possible, but don't move him if you suspect spinal or neck injuries. Cover him with a blanket to help offset chills or shock. Remember to talk reassuringly to him.

The chief emergency concerns in SM include: fainting, sprains and bruises, eye injuries, drug misuse, blood injuries and burns. Fainting, especially among beginners, is a common medical emergency. Eventually, every SMer encounters it. This is a good one to run through as a disaster practice. Fainting has a variety of causes, some preventible, some not. Its preclusion lies within the control of both top and bottom. Everything in SM play should revolve around mutuality but for some strange reason, bottoms seem to think that safety issues are strictly concerns for the top. Universally, tops feel a sense of culpability, bordering on guilt, when a bottom passes out. While a top has a duty to protect his partner's well-being, too many bottoms simply will not speak up when they feel woozy or a little out of sorts. Never hesitate to inform your partner when something feels amiss. If your arms feel tingly or if your bonds are abrading your wrists, speak up immediately. I had a teacher who was fond of saying, "If nothing is said, it is assumed that nothing is wrong." The top may be obliged to monitor things as best he can, but a bottom has the duty to alert him to anything that seems off kilter. Keeping quiet because you fear that the scene will be ended or that you'll be seen as too wimpy is unsafe behavior.

Fainting is the biological equivalent of a re-start button on a computer. It's nature's way of removing you from overly stressful situations. Please recognize that the onset of a faint is a sign that you've reached a limit and need to back off before your body and brain automatically shut down. Call for a short break or intermission after which you can resume your scene. Just remember that if you do faint, your body will need about forty minutes to reset itself.

Fainting can be triggered by:

—Too tight collars. These do not have to be choking, just tight enough to hinder blood flow to the brain.

—Standing without flexing the legs. The contracting leg muscles help pump the blood back to the heart. Without this pumping action, gravity keeps the blood in the lower limbs at the expense of the brain.

—Arms suspended above shoulder level. This position creates the crucifixion effect as it restricts breathing and puts a load on the heart.

—Drugs which lower the blood pressure. These include prescribed drugs such as beta-blockers (Tenormin) which slow the heart beat, legal depressants such as alcohol and illicit ones such as poppers or marijuana.

—Drug overdose. If so, get immediate professional help either by calling for an ambulance or getting the person to an Emergency Room. Either identify or bring a sample of the chemical substance for the ER personnel. Don't dump the person at the hospital door or pretend you haven't a clue. The hospital's lab will eventually identify the drug, but the wasted time could result in your partner's permanent disablement or death.

—Prolonged pressure on the abdomen. Bending over a side-horse, for example, restricts blood flow in the aorta (the major artery) and the vena cava (the major vein).

—Hyperventilation. Most people have experienced that woozy feeling after blowing too hard on a campfire. Rapid breathing sets up an imbalance between oxygen and carbon-dioxide within the body. Monitor his breathing. If it's too rapid, use a paper bag (never a plastic one!) into which he should inhale and exhale.

—Fainting can also be triggered by a reaction to a lot of sensations in a short period. An over-stimulated nervous system simply shuts down in some people. The physical and mental stresses can overwhelm with little warning. Reddening of the skin over a large area from abrasion, scourging, spanking or whipping diverts blood to the skin's surface and may dramatically lower the blood pressure.

Signs of an approaching faint often include some or all of the following:

—The bottom's hands feel cold to the top's touch. The bottom feels a tingling in his extremities, especially in the fingers. He sways or wobbles when standing upright, experiences shaking unrelated to room temperature, feels woozy or dizzy. Amazingly, most people don't recognize any of these as a prelude to losing consciousness.

Immediate actions to take:

—Tell him you're going to take him down. Keep talking to him. This gives him something to focus on even if he does appear to faint. Remember, hearing is the last sense to go.

—Free the feet first *only* if they're bound so tightly that your partner risks injury to his leg joints should be topple over in a faint. Otherwise, free the hands and arms as you brace him up.

—While supporting him, get him flat on the ground. Don't even think of trying to walk him anywhere. Odds are, he won't make it. You just want a gentle landing at this point.

—Put a pillow or rolled towel under the knees to help elevate the legs and get blood back to his brain.

—If he does pass out, remember your *ABCs*. Check the airway. Turn his head sideways so that he won't choke on his tongue or, if he vomits, nothing is inhaled. Make sure he's breathing. Check his heartbeat by taking a carotid pulse or by listening to the chest. Do you need to call 911 or start CPR? (Now, aren't you happy you practiced on that mannequin during first aid training?)

—If he's passed out, now's the time to quickly remove those clothespins and tit clamps. If you have to begin CPR, you'll need them out of your way. If he has a pulse and is breathing, he'll appreciate their removal before he awakens. Fainting inhibits any feeling of pain, similar to being put to sleep with an anesthetic.

—Be prepared to restrain and calm the person when consciousness returns. Some people will suddenly flail about when coming to. Be ready to grab his wrists. Hearing may be the first sense to return, but unfortunately speaking rationally is one of the last. Some pretty wild things often pop out of people's mouths at this time. Hush the poor thing until he has had time to recover some sense.

—Relax where you are for at least half an hour and stay with the person. Whatever scene you were involved with is officially over. It's now time for role-playing of a different sort. You are now "Nurse Top" and he is your patient. Render him your tender mercies. Keep him warm. Ply him seductively with fruit juices. *(No Alcohol!)* Don't let him get up or attempt to leave. Allow him to suffer from your devoted ministrations. You may be playing nurse but you are in charge!

EYE INJURIES

Regard any eye injury with the utmost seriousness. If he has something in his eye, get him to cry but don't let him rub. Tears may remove the irritant. If he's wearing contacts, remove them carefully. If it's abrasive material like sand, try removing it by blotting with a clean tissue. If not, see if it will wash out with water. If a chemical or salve like Tiger Balm has gotten into the eye, flush immediately with water for two to

112

ten minutes. Cover with gauze and get immediate medical care.

Contact lenses pose a particular hazard if you're blindfolding someone. If the person has hard lenses, either remove them or don't put a blindfold on. Corneal abrasions (a nice way of saying scratches on the eyeball) will almost certainly result. The newer soft lenses, which are mostly water, seem to do fine if the blindfold is free of any loose fibers and if it's tied loosely so as not to put any pressure on the eye. Consider using a well-made hood with a snap-on blinder instead.

If a blindfold is tied too tightly, the eyeball may be squeezed out of shape. If this happens, the person's vision will be distorted for up to several hours until the eye regains its normal shape. Take this as a warning that you're being too vigorous with your blindfolds. Pressure strong enough to distort the eyeball could also permanently damage the optic nerve and blind the person.

BLEEDING OR WEEPING ABRASIONS

Always assume that any body fluid, especially blood, is infected. I don't care if you're tricking with the Pope or someone you-know-better-than-anyone-in-the-world, always act as if HIV or hepatitis is present and take proper precautions. If possible, let the person who is bleeding bandage himself. If he can't, then you should wear latex gloves when tending to the injury. Have at least one pair in your First Aid Kit. It's a good idea to place them in a zip-loc bag to protect them from the air. Modern cities are so polluted that latex gloves will disintegrate within weeks.

For severe bleeding, send for help. Cover any wounds or severe abrasions with sterile pads or the cleanest cloth you have. Never use cotton balls or wadding. Press firmly and steadily. Don't resort to a tourniquet. Elevate the bleeding limb. Maintain both the pressure and elevation until the bleeding stops or help arrives. Disinfect or retire any equipment splattered by blood or body fluids.

HEATBURNS

Burns can result from scalding, contact with a heated object, a flame, a live wire, or boiling oil. Burns are classified according to severity. First degree burns are surface-only. Although they will be red and painful for several days, there is no blistering. Sometimes mild swelling occurs. Second degree burns destroy the immediate underlying tissue and form painful blisters. These generally heal in about two weeks. If the blisters burst and an infection sets in, scarring and skin grafts could be in your future. Third degree (or higher) burns destroy all skin tissues including the nerves. Generally, the skin is charred, dry and cracked, yet strangely painless. Don't waste time. Get immediate qualified medical attention. Shock and massive infections are likely. Death can result from some massive burns.

For first aid, immerse in cold water only if there are no broken blisters or skin. Don't apply ice to a burn and never apply oils, butter, creams or salves. Cover with a telfa pad or the cleanest non-shedding cloth available but don't put cotton balls or bunting on a burn wound. Never pop blisters since that will open the burn to infection. Avoid using pain-killing sprays. Many anesthetic sprays contain alcohol which causes severe stinging as it kills the exposed and damaged tissues. He doesn't need a chemical burn in addition to a heat burn!

FALLS, SPRAINS OR BREAKS

Stabilize the person by carefully freeing the limb. Have him stretch out and cover him with a blanket. If there is no break, elevate the limb. Apply ice to sprains, bumps and bruises. If you suspect a break, call for help. If someone takes a severe knock in the head, keep an eye on them for several hours. Should they complain of dizziness or blurred vision, it may be a sign of brain damage. Get them to qualified medical help.

ELECTRIC SHOCK

Have someone get help. Remove the person from the electric source by turning the power off or disconnecting it safely. Protect yourself by using a non-conducting tool to remove any live or hot wires. It's *ABC* time again. Check pulse and breathing.

DRUGS

In SM, the chief liability of drug use is a calamitous loss of reasoning. Drugs render clear thought impossible. Whether it's a few beers, a pill or some powder, with your judgment impaired, you just cannot make sound decisions based on the principles of safe, sane and consensual. I've intervened in play sessions where the participants were unable to follow basic safety rules such as being sure that they used a condom. SM can only be safe, sane and consensual when you have full use of your mental faculties.

Hospitals are required to obtain your written informed consent before you receive any medication, even Valium. Once any drug, which alters your judgment in the slightest, is administered, the law considers you legally incompetent to give full and knowledgeable consent. Reputable piercers, such as Gauntlet on the coasts and Mad Jack in Chicago, adhere to this general principle, turning away clients whom they suspect are under the influence of chemical substances. SM would be better off if participants adhered to a similar standard.

Current written SM opinion seems to be running against use of chemicals. Without doubt, some use drugs as anesthetics, deliberately and

114

routinely dulling their senses in order "to push their limits." Others are addicts, using drugs as a crutch or as the only way they can partake of SM play. Such chemical dependency defeats the high that SM play can provide. I do disagree with the blanket condemnation of the purists who demand absolute chemical abstinence. Throughout history, people of every culture have discovered and employed various drugs for religious, social and ritual use. Over the ages, humans have changed their definitions of what constitutes a dangerous substance. In the twentieth century, alcohol was banned at a time when marijuana was legal. Some drugs, nicotine for example, are currently being stigmatized as deadly. In and of themselves, drugs are not evil. The misuse of drugs, as in addiction, is the problem. A sense of balance is needed. A single beer is not on the same order as chronic alcoholism. Someone who employs a hallucinogen for a ritual insight operates on a different level than someone using it hedonistically. A person growing his own grass does not aid the drug trade whereas the crack-cocaine user funds the drug cartels. Ethics, the code of conduct by which you interact with society, must come into play.

I believe that a person should never top when partaking of chemical substances that impair his ability. A top needs his full judgment, skills and physical coordination. With drugs, there's just too much potential for mayhem and mischief. Someone who's apt to pass out dead drunk while you're in heavy bondage puts you at as much risk as someone who slips into a drug induced psychosis. In either event, severe trauma and permanent damage to you could result. I'm amazed how many bottoms let a drugged-out top work them over. No one in their right mind would let a drunk surgeon near them, but they don't seem to fear an inebriated top. I hate to sound repetitious but when you play with someone, you literally put your life in his hands. If he is whacked-out on drugs, it may result in the fatal mistake that gives you AIDS or allows an ill-placed rope to choke the life out of you.

If you decide as a bottom to imbibe, be extremely confident of your top's concern and ability. I personally find it impossible to depend utterly on someone whom I have just met in a bar. Responsible SM requires that you have absolute confidence that this person will do nothing to compromise your safety. Before taking anything—even alcohol—that alters your reasoning powers, talk with your top and make any and all decisions while you are clean and sober.

Selected trust-filled, intense and wonderful sessions can be intensified by altered perceptions. But while drugs can enhance your experience, they readily diminish it. It's always a trade-off. Rational thought often goes out the window; sensations are deadened; the ability to communicate problems is hindered. There's an additional risk of side-effects

115

from headaches to heart attacks. If you are going to bottom while under the influence, consider having a third person, who is clean sober, monitor the activity. Many play parties designated a dungeon master or official host whose duty is to enforce the safety rules of the house. With someone else watching out for your well-being, you'll be able to relax and enjoy the experience, comfortable that the guidelines established for safe, sane and consensual play are being monitored.

Any use of chemical substances must assure that no harm occurs to anyone, including yourself. If you're going to get plastered, you take a taxi home or sleep it off before driving. Avoid chemicals that will damage your brain or body. Never slip anyone a drug without their consent. Don't bring illegal substances into someone else's home or clubhouse. Drug laws allow the government to seize both the premises and furnishings wherever drugs are found. Your craving for a high could cost someone their property. It's a selfish attitude at odds with SM's goal of responsibility and accountability to others.

Drugs that you're likely to encounter fall into six categories: inhalants (poppers), marijuana, hallucinogens, designer drugs, cocaine and opiates (heroin). The recreational drug of choice changes rapidly, some falling out of use, others being re-discovered, another being newly synthesized. Still this list will give you knowledge of general groups of drugs and their reactions and side-effects. This list is only to provide information. To quote a former University of Chicago president, "We also teach cancer, but we do not advocate it." I don't include legal drugs such as alcohol, cigarettes or prescription drugs such as Valium. Enough information is available from other sources such as the Physicians Desk Reference.

INHALANTS

Poppers contain amyl, butyl or alkyl nitrites that produce a quick rush when inhaled. This results from the dilation of blood vessels throughout the body with a resultant relaxation of muscles. Hedonists found that poppers heightened sexual pleasure. Fuckers and fisters alike discovered that poppers allowed for deeper, more comfortable anal penetration. Before the prohibition of poppers, federal laws required labels that listed ingredients. You knew what chemicals went into the formula even if you never bothered consulting a book on toxicology for undesirable side effects like, oh, cardiac arrest. Under federal regulation, government standards of purity applied. Nowadays, underground labs produce poppers in unmarked brown bottles. Understandably, they don't want to label them, but who knows what's in them?

Since the sales ban of room odorizers, users have been confronted with lack of quality, inclusion of untested substances and out-right

fraud. While I've chanced upon the old standbys of amyl and butyl, I've stumbled across some pretty nasty formulas. Among them are:
—Petroleum by-products: One bottle contained nothing but a fuel oil additive.
—Plasticizers: These are chemicals used to impart flexibility to resins and vinyl. For a good fright, read their side-effects in toxicology books.
—Industrial Solvents: Acetone and other chemicals can give a high but they also rapidly destroy the liver and kidneys.

In short, we're in a new era of bootlegging and it's time to revive the lessons learned by our grandparents during the Prohibition. 1) Always ask what's in it. You don't need to know proportions or recipes but you should insist on knowing what chemicals you're inhaling. 2) Deal with people you know and trust. They're less likely to poison you for a few bucks. 3) Inspect the bottle for floaters or oiliness. Any of these are a sign that the lab is sloppy. 4) Trust your body's reaction. If something tastes or smells odd, or if you have an adverse reaction like coughing, chemical burns or dermatitis, don't use them. 5) Ask a trusted friend for a recommended source. A reputable dealer will guarantee his product and refund your money if you aren't satisfied. If he won't, don't deal with him. Remember, it's your health. Don't risk permanent brain, lung, liver or kidney damage with poppers that are "better than nothing."

Ethyl chloride is another inhalant. It is an extremely flammable color-less liquid or gas with an ether-like odor and a burning or bitter taste. First described as an anesthetic in 1847, it was abandoned as an inhalant when drugs with fewer side-effects became available. It's still used as a local anesthetic that numbs the skin by freezing it. It's also important in the manufacturing of dyes, drugs and lead products. EPA documentation shows that increasing levels of exposure through breathing causes euphoria, inebriation, uncoordination, noisy talkativeness, unconsciousness and finally death.

Common side effects include headache, dizziness, stomach cramps and nausea. Since it's a respiratory tract irritant, those with asthma or smoker's cough will find these conditions worsened. The next day, users may have a raspy voice like Bette Davis on a bad day. Ethyl chloride causes irregular heartbeats and heart attacks have been reported. Over-inhalation can induce what's euphemistically called the fifth state of anesthesia—death.

Ethyl chloride produces auditory and/or visual hallucinations. Often a person who inhales too much will simply carry on silly conversations with persons not present. But sometimes, a normally restrained individual can become overly aggressive, even violent. He may suddenly start yelling and swinging at imagined persons. Since the short term memory is affected, it's very difficult to convince him afterward that psychosis did occur. It also produces an effect known as "twilight sleep" during which the recipient recalls nothing between the drug's onset and its wearing-off. To him, that time was spent in unconsciousness or pleasant sleep although to any observer, he seemed fully awake and feeling everything. A person in "twilight-sleep" remembers nothing done to him—whether pleasurable or not!

CANNABIS

Marijuana is made from the crushed leaves and flowerets and is either smoked or baked in cookies or cakes for consumption. Hashish is the resin from the flowers which is smoked, eaten or made into a beverage. Both are from the Cannabis plant grown throughout the world. Traces of the plant have been found in prehistoric sites from ten thousand years ago. Every culture has found valuable uses for it in medicine, religion and industry, breeding plants for specific qualities. During the previous century, it was a standard part of herbal gardens and was used to treat everything from migraine headaches to Queen Victoria's painful menstrual cramps. Until 1941, it appeared in the pharmacopeia of the National Formulary which lists all the officially approved drugs. Marijuana was finally outlawed in the US by a combination of the alcohol lobby, which viewed recreational use as competition, and the drug manufacturers who had expensive new drugs that home-grown marijuana would undercut. From the La Guardia report of 1944 to the National Commission on Marihuana and Drug Abuse, commission after commission has argued against its criminalization, urged the removal of penalties for individuals and called for expanded research into its medical uses. Considering that the plant has been used for over ten thousand years by millions of people, it's significant that not one death from overdose or addiction has ever been reported—unlike alcohol or nicotine. The public debate remains steeped in emotionalism and ideology with deliberate distortions and half-truths by special interest groups.

When smoked, the effects begin in about ten to fifteen minutes. Ingestion takes about thirty to forty. Cannabis initially increases the heartbeat and raises the blood pressure, though it will soon lead to lowered blood pressure. Other effects are: a sense of well-being, a floating sensation, dry mouth, increased appetite, an altered sense of time and a heightening of the senses so that one becomes engrossed in music or the flashing of colored lights. Sometimes it can produce undesirable effects such as vertigo, depression, lack of coordination or anxiety. Cannabis is not physically addictive. Use will not lead to increasingly larger doses to obtain the same level of intoxication, nor to a craving and habitual use, nor are there any physical indications of withdrawal symptoms. Experimental occasional use appears to be safer than caffeine or nicotine. The danger in SM play is to get so high that you become completely intoxicated or "stoned stupid." Intoxication, whether by alcohol, marijuana or some other chemical, leaves you without judgment or ability. If you are going to render yourself this vulnerable, arrange to do so among trusted individuals in a safe environment.

HALLUCINOGENS

These are nonaddictive substances which are often poisonous but which in nontoxic doses cause hallucinations and alter the state of consciousness by producing changes in perceptions, mood and thought. The hallucinations produced by the drug may involve any or all of the senses. They act directly on the central nervous system producing a dreamlike state without depressing brain function. They may dredge-up forgotten and repressed events or reveal subconscious thoughts. Artists, philosophers, writers and mystics have employed them to break free of reality and discover other horizons. There is evidence that these drugs only initiate the conditions for hallucination and that a person's cultural background determines the response. On the same drug, a Catholic might chat with the Virgin Mary while a radical fairie-shaman soars the forest as a hawk and a fundamentalist visits Hell. Although the altered perceptions are normally temporary, some individuals may suffer permanent physical or mental damage. Many hallucinogens are similar to neurocompounds in the brain and have been useful in psychiatry. They should not be regarded as harmless toys but as powerful tools. Every culture has discovered some substance from a plant, mushroom or animal that produces visions and connected it with religion or magic before secularizing it. A priest noted that the Spanish soldiers who tried to stamp out the Aztecs' ceremonial use of peyote as devilish, ignored their own ritual use of wine in the mass.

Peyote gives visions of brilliant kaleidoscopic colors accompanied by hallucinations. There may also be a feeling of floating, a sense of being outside one's body, seeing things with telescopic vision and a change in the perception of time. Peyote is an important ritual part of the Native American Church. In the face of great opposition over five hundred years they have preserved its use as part of their heritage. The cactus button is eaten but it often induces nausea and vomiting since it contains several toxins among the over three dozen different chemicals present in the plant. The principal chemical is the drug mescaline which can be synthesized and is often combined with amphetamine derivatives (see *Designer Drugs*). Don't contribute to peyote's extinction by using it for mere pleasure or experimentation. Parts of the Southwest have been picked clean by collectors.

LSD, lysergic acid diethylamide, was synthesized in 1943 from a chemical obtained from a fungus called ergot. It can also be made from seeds that the Aztecs used in their religious ceremonies in the belief that they bestowed powers of prophecy and facilitated union with the gods. LSD produces a floating, almost weightless feeling. Objects seem to change size, shape and color. Fantastic visions of bright intense colors and plastic shapes may appear. Hallucinations of all the senses may occur, including feelings of temperature changes. It's been said that LSD opens the gates of both heaven and hell with the person's emotional state determining which is entered. LSD should not be treated lightly. Effects can range from excitement to panic and fear. Army experiments inadvertently determined that LSD can at times produce permanent psychosis.

Many mushrooms, such as Europe's Fly-agaric or Mexico's Psilocybe, contain complex compounds that can alter the perceptions. Mushrooms pose several difficulties. Many species have poisonous look-a-likes that even experts find difficult to tell apart. Every summer the media carry stories of people who die after their livers have been destroyed by ingesting the wrong mushroom. Different environments can also affect the quality and kinds of chemicals within even the correct fungus. And of course, the hucksters are ever ready to defraud the gullible. How can you be sure you're not paying premium price for grocery store mushrooms laced with a little LSD or nothing at all?

DESIGNER DRUGS

Designer drugs are a special class of synthetic drugs. By slightly altering the chemical formula of controlled or illegal drugs, make-shift labs created drugs for recreational use that were beyond government regulation. After a series of deaths and disabilities attributed to designer drugs, Congress passed an omnibus amendment which outlawed future formulations. These drugs fall into two divisions, the synthetic opiods based on demerol or sublimaze, and the mescaline-methamphetamines derivatives.

The drugs based on demerol (meperidine) are often referred to as synthetic heroin which is a misnomer since heroin itself is derived from meperidine derivatives. MPPP is the ingredient of the drug which is injected to give a heroin-like euphoria. However, due to the sloppy nature of the underground labs in producing MPPP, the drug is commonly contaminated with a by-product, MPTP, that causes permanent Parkinson's symptoms of drooling, muscle rigidity, tremors and a jerky mechanical movement of the limbs. The damage is irreversible.

The group of opiods based on sublimaze (fentanyl) are generally short acting but extremely powerful. China White is over 1,000 times stronger than heroin, making the difference between a pleasant buzz and death miniscule—especially since the potency of a street drug is always unknown.

Drugs based on amphetamines (AKA speed) seem to be the most popular designer drugs. Sometimes mescaline, the main active ingredient of peyote, is combined with speed to create a hybrid group of drugs. Oddly, many amphetamines have been around for a long time. MDMA, commonly known as Ecstasy or XTC was first made back in 1914 as an appetite suppressant. As a white powder in pristine form, speed can be packed into gel-caps with the onset of effects occurring within thirty minutes and lasting six to eight hours. Crystal, also known as ice, was synthesized in Korea shortly before WW II for use in "pep pills" by occupying Japanese troops. Kamikaze pilots often were given a good dose in their ritual drink of sake. It has become extremely popular among fisters in the US. The effects of crystal may last up to three days.

Ecstasy, crystal, Adam, Eve, Love drug, M&M, Hug drug—all produce similar effects. Their popularity resides in the positive feelings that they generate in the user's mind, a drug induced elation that increases self-esteem and heightens the user's perception of interpersonal relations. This drug-induced awareness of people includes: a feeling of closeness to others, a desire to be with people and a marked need to talk with them (known as speed rapping). Unfortunately, this induced elation brings with it a wandering mind that's unable to focus. Thus users perceive an unending discussion of their weekly grocery list as an incredibly intimate, important and fascinating conversation. A real let-down when you're trying to work a scene of sexual magic and your partner is in the midst of Short Attention Span Theater.

Speed derivatives also have some nasty side-effects. They affect the ability to make sober judgments. They can be addictive. They dangerously speed up the body's metabolism while suppressing the appetite. (These were Judy Garland's infamous "diet" pills.) Many abusers of speed-based drugs look anorexic, tend toward repetitious, euphoric and empty talkativeness. Physical and psychological mayhem may also take place. Hallucinations, panic attacks, anxiety and paranoia have been commonly reported. Hyperactivity, manic behavior, hypertension, rapid and irregular heartbeats, involuntary jaw-clenching, tremors and hyperthermia are also common. Deaths due to hyperthermia (a fever-like overheating) and seizures are being reported with growing frequency especially among those under-thirty years old.

COCAINE AND HEROIN

These two white crystalline powders are the classic drugs of abuse. Chemically, both are alkaloids having a bitter taste and a profound effect on the nervous system. Heroin is an opiate derived from the resin of the opium poppy. Created from morphine by Frederich Bayer, the same nineteenth century German chemist who also synthesized aspirin, heroin is six times more addictive than morphine and produces a greater euphoria. Off-white or brown as a powder, it may also be a tar-like substance. Most often injected, it acts first as a stimulant and then as a depressant, producing a stupor inducing sleep. It can be free-based, heated till it boils with the user inhaling the fumes. Heroin is a powerful narcotic. Addiction to it involves three features: an intense craving for the drug, an increasing tolerance that requires greater and more frequent doses and withdrawal symptoms. The withdrawal from heroin is so severe that patients have died quitting it cold turkey.

Cocaine is extracted from the leaves of the coca plant grown on the eastern Andean slopes of Peru and Bolivia. The leaves were chewed by the Incas who discovered that it made them feel better by relieving fatigue and increasing their endurance. Refined cocaine acts as a stimulant producing a rush. The drug accelerates the heart beat, increases the rate of breathing and raises blood pressure. Cocaine is most often snorted as a white crystalline powder into the nose, though it can also be injected or smoked. Crack-cocaine is a very powerful new form multiplying the problems of coke abuse. (Thank the far right for introducing this form to the US in order to fund the Contras in Nicaragua.)

Cocaine is an anesthetic that can put your heart to "sleep" and no medicine can counter the effect. It is the only drug that addicts can identify the exact dose that tripped them over the line from casual user to addict. Unlike heroin, cocaine does not require ever increasing doses nor does it trigger violent withdrawal symptoms. Crack coke addiction produces a craving for the drug so intensely powerful that the addict will literally do anything to obtain the next dose. Women in crack houses prostitute themselves for a single hit. To be an addict is to live in the thrall of a drug, condemned to a zombie-like existence devoid of any hope or joy except for the next fix. Cities and communities are under siege from addicts who rob, kill and steal for the drug.

The cocaine and heroin trades have destroyed entire cultures, environments and countries throughout the third world. The fault resides principally with the unbridled appetite for coke and heroin in the United States. The concentration of immense wealth into the hands of people with no ethics and no regard for human life has led to an unprecedented wave of corruption and terror. Dwellers in rural Peru tend to their daily activities fully armed, living in fear of narco-terrorists. What sort of SM relies on the misery of thousands for a few moments of drug induced bliss? Extend the dictates of safe, sane and consensual beyond the walls of your playroom.

Chapter 7: Invasive Specialties

With no fear of blood
I find you
so beautiful
kneeling
        from "Apostrophe to Stanley"
                —Jeffery Beam

I didn't intend to write a how-to sex cook book. "Now squeezing the
Bottom's left tit between thumb and forefinger, gingerly apply clamps
and leave until tender." Instead, I've tried to reveal the thinking behind
good SM, to help you understand it and be creative about it. Dieticians
are fond of pointing out that the average person has less than ten recipes
and cooks the same meals over and over for most of their lives. Add just
a few new ones or alter the existing ones, and you can transform a person's life. Our sexual repertoire tends to reflect the same sort of self-
limiting blandness, although the choices now available are far better
than they once were. Back in 1965, pierced tits and Prince Alberts were
so rare that an English friend of mine drove a crowd wild in a San Francisco leather bar when he put people's earrings through his tits and dick
during a contest. Many actually thought that he was piercing himself on
stage! It's hard to imagine a time when body piercing was an unknown
art in California. Now, piercers are almost as common as convenience
stores and tit rings as plentiful as earrings.

Why do I choose the following from a range of activities? My own
personal taste is a major reason but concern for safety issues, debunk-
ing of myths and spreading word on pleasurable activities have provided
reasons for inclusion. Partly too because, as with everything in the
modern world, different aspects of SM play come and go in fashion.

In a burgeoning SM press which professes to explore techniques and
practices, certain activities are either passed over quickly or spoken of
with an air of disapproval. One famous handbook wrinkles its nose in
distaste when discussing fisting while another repeats erroneous information without double checking facts. This can result in personal bias
and hear-say being presented as gospel. SM is a very personal exploration that ought to be conducted with a mind uncluttered and unfettered
by ignorance or prejudice. All the activities listed in this chapter are in-
vasive which means that they may involve either breaking the skin's protective barrier or inserting something into the body. Both therefore put
the person undergoing the activity at some sort of risk for disease trans-

123

mission. Because most people do not intend to break skin while whipping and flogging, I placed those in the non-invasive section of chapter nine. It is a difficult call but since advanced practitioners make a conscious decision to proceed to that stage, I chose not to view splitting the skin as intrinsic to those activities.

ABRASION

Abrasion is a subtle exploring and exploitation of the sense of touch which ranges from a feather-light stroking of body hair to dermabrasion (scraping-off of the top skin layer). Rarely can the genesis and popularizing of specific SM practices be attributed to one person. Although others had also practiced forms of abrasion, the credit for establishing it as a scene in itself belongs to the late Bob Buckley of Melbourne, Australia. Having first thought of the idea back in '78, he initially used it as a prelude to relax his partners before other activities. Gradually, he observed that the more he prolonged the abrasion, the more intensely they responded. His abrasion demonstrations at Inferno XIII caught the imagination of attending SMers from around the world. He could, with just a pair of toothpicks and an incredibly keen reading of his partner's tender and erogenous zones, stroke, prick, jab and tickle them into jelly.

Buckley emphasized several things in his numerous demonstrations: subtlety and lightness, rather than heavy-handedness; intense concentration, not dramatic flair; and an understanding that you're trying to create a cumulative effect, rather than a series of isolated sensations. Abrasion is for the patient disciplined top and demands sensitivity and inventiveness or it will not work. Anyone lacking these qualities ought to seek some other activity. Buckley wrote down a number of his talks. Unfortunately, he never published a collection of them. He was in the habit of depositing copies with the different groups to whom he spoke. If you want to read his talks, inquire of GMS/MA in New York City or Dreizehn in Boston.

For those unacquainted with the practice, the word abrasion tends to suggest that you're either intending to flay them alive or spend a long dull evening boringly scraping their skin. Tops may use a less foreboding word with people unfamiliar with abrasion. One friend calls it skin sensitizing, another erotic rubbing or SM massage. I prefer the term texturing. They all describe the sensations that result from the skin's contact with different surface textures of assorted utensils. The varying names are just descriptive hooks to encourage curiosity and lead to further investigation. Once individuals are comfortable with the sense of the scene, I'll begin to refer to it as abrasion. Since it involves playing exclusively with the sense of touch, you can heighten concentration by depriving the other senses through blindfolding and earplugs. Music through a good set of isolating headphones can work well especially if it's a collection that you've arranged to coincide with the progressive intensity of your abrasion.

Among the implements that you can use for abrasion are your own hands, fingers and nails. Take a really good look at your nails. They're hard; the flat side is smooth, yet the edge is narrow and capable of painfully scratching the skin. By varying the pressure and angle of your nails, you can trace delicate lines or raise welts with a heavy claw or tickle with a light wavy motion. With your fingers, you can tap lightly on his forehead or drum staccato rhythms on his chest. You can massage the fur on his belly with the palm of your hand or rub his balls so hard that the friction burns the skin of his nut sack.

Abrasion works best if you work with the anatomy. There's a special model that physicians have made which sculpts the human body according to the number of nerve connections to the brain. Called a humunculus, it looks like an imp or a goblin with bandy legs and arms but huge hands, eyes, lips and obscenely large genitals. It's a model of how our minds perceive our bodies and of how much importance we place on each part of our anatomy. Abrasion allows you to exploit these perceptions to a high degree. Make use of your local library and look through the illustrations in *Gray's Anatomy* to learn where your muscles and nerves are located beneath the skin.

Follow the contours of muscles, natural curves, bones and limbs. Trace the lines in the palms of the hand with a toothpick. You can play with the head, but do it delicately so that the person doesn't worry about marks or scratches being left. Ears are often sensitive and erotic. If you play lightly and cautiously, this may be one of those rare times you can safely involve the face without risking emotional or physical trauma. There are six major nerves that service each side of the face. Just trailing your finger along their path will latch his entire concentration onto your fingertip.

Learn areas of special sensitivity or eroticism like the back of the neck. Make him dance and squirm as you prick the hollows of the knees with toothpicks or deliver mosquito-like bites to the soles of his feet. Above all, experiment on yourself. Abrasion is one of the few activities that I don't need caution you to learn from someone with experience before you try it yourself. I would strongly suggest that you test all of your implements on yourself before you use them on others. This way you'll know first-hand just how hard or light you should drag that grit pad across the inner thigh.

Position your partner as you like. Whether he's upright, prone or slung in a sling, you want quick and easy access to the different parts of his body. I like to use a woven leather sling for several reasons. It allows the bottom to relax and float safely while blindfolded. I can move around the sling easily and the open weave gives me an opportunity to attack from underneath. Think of ways to make the surface on which he rests stimulating. If he's lying down, put plastic bubble wrap or a wooden bead car seat between him and the surface. Securing him to a taut rope spider web provides an intriguing texture as well as vibration possibilities from the anchoring lines.

IMPLEMENTS

The beauty of abrasion is that virtually any object can be used. Household items such as a nail brush, toothpicks, vegetable brushes, a bath brush, forks, chopsticks. Any kitchen or bathroom drawer is an unexplored toy chest. By rummaging around your tool box or sewing kit you can discover specialty tools. Dab wire brushes, run pattern wheels or neurologic wheels over the skin to trace a prickly outline of his muscles. Look in the kitchen for textured foods. Use tortilla chips to "shave" his armpits. Swirl grapes beneath your hand like soft ball bearings. Try dragging a handful of cold spaghetti noodles from his feet to the hollow of his knees, over his butt and up his back to the nape of his neck. Crush eggshells against the soles of his feet. If you need inspiration, you really ought to play with your food more often.

Natural objects such as feathers, twigs, stinging nettles offer some interesting sensations. Insects are a bizarre possibility, but don't try this unless you really know that your partner is free of phobias. Bugs scare the bejesus out of many people, touching such a chord of terror that you may risk a grand emotional disaster. Even among the self-possessed, their little barbed feet do cause hackles as they crawl up a person's back. Avoid stinging or biting beasties. Remember that bugs are affected by temperature. The colder it is, the slower they move.

Always trick expectancy. Vary the touch from ultra-light to near skinning with unpredictability. In general a feather-light touch will hypersensitize an area of skin, cocking the nerves, while a swift rough stroke with lots of pressure traveling the length of a given body part will seem to fire them off. Bring other senses into rapid play. Try suddenly drumming cardboard tubes from empty rolls of paper towels over his body. Make it loud, fast, furious and short to produce a perception of violent force in both touch and sound. Plastic fly swatters also work well.

Abrasion has a variety of uses. You can calm an anxious partner through a reassuring massage. You can use it as a springboard from which to launch into various activities such as flogging or clothespinning. Use it to sound out other activities by talking about different fantasies. That toothpick poking the tits becomes a needle in a make-believe piercing. A butter knife becomes a scalpel in a cutting ceremony of ritual scarification. Of course you may just do abrasion as the sum of the scene.

TACTILE MYSTERY
Ted, Philadelphia, Pennsylvania:

Abrasion is a very personal and individualistic extension of my touch and special handling. No matter what part of the body I fiddle with, it's always the mind that I'm really playing with. I try to combine sensations like sweet and sour. I like to run a pattern wheel inside a feather duster. For the person undergoing abrasion and savoring the textures, the stabbing metal intermingles strangely with the tickling plumes.

During abrasion scenes, I'll blindfold the person I'm working on, but I never use headphones or earplugs. I like using my voice too much. It's a way of being in greater control of what he hears. I often will have music playing in the background, usually some pieces that I've specially recorded to complement the scene. Sometimes I'll play different classical pieces low in the background. But I think of my voice as the main instrument that's guiding my partner. I purposely lower my pitch so that the words rumble and roll with a rhythm that people seem to latch onto. It starts a synergy where the words, the action and his reactions affect me and what I say and it continues to roll on like that. After the scene is finished, some of the things I've said, in retrospect, sound pretty stupid, but at the time they're spoken, they really were pretty effective.

When I'm running my hands over someone's skin, I use talk to probe and guide him. I really do feel as though I'm doing a Vulcan mind meld. I've been known to murmur, "From my mind to your mind, my hands control your sensations." Corny, but the bottom in this instance began to writhe with the rhythm of my words and hands. I had him mummified and hooded so he wriggled like a moth struggling in the cocoon. Only his tits and cock and balls were exposed. And I pricked and tormented those with a dried rose stem. Deprived of sight, he retreated to his own fantasies to identify the cause of his sensations. He squirmed, convinced that the gentle tapping of the thorns was an electric wire sparking on his bare flesh. I also had a soup ladle that I had filled with ice cubes and ran this over his genitals, nipples and along his plastic wrapped limbs. He's never figured out what the cold metal was and I've never told him. All he's got is the memory of a mysterious caress to go on. But it ensures that he focuses on his sense of touch. For most of the people I do abrasion with, that tactile remembrance is amazingly sensual. Almost everyone says that they'd like to do it again.

▼

Finally, to keep from spreading disease, keep your implements clean. Don't risk transmitting HIV, hepatitis, skin infections or scabies from one person to another. If you've any abrading or pricking items that aren't disposable, wash them in a 10% bleach solution or a strong detergent, rinse and let air dry. Scrub pads, sandpaper, emery boards, toothpicks and the like are disposable, so use on only one partner and discard.

BODY MODIFICATION

An essential component of initiation rituals is the permanent marking of the initiate's body. This involves tattooing, piercing, scarification, mutilation and amputation. Sometimes the dividing line is hard to draw. Circumcision of the foreskin involves scarification, amputation and mutilation with cultural attitudes shaping one's view. My European friends wonder why American men are routinely, radically and unnecessarily clipped of their foreskins. Western feminists are befuddled when African women staunchly defend clitorectomy. One group's sacred ritual is another's barbaric act.

TATTOOS

Tattoos have an ancient history. A stone age body discovered in an Alpine glacier bore mysterious markings on its back. The Old Testament forbids the practice. Certain eastern Native American tribes covered their bodies and faces with ornate designs. Japanese and Chinese have long used intricate figures from their traditional folklore. The modern fascination with tattoos emerged from the mingling of western sailors with Pacific Islanders. From them, the practice took hold among the working class, with the occasional war acquainting more men with the art of tattooing. Polite western society has unceasingly frowned on them as vulgar and a sure sign of the lower classes. Yet its symbolism of ritualistic initiation persists, especially among the military. The peer pressure within segments of the armed forces is tremendous, as though that first tattoo confers rather than confirms a man's macho identity. More tattoo parlors exist near military bases than anywhere else.

Tattoos are a matter of taste. They've been likened to bagpipes, you either like them or hate them. Some love tattoos on others but find the idea of getting one themselves abhorrent. For many, a tattoo is private and they want theirs where only sexual partners will find it. A few love it as an art form in itself, decorating their bodies as living canvases.

Tattoos are strictly visual enticements. A properly designed and well-placed tattoo can complement and enhance a good physique. A sweaty rock hard chest decorated with a crisp intricate design looks great on a sun bronzed twenty year old, but take a look at the WW II vets to get an idea of how that tattoo might look in the future. When your tits have sagged and the tattoo has blurred beneath gray hair and age spots, the visual sexiness may dim. Since a tattoo is permanent, pick a design with which you'll still look good when you're on your retirement pension.

Think about tattoos very carefully. For a mere sixty dollars, you could make a mistake that costs over three thousand to correct. Lasers can zap some tattoos by evaporating the dark pigments, but those exotic colored inks present a problem. Complete removal requires surgery, often with skin grafts.

Avoid putting anyone's name in your tattoo. Most relationships don't last forever and a future lover may not enjoy reading your ex's name every time you strip. Consider also that you still have formal occasions where displays of lightning bolts around your neck just won't do. As a rule, refrain from tattoos that can still be seen when you're completely dressed. Tattoos on the hands, neck and face will almost guarantee your lifelong unemployment.

Several firms make temporary tattoos. Applied with either water or alcohol, these last up to a week, although they can often be scrubbed off sooner. It's a good way to experience the pleasure without the permanence. They also help to dampen your compulsion long enough for a cool-headed deliberation before undergoing the needle. There are some inventive ways of concealing a tattoo. One enterprising fellow had a circle of stars tattooed in white around his butt. They blend in with his pale ass until he gets a good spanking and then, to the delighted surprise of his top, a cluster of white stars emerges from the reddening cheeks! Some of the newer inks glow under black lights. If you happen to strip your shirt off at the disco, it's sure to get you noticed.

Seek a reputable artist. If you see someone with a great tattoo, ask who created it. When you pay the parlor a visit, request to see pictures of their completed and healed work. If they haven't a collection to show you, don't risk a botched job. Most have a pattern book if you've nothing specific in mind. Artists are quite happy to modify a design or work with you to create a special one. Also ask about sterile technique. New needles should be used for every client and the instruments sterilized after every customer. Hepatitis is a problem in substandard parlors. So far, there's no documented case of HIV being transmitted, but don't chance it.

There's a bit of painful stinging as the needle pushes the pigment just below the surface of the skin. The waist, genitals and buttocks are the most sensitive areas. If you happen to have a design, such as a tiger, which takes a lot of coloring, it may feel like ground glass rubbing into your skin. Elaborate tattoos may take several visits to complete since the outline and details must heal to assure accuracy. Discuss this with the artist.

A well-chosen, well-placed tattoo can enhance your body as well as revealing something of your personality. An ill-considered tattoo, however, might inspire you to undress strictly in the dark.

SCARIFICATION

Scarification relies on the formation of scar tissue or raised keloid bodies where ritual cutting of the top layers of skin has occurred. Many tribal groups throughout the world use scarification. These aren't brutal or deep mutilations, but rather intricate traditional patterns with deep social and religious significance. Often, a special irritant is rubbed into the wound to insure that the tissues inflame enough for adequate scarring. In the SM community, scarification shares many of the same functions as tattooing. But unlike a tattoo, it is palpable and you'll know it's there when the lights are out. As with tattoos, make certain that you've thoroughly checked out the qualifications of the person who will be doing the cutting. Plastic surgery or re-cutting is required to undo a poor scarification.

PIERCING

Until recently, good piercers were located in a few major metropolitan areas. Now, many experienced professional piercing businesses operate. SM/leather events, which invite vendors, will usually have an accomplished piercer in attendance. Quite a number operate on a freelance basis. Some charge a fee; others do it free as part of a scene. Backgrounds vary from tattoo artists to medical personnel who have discovered a second use for their skills with a needle.

Credit for the popularity of body piercing in the United States belongs to Fakir Musafar, an advertising executive in the everyday world, and Jim Ward of Gauntlet. Fakir's explorations with piercing rituals and technique began in his teens and continued quietly for thirty years before he began sharing his discoveries and explorations with others. Jim Ward also went very public with his piercing fetish when he founded Gauntlet Enterprises in the late seventies. From the coast, piercing knowledge spread throughout the SM world and is beginning to spread into the non-SM communities.

As statements, piercings do not mean today what they did thirty years ago, nor what they will ten years from now. Piercings are done for two basic effects, as adornments or sexual intensifiers. Though they may be handy for tethering and some find them visually exciting, I would list nasal piercings as adornments. A ring in the nipple, however, has a function beyond mere looks or utility. It provides added stimulation, acting as a sexual enhancement, an intensifier of erotic feeling.

A Prince Albert penetrates the urethra just below the cock head with the ring entering the hole and exiting from your piss slit. It's sometimes called a dressing ring and was purported to have been used to fasten the penis out of the male bulge when tight knickers were the rage. (Check out those portraits of men in white pants from Napoleon's era—balls but no cock.) I ran across a statement in a German magazine which mentioned that the ring helped keep smegma from building up under the foreskin but the article didn't elaborate. Supposedly, Queen Victoria's husband, Prince Albert, who was from the region of Saxony where this piercing is said to be traditional, had one; hence the current name. The PA was the only piercing practiced in modern Western Europe until recently. Its origins may extend back to Ancient Rome. The British Museum has several brass Roman wind chimes (tintinabula) whose figurines sport enormous penises and dildos with rings from which bells were hung. While it's not proof that the Romans themselves sported PAs, it's hard to imagine that, confronted with these representations, no Roman took the idea into his head.

A frenum is done slightly lower than the PA and perpendicular to the penile shaft. The frenum anchors a ring that flips over the glans of the penis and serves as a cock-ring for the dick head. The guiche occurs on the mound behind the ball sac. Weights can be hung from the healed guiche to bounce against the nuts when fucking. It's also known as the fister's piercing. When a fist is inserted into the butt, the prostate is pressed against this region of the guiche and manipulation of the ring can be quite erotic. If someone has a guiche and either a PA or a frenum, it's possible to lock them together with the penis separating the balls.

The nipple is made of the same sort of erectile tissue as the head of the penis. Far from delicate, this tissue is like football leather. It's very tough to push a needle through. Single tit piercings are left for tops and right for bottoms, but if it's a pleasure in itself, why not do both and screw the signals. Nipple piercings are especially good for involving tit play in bondage situations. New jewelry designs fit quite close to the body and keep your piercings private.

Scrotal piercings are less common. Some interesting scrotum piercings were on a fellow with a generous ball sac. He had series of small rings set along the margin of his sac. His chaps were outfitted with small D-rings along the crotch. When he laced the corresponding rings together, his ball sac formed a living codpiece.

Ear, eyebrow and nasal piercings have been the traditional "in your face" piercings of the outsider. Only recently have male ear piercings become trendy rather than socio-political statements as nasal piercings still are. Tusks and rings are the favored adornments for the nose. There are other piercings which I haven't mentioned because they aren't that common. Gauntlet has a catalogue as well as videos that illustrate the various male and female piercings in detail.

There's a traditional Japanese technique of implanting tiny ball bearings into the foreskin that is becoming popular in Europe. Supposedly the members of the Yakuza, the Japanese Mafia, had a tiny bronze ball inserted for every year they spent in prison. Stainless steel balls of about a quarter inch diameter are generally used. Since most North American men are shorn, this may not prove as popular as in Europe.

The best places are those that protrude from the body surface such as the nipples or penis. Piercings on sites that do not protrude generally take longer to heal and have more problems. The guiche is particularly troublesome since it lies between the anus and the genitals. Lack of air, chafing from walking and fecal contamination make healing especially difficult, sometimes taking up to six months. The Prince Albert heals the quickest since it's frequently washed by sterile urine and hangs from an appendage.

Healing time normally varies from six to ten weeks. Plan on some restrictions. Even without problems, the site may be sore for weeks, curtailing sexual play. Care needs to be taken during healing. Not all considerations are necessarily sexual. You wouldn't want to have a guiche done the week before you leave on a backpacking vacation. If you have a partner, discuss it with him first. You may find he has a strong aversion to metal in flesh. On the other hand you may be lucky and find that you've an eager companion on your discovery of a new fetish. My lover and I were driving back from Washington D.C. when I blurted out my desire to get a Prince Albert. I was babbling on about how I was fascinated by a friend's PA and that I found the thought of a metal ring in my dick exciting and if we didn't like it, I could always take it out and the hole would heal up and no one would ever be able to tell that it had ever been pierced, when my lover silently took my hand and placed it over his hard-on. "Does that say anything to you?" he said grinning.

Your choice of piercer is crucial. Make certain that the person is qualified. Always get references and see what healed piercings done by the piercer look like. Asymmetric tilted tit rings may not be what you really had in mind. The skill of the piercer not only assures aesthetic looks but minimizes your pain. Experienced piercers are so quick that most piercings are slightly more intense than a jab from a needle in the doctor's office. Few really want to experience the pain of having a tit poked at from the inside by a fumbler trying to get the piercing straight. Safety and sterility should be primary concerns. A decent piercer will be happy to discuss your concerns with you. He should be willing to show you his sterilizing equipment and explain his efforts to make your piercing as sterile as possible. Needles should never be re-used. Cleanliness of the place ought to equal a physician's office. If anyone ever attempts to use a piercing gun, like those once used by ear piercing clinics, run away. Those things are unsafe and can spread infection. An abscess in your genitals or HIV could result from being pierced by one of those things.

Only licensed medical professionals should ever inject numbing medications. Some people have a drug reaction that stops the heart. Besides, what's the point of getting stuck with a needle and injected with a stinging medication just to numb you from another needle's jab? PAs are the only male piercing that topical ointment can be used for. Usually, it's placed into the urethra several minutes before the piercing is done. It doesn't eliminate the pain, but does lessen it. Its major value seems to be as reassurance.

JANET BLEVIN'S JOURNAL (EXCERPT)
Greensboro, North Carolina:

Today, we're on our way to Norfolk, VA. I am driving Kevin to get his "Prince Albert" (his dick piercing). I received a piercing several years earlier at the Gauntlet in San Francisco, so I'm having a hard time imagining this—me driving Kevin up from down South to some guy's house where another man comes down from up North to pierce on the weekends. "Needles" to say, I have my doubts but I don't convey them to Kevin.

Having arrived in town, we turn down the right street and begin looking for the house. It was a strange, seedy sort of neighborhood. My eyes opened wide as I pulled to a stop in front of the appropriate house. I looked at Kevin and he looked at me and we looked at the house and we looked at each other. I suddenly lost it and burst out laughing. I said, "I feel like I'm taking you to have an abortion in one of those illegal clinics." He mentioned the scene from the movie *Dirty Dancing*. We laughed some more, gathering up the courage to venture forth out of the jeep. We finally do to be greeted by three men and two dogs, one of which has a serious underbite.

After Kevin signed the paperwork giving them permission, they made him lie down on the dining room floor. Another oddity. I pulled up a chair to watch the proceedings, voyeur that I am.

They numbed him with a shot of medicine. No problem there. They put the piercing needle through the head of his dick. No problem there. They started to put the ring in. Big problem there. The needle they used was too small for the size of his ring. The one guy, a trainee, pushes and prods to try and get the ring in. He only succeeds in getting a lot of blood out. I was getting concerned at this point. Not that I wasn't already concerned after driving up and seeing the neighborhood scenery.

The third guy, visibly frustrated, goes to get another ring. He hands it to the trainee, who then tries to put it in, what looks like backward to me. I keep asking Kevin how he is doing and if he's alright. He says yes. He says the numbing is working and he doesn't feel anything. All the while this guy is smashing Kevin's penis trying to get the second ring in. I lie and tell Kevin how good it looks (this while more blood is rush-

133

ing out).

After much torment on my and the trainee's part, the ring is in. Yeah! It does indeed look good. The bruising hasn't yet shown up but once it does, it takes a couple of weeks to go away. We're outta here. That is, if no one stole my tires while we were inside for a whole hour. At Gauntlet, I was pierced and gone in fifteen minutes and that included watching an aftercare video. Maybe that's because Jim Ward pierces a lot of people. When I asked how many people this guy has pierced, he snapped, "Enough to know I'm doing it right." Hmmm, oh well.

We get back in my jeep. As we're riding back home, Kevin gives me a few clues that with a new hole in his dick, he's feeling the jeep's bumping up and down. It almost brought out the sadist in me.

▼

The choice of jewelry has increased lately. Several firms, US and European, now make a variety of attractive and functional designs. The composition of materials has increased from the traditional surgical stainless steel and high carat gold to include newer, inert metals and materials. Avoid silver and base metals. They oxidize forming rust and tarnish that may adhere to your piercing, cause allergic reactions or poison you.

A practice has been to have piercings done in scene as a rite of passage. A bottom in training may have various piercings done as levels of training are completed. I had my tit pierced during a commemoration ceremony with my club members. It's a very intimate and meaningful ring that reminds me of those friends. A number of Radical Faeries practice rituals and ceremonies that use temporary piercings as a way of attaining some sort of ecstatic consciousness. Read *RFD* magazine for organizations and information involved in reviving ancient rites. Of course, some enjoy piercing for the extreme erotic sensations that they provide during SM play sessions. I know quite a few people whose first piercing occurred during a solo SM masturbation session. They seem to be the ones who retain the desire to receive temporary piercings as part of a scene.

Temporary piercings usually occur in multiples. While someone may want to have his dick nailed to the floor during a scene, more often a series of insertions are done since the thrill comes from the sting of the needle entering flesh, so that instead of a single temporary PA, a row of hypodermic needles decorates the length of the penis. Janet has told me of women SMers who attach black fabric with straight pins to their arms and torso like bat wings and then go out on the town. This sense of fun fantasy is missing, by and large, from male SMers who tend to prefer a scene of grim and grave ritual.

134

T.S., Portland, Maine:
Having just pledged the club, TJ wanted to mark the occasion with a public temporary piercing. With a hood that blinded him, he was led naked into the club's playroom and stretched spread eagle on a mat. Four men stood by with plastic inflatable casts that they slipped over his arms and legs. At George's signal, they were inflated, preventing his limbs from bending. As the four men held his arms down, George prepared a sterile set-up on a small table. As a nurse anesthetist, he could obtain a wide range of needles and he knew how to use them safely. Swabbing the area with a skin disinfectant, he donned a pair of surgical gloves. He clamped each tit with triangular-tipped forceps with a rubber-band wrapped around their handles so as to better control closure without cutting off blood circulation. He handed the forceps on TJ's right tit to a club member. Grasping the other with his left hand, he lifted a long thin steel wire from the sterile cloth with his right.

"I think it's a guide wire from a cardiac catheter," someone whispered to me. Turning to TJ, George asked him what he desired. TJ answered him. George asked, "Why?"

"I've jacked-off dreaming of having my tits pierced. It excites me and scares me. I want it. I need to face the fear and pain. If I can go through with this, I'll always remember pledging the club."

Sweat beaded on TJ's belly and his heart pounded rapidly. George leaned down and whispered something in his ear. Sitting up, he poised the needle parallel to TJ's chest.

"Steady," and the wire stung into the nipple.

With a bellow, he bucked, throwing one of the men holding him but the needle was through. Drawing it like silver thread, George poised it at the next nipple.

"Still determined?" Pale and panting, he assented. George drove the wire through. With a single strand of metal threaded through both TJ's tits, George twisted it gently but exquisitely, giving him what he had craved. At his request, they left him alone with his own thoughts.

URETHRAL PLAY

Christopher "Parusha" Larkin in *The Divine Androgyne* said that men have three erotic orifices: the ass, the mouth and the urethra. Of these, the opening in the penis is perhaps the least thought of.

Many men have experimented with masturbating while sticking something down their dicks. From collar studs to old fashioned hat pins with pearl ends, from knitting needles to wooden spoon handles, to just trying to work their little finger down the piss slit, men have endeavored to fuck the insides of their dicks. Part of the pleasure of a Prince Albert piercing is its heightening sensations by rubbing a small portion of the urethra.

Sounds are blunt, highly polished metal rods that are inserted down the urethra by medical personnel to stretch open constrictions that inhibit urination. Unless you've a way of insuring sterilization, you should never insert them into the bladder. A severe infection could result. Van-Buren sounds have curved ends and Dittel have straight. They range in size from 8 to 40 French. French gauges measure the outside circumference in millimeters. A standard size is 16 French which means that the sound is 16 mm in circumference which is a diameter of about 5 mm or 1/5 inch. Often used in place of sounds are uterine dilators. Haggar dilators are about seven and a half inches long, whereas Pratts are nearly a foot in length. These have the advantage of being double ended with a different size at either end. Dilators also have less of a curve than Van-Buren sounds and are usually flattened in the center to provide a gripping surface. This makes the business end of them shorter than sounds and lessens the possibility of insertion into the bladder.

As with most SM, bodily damage can occur from inexperienced use. I would advise anyone who is interested in playing with sounds or dilators to learn it from someone experienced. Runs and SM events frequently offer demonstrations on safe urethral play. Demonstrations, however, just cannot capture the energy and the eroticism that a scene creates. Consequently, extraordinary activities often look like cold, clinical procedures. In the hands of a good top, sounds give deliciously pleasurable feelings from both the pressure and the motion within the urethra. If these sensations are marvelous on the outside of your member, fantasize about stroking it from within.

Catheters are flexible tubes which medical personnel insert into the urethra and into the bladder in order to drain it of urine. Catheterization must be done with examination gloves under sterile conditions since the chance of infection is high. Forty percent of all hospital acquired infections are catheter related, mostly from a break in sterile technique during insertion. Improperly done, it could result in a bladder infection that can rapidly spread to the kidneys where it could cause havoc. A low grade fever is generally the first sign of a bladder infection, followed by cloudy urine and a feeling of needing to urinate frequently. Get medical attention right away.

If you've never done catheterization, learn it from somebody competent. You may also want to consult back issues of *Dungeon Master*. ["You're going to put *what* up my *what*??" by laFarge, *DM* 34 and also "Catheters," J. Roman, *DM* 37.] Though often done as a scene in their own right, catheters may be part of a control scene since the top determines whether and when urine flows from the bladder. It's also done in conjunction with prolonged bondage so that someone mummified in a deprivation scene hasn't even the distraction of needing to take a piss.

Catheters should be used once and then tossed in the trash. They're quite cheap and reusing them is not worth the price of infection. Even if you do have an autoclave to resterilize them, the heat will weaken the rubber and may cause the inflatable balloon to burst.

When prepping for catheter insertion, wipe the head of the penis with Benzalkonium antiseptic wipes and then swab with a betadine solution. Don't use alcohol; it's too harsh on the glans and not as effective against germs. KY is still the best lubricant. To preserve sterility, use only from a new, unopened tube or from a single use foil pack.

Chapter 8: A Special Specialty

Does it hurt

> *He moves again*
> *The deeper regions*
> *yield more*
> *and more*
> from "The Beautiful Tendons"
> —Jeffery Beam

FISTING

Fisting, also known as handballing, is in a class by itself. This is big-time penetration. There are many misconceptions and myths: that fisting is the brutal ramming of a hand up your ass; that it will damage your gut; that it will guarantee your catching AIDS; that repeated stretching of your ass will cause loss of control over shitting; that your bowel movements will become irregular and your turds misshapen; that you'll be prone to farting. Some of these are interesting variations of the heterosexuals' contention that a dick up the butt leads to incontinence. Properly done, fisting isn't a traumatic forcing of the hand into the rectum but instead more like a swallowing of the hand by the butt. There are still quite a few doctors who won't believe fisting is possible, yet they themselves use speculums, anesthetics and muscle relaxants to open an asshole just as wide during rectal surgery. My personal favorite is the holier-than-thou attitude of some SMers that fisting is not really SM because it's too pleasurable. I wish the authorities were so discerning.

Fisting has few exclusive tops or bottoms. The recipients of a fist are more inclined to retain a bottom-only preference without the drift that tops have. Among exclusive tops, health problems, anatomy and psychological factors are largely the determining factors in their preference. Among fisters, there are constant rumors of "exclusive" tops who bottom in private. While it's just wishful thinking in most cases, there's too many rumors for just idle gossip. Being one of those people who topped for years before throwing my butt into the sling, I can vouch for the emotional and mental difficulty of becoming comfortable with taking a fist. The physical ability to take someone's hand is just one aspect of fisting. It's probably more important to be completely at ease with your partner and fully comfortable with yourself. Not only is the receipt of a hand into your rectum and lower colon the deepest, most intimate penetration you can have, but it makes you extremely vulnerable on every level. In any event, respect privacy. Outing an "exclusive top" as a "closet bottom" only prolongs his process of self-acceptance and needlessly hurts him psychologically and emotionally.

Fisting has less of the body beautiful cult than most SM. Skill, ability and rapport count more than image. Choice of partner is critical. Find someone who knows what he's doing, someone you can trust. If you don't have absolute confidence in the person topping you, you'll find it difficult to relax enough to take his fist. If you're at all uptight, your stress will reveal itself by solidly clenching your sphincter shut. Just because he's flying a red hankie doesn't mean he knows safe and exciting play. Not everyone has a knack for topping; some are just plain boring. Their routine is either limited to a few special tricks or their technique is rather mechanical. And as with any SM activity, an egotistical top with an attitude is dangerous. This isn't the sort of play for violence or forcing—too much damage can be done to your internal parts.

The best tops have a talent for reading their partners, pushing them a bit and backing off just before things get too intense. They're adept at negotiating that boundary line between pain and pleasure. With a definite rhythm to their actions, they do seem to have a direction in mind when they take their partners for a ride. You want someone who knows how to take his time, tease your ass, relax your sphincter and play with your hole to the point that it sucks his hand in. Many of the best tops bottom as well. They know first hand what you're feeling.

UNFOCUSED FEELINGS
Jay, Detroit, Michigan:

Although I've bottomed as often as not in leather sex, I'd only topped in fisting activities. I intensely enjoyed the pleasure that I gave to the fistee. For three years, I only topped, rationalizing that I was still learning. When my lover began exploring the fisting scene, he wanted to learn as both top and bottom. We began mutually reversing roles as he learned the art of fisting. I was of course the ultimate pushy bottom giving stage directions even while my ass hung from the sling.

He gave himself over to the pleasures with abandon, losing himself in the oblivion of the sensations. Although I found the extreme sensations overwhelmingly satisfying, I afterwards felt vaguely uneasy—an odd contrast to his utter relaxation both mentally and physically.

One session finally brought an end to my teacher-as-the-bottom role. I had grabbed a handful of lube and was greasing my own butt-hole when he blurted out in exasperation, "Don't you think I will put enough in? When are you going to let me do things to you in my own way? When you insist on telling me what to do, I get the message that you don't trust me." It took an effort, but I relinquished control when I bottomed.

But while he continued to revel in ecstasy, I began to crash emotion-

139

ally at the end of any scene in which I bottomed. I felt vague but over-powering guilt, but could not say why. I found that more and more my "head wasn't in it." I began to be plagued by spasms of my prostate that precluded accepting my lover's fist. Even on those occasions when every-thing was OK in my head and no psychosomatic spasms occurred, at the session's end I still felt an upwelling of guilt and a vague sense of disapproval.

I stopped bottoming for my lover. Strangely, I could bottom for some-one who wasn't particularly close as a friend and not have emotional crashes. My lover felt rejected. He couldn't understand why I couldn't even talk about it with him. We had tried to discuss it, but I just couldn't verbalize the problem. Hell, I couldn't even define it to myself. As far as he could see, my Catholic upbringing was getting in the way. Simply put, if the Church teaches that pleasure is bad, fisting must be evil, evil, evil, and I must be experiencing the classic Catholic guilt trip. The expla-nation was too simplistic. I couldn't talk about it mostly because I had no locus for the feelings. I hadn't a handle on why they occurred nor whose disapproval I should fear. There was no sense of sin. So why the guilt?

I have a friend with whom I am very close and whose background closely resembles my own. When I last visited, we had a session with a third friend and I took my turn in the sling. He knows me well enough to sense my mood. While our mutual friend worked me over, he worked on my head, coaxing me to let go, guiding my mind and psyche. I managed to break through some major mental barriers. At one point ac-cording to them, I screamed out my lover's name repeatedly, yet I have no clear recollection. At the end of the session, he stroked my head and chest talking me down and reassuring me. He acknowledged and praised me for having let go of the mental and emotional anchors, but he put off any discussions till later.

The next day, we talked. After he recapped my emotional and psy-chological highs during the previous night's activities, he asked me to describe my vague unease and feelings. Then, he had me summarize my family background. I had grown up in a large Catholic family with a cold domineering father who crushed any sign of independence. Displays of emotion were belittled—except for anger. But even that emotion was reserved for him. We were punished if we lost our tempers.

We discussed things over coffee for a long time. In conjunction with the previous night's experience and the professional savvy of my ther-apist friend, I could at last find words for what the emotional side of me was trying to communicate. I have three deep fears: of being vulnera-ble (physically and emotionally), of relinquishing control, and of losing myself and loved ones. Since I grew up in an environment where any

140

openness or apparent loss of control would leave me vulnerable to attack, to relinquish control was to court disaster and loss of approval. SM, especially fisting, is the ultimate relinquishment of control. With the pleasure/pain ratio at maximum, many of those scarred-over family traumas popped open leaving a jagged wound but no remembrance of the original injury. Scars being non-elastic, cannot stretch. My response to that bursting of emotional scars was an irrational dread. Since then, I've been concentrating on accepting my vulnerability. With the help of my lover and of my friend, I am paradoxically gaining control over my life by trusting enough to give up control.

ANATOMY AND PHYSIOLOGY

The Red Queen advised Alice to begin at the beginning, continue on to the middle and stop at the end. In the fister's wonderland, learning anal anatomy means beginning at the end of the digestive tract and working towards the beginning.

The lip of the ass's pucker hole is a special ring of muscle called the anal sphincter. Its job is to stay clenched to prevent shit from dropping out of the chamber just above it. It's given some help by a generous supply of blood vessels that help inflate it somewhat. The chamber within is the rectum and is where feces is temporarily stored until you find a convenient place to drop it. The size of the rectum varies considerably from one person to the next. Like the size of the penis, it isn't always in proportion to a person's overall body size. Most rectums will stretch over time to accommodate a fist. At the upwards part of this chamber is a sharp little "S" turn which marks the divide between the rectum and the descending colon. This turn is where the bowel is attached to the body cavity. Care must be taken not to rip this adhesion. The colon is where any remaining water or nutrients are absorbed from shit and the familiar turds are fashioned. (Diarrhea is the watery shit that hasn't had this processing.) The colon rises from the rectum along the left side of your body before it makes a sharp turn to the right. When the nurse in the doctor's office gives you an enema, this is why you lie on your left side to help the water flow into it. Most people only take a hand into the rectum or in the first part of the colon. Deeper fisting the length of the descending colon is possible but not something for beginners.

Your body organizes its nerves into distinct networks like regional phone systems. Quite often, different organs share the same lines of communication to the brain and some parts of your body lack a way of directly talking to the brain. It's similar to someone without a phone having to use a neighbor's phone during an emergency. When a person has a heart attack, they often feel a pain shooting down the left arm. Someone with appendicitis may have flu-like symptoms or may com-

141

plain of a backache or even of a sore bladder. The most familiar example of a shared neural network is when you eat ice cream too quickly. Instead of a cold tongue, you get a headache. It's a phenomenon known as referred pain. But since pain and pleasure are so closely linked, what applies to one, applies to both. It's not so strange really. You already take for granted that stroking your genitals begins a series of reactions and responses. Why should it increase your breathing and pulse rates and make you grimace so bizarrely? You don't do it when your hand is caressed.

Fisting's pleasure arises from the inter-connection of neural inputs from the entire pelvic area, known as the ano-genital region, that plug into the spinal cord. Medical texts once called the solar plexus the abdominal brain. This network of nerves is so extensive that it's capable of operating independently from the brain. People with spinal cord injuries may have no feeling or use of their bodies below the injury, but their dicks still get hard and shoot when stimulated. Think of these nerves as one vast party-line where everyone can participate in any phone call to the brain. The trick is to entice everyone to pick up the call.

Shared neural networks mean shared pleasure centers. For example, taking a really good piss can give you a feeling similar to a minor orgasm. You've heard those sighs and grunts of minor ecstasy from men pissing. To fist is to tap into the body's pleasure party line and overload the network. The result is often a state of ecstasy with its attendant lack of control over physical response and an extreme inward focusing. There are often intense interactions between the partners, but fisting is really the bottom's scene. I've often found that slapping a blindfold and a pair of headphones on the fistee helps send him on these ecstatic transports by freeing him from any feeling of needing to stay in touch with me. When I top, I want him to go off on a flight. I get my pleasure from sending him into uncontrolled grunts and shudders. The phones and blindfold give him my permission to take rational leave of me without guilt. It's my gift to my partner.

The best tops are those who understand how to bring the variety of sensations into play. Contrary to common assumption, the prostate is not the exclusive source of pleasure during fisting. The bliss comes also from massaging the lining of the bowel, from stimulating the lips of the anal sphincter and from incidental rubbing of the bladder. Stimulation isn't just internal; kneading or slapping the buttocks, rubbing the perianum, sucking on the balls or even jacking the dick feeds more signals, more energy into the neural network. When this neural system is powerfully aroused, it triggers a complicated physiological process that releases endorphins, the body's natural opiate (Geoff Mains explored some of these chemical processes in *Urban Aboriginals*, Gay Sunshine Press,

1984.) Words are inadequate when explaining such an intensity of sexual stimulation that an erection becomes inconsequential. The term ecstasy is the only satisfactory one that describes the physical, emotional and mental states that the fistee experiences. Some Eastern religious cults have used ritual fisting to bring on this ecstasy as a way of communing with the cosmos. Some Californians have forged links to yogin thought, but as a Midwesterner, I prefer a more practical and less mystical explanation. Suffice it to say that fisting allows men to have multiple orgasms without ever cumming.

SAFETY

The insertion of anything into the body brings risk. Fisting can indeed be risky but those risks can be reduced dramatically. Although initial AIDS studies placed fisting in the riskiest category for AIDS infection, those reports had some flaws and reflected the shock of the investigators at such "extreme" behavior. Considerations of co-factors (such as unprotected anal intercourse or feces and mucous spread from one person to another via shared lubricant or by tops who didn't wash their hands) were not examined. Bottoms, in those days, were often opened up by fucking them and it was fairly common for a top to jack himself off inside the fistee's hole. Re-examination of data and new studies have affirmed that the current safety precautions are effective against HIV infection. In the newer guidelines, fisting has been removed from the dangerous list. But don't relax your vigilance. Play as safely as you can.

Follow these five guidelines religiously. If you skip any of these, you're increasing the likelihood of bodily damage or infection by the AIDS virus. Insist that your partners play by the following rules.

1. At least one of the participants should have had some experience in fisting. It can be safe and pleasurable, but it could also be extremely risky. Know what you're doing!

2. Each fister must have his own personal container of lubricant on which his name is clearly marked and from which only he will have his butt lubed. Never share lube. Bits of your mucous, feces and blood get into your lubricant. If your lube is subsequently used to grease another person's ass, viruses, bacteria and amoebas could hitchhike along and infect that person.

3. The top should always wear a brand new pair of latex gloves. This protects him from any infection of yours and you from any of his. In cases where more than two people are playing, it keeps germs and viruses from hitchhiking on his hands from one butt to another. Latex gloves also provide additional protection from scratches that could be caused by fingernails on the bowel lining. A box of fifty costs less than five dollars at the discount drug stores.

4. Keep your secretions from getting into his hole. Many people love to jack-off while fisting their partner. If you do this, you must make absolutely certain that no pre-cum or cum gets into his butt or into his lube. Some solve this by fisting with their one gloved hand and keeping ungloved the hand with which they're masturbating. If you're playing with more than two people, then let someone else wank you off. Mid-America Fists In Action requires that tops at its officially sponsored parties wear some sort of genital covering.

5. After each session, the top must scrub his hands, preferably to the elbow, with a solution of grease cutting detergent (Dawn in the US; Fairy Liquid in the UK) and green soap, then thoroughly rinse. Make certain that you're completely degreased. Dry hands with either paper towels or a fresh clean cloth. Don't let your hands spread diseases from one person to another.

PREPARATION

If you're topping, you should clip and file your fingernails. A number of people perform the tongue test. If your nails are long enough to scratch your tongue, they need additional filing. This isn't as critical as it was in the pre-AIDS days since safety now demands that the top wear gloves. Protect yourself and your partner and wear latex gloves. If you have cuts, abrasions, burns or sores on your hands, you shouldn't fist even with a glove. In the medical record, there is a case from Australia where an exclusive top, who never wore gloves, was infected by his HIV-positive lover. This was a special case because the top in question had a chronic open sore on his hand through which the virus was able to enter his body. The study does serve as a warning that HIV can infect the top if there are any breaks in the skin. Since most of us suffer from hangnails and get minute scratches and punctures on our hands, it's best to play safe and wear gloves.

Some researchers are concerned about the ability of vinyl to block HIV. If you or your partner have an allergy to latex, then you might consider wearing two gloves on each hand (double-gloving) with the vinyl towards the person with the allergy and the latex as the barrier for the person without the allergy. If you've no evident cuts, abrasions or hangnails, the vinyl gloves will probably offer adequate protection.

Gloves also assist in clean-up. Even with short nails, some fecal and mucous material still gets under the fingernails. Unless you really scrub well with a good stiff nail brush, a degreaser and green soap, you probably would carry a few relics under your nails. If you're in a situation where you may be fisting several people, you could transfer disease from one to another. Play safe; wear gloves.

The person who is planning to receive a fist undergoes an extensive

144

enema to clean out the lower bowel. Fisters refer to this as "douching" or "hopping on the hose." This isn't a quick little squirt into the rectum like the one you get at the doctor's office. This is more akin to a high colonic that cleans the colon out. Plan on taking half an hour or longer. Everyone's body responds differently. My lover can usually finish in less than thirty minutes; I've never taken less than ninety. In general though, warm water allows a more relaxing douche while cold water causes contractions and cramping. The two methods of accomplishing this clean-out involve using either a hose and nozzle connected directly to the tap or that old stand-by, the enema bag. Most find the enema bag far gentler than the hose. Either way, be sure that the nozzle and the system have been thoroughly cleaned before you use them. (Wash in hot soapy water, dunk for several minutes in a ten percent bleach solution—one ounce of bleach to nine of water. Rinse well and let air dry. For metal nozzles that may corrode, soak them for five minutes in a three percent bleach solution—four ounces of bleach to one gallon of water. Rinse and pat dry with a clean cloth.) Use a lubricant of some kind to avoid irritating the anus. If you're using a rubber hose, avoid any petroleum-based product since it will break down the rubber.

As you guess, fisting is not often a spur of the moment activity. A douching session will go easier if you've watched what you've eaten the day before. Stuffing yourself at a buffet makes for a long nasty douche the next day. Stay away from laxatives since these stimulate your entire digestive tract. The goal is to rid the colon of feces, not to open the sluice gates all along the passageway.

Enemas can cause some problems. If you douche too frequently, your body may come to rely on the flushing action of the water and simply stop its normal bowel movements. Your body will eventually restart itself, but the interim could be a bit uncomfortable. During a prolonged clean-out, you may notice a tingling in your fingers. Don't ignore it! It means that your body's fluid balance is seriously out of whack. You could faint or even trigger a heart attack. Take a break and drink real fruit juices to restore your electrolyte balance. If you prefer sodas then drink 7-up. I'd also recommend that you eat a banana. They're high in potassium, a necessary element for your heart. If you're using an enema bag, you can avoid this electrolyte imbalance by adding table salt to the water to make about a ten percent solution.

Most people wait for about thirty minutes after the big clean out to allow the colon time to absorb any remaining water. They'll generally have an additional squirt into the rectum just to be sure that things are feces-free. After your douche, you may notice a mucous discharge or a wet fart. Don't be alarmed, it's just your body restoring the normal mucous coating to your bowel. The douche will also cause farting the next day which many people mistakenly attribute to the act of fisting. It's actually due in large part to the water having flushed out many of the bacteria that assist in digestion. Without these microorganisms to help break your food down, a lot of gas can build up in your gut. Eating some yogurt with active cultures can help. Cottage cheese and buttermilk can also offer relief. Unless you want more gas than a blimp, avoid certain foods like refried beans or mustard greens such as broccoli.

Douching creates a special risk for disease transmission. Whether you fist or fuck, your chances of catching or passing-on an infection rise dramatically when you douche, and this also applies to those who use those little bottles of prepackaged enemas. Your rectum and sigmoid are blessed with a myriad of tiny blood vessels very close to the surface. These work to prepare your turds for elimination, absorbing the last bits of water and nutrition before you take a crap. To protect itself, your gut has a slimy coat of mucous. The douching action of the enema strips off this protective coating, removing a natural barrier to infection. Further, the douche may also rupture some of these exposed capillaries which leaves an even better opening for disease.

But this also means that if you are already infected with hepatitis, AIDS or some other organism, your "clean" butt hole may really be swarming with germs to pass on to others. An unwashed, ungloved hand that's inserted into different rectums is the perfect way to spread disease from one butt hole to another. Some folks who are HIV-positive become fatalistic about safety. After all, if you already have the BIG one, what does it matter? Well, it matters a great deal. The virus that you have may be currently inactive and, without protection, you could be exposed to a very active and virulent dose of HIV. Further, if your immune system is impaired, now more than ever you need to safeguard your health. A friend of mine, who was HIV positive, contracted a case of herpes that turned his asshole into a bloody mass of excruciating weeping blisters for the last ten months of his life.

LUBE

Crisco remains the lube of choice. It's natural vegetable oil that melts at a slightly higher temperature than that of a person's normal internal heat. It's also ridiculously cheap and comes in personal and glutton sized containers. For safety, each person should have an individualized can or container with his name on it for his and only his internal use. This prevents the germs and viruses of one person from infecting another, also known as "cross contamination." Crisco does break down latex but this occurs at a much slower rate than for the extremely thin and tightly stretched condoms. I've never had a glove break, even during long sessions. Your hand can feel the glove get looser as the latex deteriorates.

146

Petroleum and mineral oil based lubes such as Vaseline, baby oil and Elbow Grease are expensive and will break down the latex in the glove faster. Some AIDS Education groups are becoming rather insistent about the use of synthetic lubes during fisting. These lubes are water based and tend to dry out. They often contain nonoxynol-9, a viricide. If you do use a synthetic lubricant, keep a spray bottle of clean water to rewet it. Don't use spit. Of the various brands, Forplay seems to stay wet the longest. Two reasons are given for using a synthetic lube: they won't break down latex and the nonoxynol will help to kill viruses. I see the use as a trade off. As noted above, latex gloves are much thicker than latex condoms so that the risk of a glove breaking is significantly lower. The hand is also more sensitive than the penis is in detecting a problem with breakage and the hand doesn't leak semen into the gut. Most of the viricides are chemically detergents and can prove a bit rough on the rectal lining during a prolonged session. Rub some synthetic lube in your mouth to get an idea of what it does to the mucous membranes in your rectum. Also, since synthetic lubes are more expensive, people tend to skimp on the amount that they use. While the synthetic lubes may kill off some viruses, the irritation caused during their use may create a situation that allows for greater access by viruses. Crisco doesn't irritate the lining the way that detergents do, is cheap and plentiful (in the US) and is something with which the digestive tract can deal. Additionally, its high lubricant properties lessen the chance of trauma by friction.

If you're planning anal intercourse, do it before fisting and use a synthetic lubricant which won't destroy your condom. After you've fucked, then you can glove and switch to Crisco. But if you plan to fuck after a fisting session, then don't use any oil based lube. Use only a synthetic water based lubricant. Whatever lubricant you do decide to use, always be generous with it. There's a saying that you can never have too much lubricant while fisting.

POSITIONS

Most fisters find cradling in a sling is best for both the fister and fistee. It affords the fistee comfortable support and a feeling of floating. The chains provide a place on which his legs can either rest or be secured by stirrups. The fister can gently rock the fistee to build a rhythm. Slings can be adjusted to control the height at which he can comfortably fist his partner.

Not everyone has a sling. Other positions for the fistee include lying on his back, on his stomach, on his side or doggie-style on his hands and knees. One additional position gives the recipient great control. The top props his elbow on the floor with his hand extended towards the squatting fistee who lowers himself onto the hand. For someone having a rough time dealing with sensations, this restores a modicum of control. In choosing any position, remember that the top must also be comfortable. Compromise!

MECHANICS OF FISTING

Think of it as anal massage. It runs a continuum from finger-teasing to double-fisting. Most people regard fisting as the insertion of a hand to the narrowing of the wrist. The desire to "take a fist" may be so compulsive that unrealistic expectations set in for the budding bottom. Most likely, he'll be in such a frame of mind that, unless he experiences his anal muscle relax around the wrist bones as his ass swallows the hand, he feels cheated. I've had partners who have apologized for failing to take my hand on their first attempt at fisting. I always tell them to just enjoy the sensations as they come and not to worry about progress.

Try to recall the first time you got fucked in the ass. Remember that feeling of having to take a dump or of uncomfortableness with pleasure building till you popped your cork? Recall too that once you came, you wanted that dick out *now*? With fisting, your body again has many different sensations to sort out. Give it time; don't rush. Remember to keep your mind, body and emotions in balance. If you want it bad, close your eyes, or get blindfolded and fantasize about it. Don't start worrying and pestering your partner with, "Is it in yet?" Relax, put your head back and enjoy the flight.

Needless worrying will only make you clench your sphincter involuntarily. The name of the game is to enjoy it, not to be so uptight that you could crack walnuts with your anus. Fisting has as much to do with your emotional and mental state as with anatomy. It's not so much that your hole is being stretched as you're teaching your body to relax it, and that takes patience. Even an experienced fister needs to be massaged and relaxed. Anyone who forces his hand past an unrelaxed sphincter will indeed cause trauma and damage to the fistee. You may want to purchase some larger sized dildos and butt plugs to accustom yourself to the new sensations and to train your sphincter to relax. Just take your time and don't injure yourself.

CHIEFLY FOR TOPS

If you are going to fist someone, wash your hands to the elbow and dry with a clean dry towel. Most people don't think of this before fisting, but it applies the same logic of scrubbing germs off your hands before eating. The mouth end has more defenses to kill them off than this end. Put on fresh clean latex examining or surgical gloves. You may want to do this when the fistee is getting in position. Rinse the cornstarch or talc off the glove. This will lessen the chance of chafing the rectum. Even with gobs of lube, the powder can suddenly cause the latex to adhere, painfully, to his rectal lining.

Take your time leading up to the entry. Begin by caressing him. Massage the peri-anum, rub the fine hairs on his butt and tickle his pucker hole. Affectionate fondling helps relax him. When you're ready to enter, be smooth and gentle. No rough stuff. Use lots of lube. Run a greasy finger around the anus to relax the sphincter. Try calmly massaging the outside of his pucker hole with your greasy fist.

Minimize any foreplay or rubbing of the prostate. Your goal is to relax the sphincter and open the asshole. Make certain that you thoroughly work lubricant over your gloves. Many tops pack grease into the butt before they begin to open the hole. Keep things well lubricated at all times. For entry, a fister's adage is the "1, 2, 3, 4, 5 and in" method. Slowly insert one, then two, then three fingers, gradually opening and relaxing the hole. Go slow and gentle, but be persistent. You'll eventually want to try folding your hand so that your index finger rolls over to your pinky, with the thumb resting on the center of your palm. This puts all your fingers in a tight outstretched bundle. Not everyone can collapse his hand into a slender roll. The bones in my palm don't move very much towards each other but it compacts my hand enough to slip past the sphincter. Some friends of mine, however, can readily roll theirs into a tube shape.

You have to be attuned to your partner. Talk to each other. He may tell you to go faster or slower. Gauge the tension in his rectal muscle and note his facial expressions and body language. If he's pushing his butt onto your hand, don't pull away. He's in rut and it's a sign that he's in the proper frame of mind. Use your voice to reassure and relax him. Restrain his impulse to masturbate while you're teasing his butt open. Often it only tightens the sphincter as the sexual stress builds, so tell him to keep the dick play under control and to concentrate on the sensations in his ass.

If he is especially tense and tight, use it to your advantage. When you have several fingers in, tell him to tighten as hard as he can and hold it. Encourage him to squeeze your fingers ever tighter with his sphincter until his pucker hole tires. Sometimes it helps to let him bear down as well and slowly push you out. This taps into a natural reflex to relax and makes re-entry easier. You could also divert his overly focused attention from his anus to another part of his body. If he's not ticklish, rub his chest and belly or massage his thighs.

Many people use some sort of chemical relaxant like poppers. I would try to encourage him to learn to fist without them. If he does poppers, you may choose to guide his use of them. Have him take a deep hit and

149

hold it till you count to ten. Then have him exhale deeply as you push things a little further. (Be forewarned that some poppers can trigger a coughing fit that can force your hand out of his butt.) The poppers will serve to loosen the muscles and the slow exhalation will relieve some of his tension. Remember, never cram your hand, just push steadily. Most people take time to stretch their rectum to accommodate a fist. If it doesn't slide smoothly in, don't force it in! You could tear his bowel.

When it does slide in, curl your fingers into a balled fist. Most beginners tolerate being "handballed" in the chamber of the rectum. Just give him several moments to catch his breath. The sensations are pretty overwhelming. Talk to him soothingly and assure him that everything is fine. If he's new to fisting, he might find things overpowering and may want your fist removed immediately. Try to dissuade him. Distract him by tapping or rubbing his torso or legs. Have him take a deep breath and then slowly exhale. Use your voice to usher him into relaxation by telling him to let first his toes, then feet, then legs, hands, arms, neck and even his facial muscles go slack. Once you've gotten him to fully relax, refocus his attention on his butt. Have him tighten, then loosen, his asshole's grip on your hand. This lets him know that he does have some control. Begin very subtle movements until he gets used to the sensations. A small motion often is amplified as a major sensation. The rectum will be tight at first, loosening somewhat as you play.

If the person is an experienced fister, he may want you to enter with your fingers extended. As you slide in, you'll be wiggling your fingers slightly to work your way around the "S" curve of the sigmoid. Some guys have stretched this so that it's been straightened out. Most will need you to tease the "S" open one finger at a time. Once past this curve, you will be able to feel the strong pulse of his aorta between your hand and his backbone. I find that it's a very erotic sensation, reaching so deep into a man that his life's blood pulses at my fingertips—talk about intimacy and trust! This is the major artery in his body and in fifty-ish, overweight men, it can develop bulges like an old rubber hose called aneurysms. Don't play, fondle or put pressure on it. I've never heard of anyone rupturing one of these while fisting, but don't take needless risks.

Many experienced bottoms will not want to ejaculate during the initial fisting, usually called the "opening." This lack of normal "demonstrable" male sexual pleasure can make novice tops insecure. If their partner hasn't shot his load, then it's easy for them to misinterpret this as meaning they've somehow failed to satisfy their partner. To compensate, they may begin handballing rather too vigorously in an attempt to bring him to orgasm. Make certain that the two of you are communicating.

After he has cum or decided that he needs a break, you need to withdraw your hand safely. First curl your free hand around the wrist that's in him so that your thumb and index finger push lightly against his anus. Get him to relax and tell him not to bear down as you begin to pull out. When you begin to withdraw your fist, press your free hand against the lip of his anus. This will help you withdraw smoothly from him without inverting his anus. If you have your hand curled up into a ball, unfold it with a slight downward motion as you pull out. If you've entered him so that your fingers are extended, wiggle them slowly as you pull back to ease his colon off your fingers. This will keep his bowel from sticking to your fingers and getting turned inside out, a condition known as prolapsed bowel from which, incidentally, I've never known a fister to have suffered. Moving slowly and smoothly will assure that this won't be a problem. Once your hand is all the way out, gently massage his butt to help bring him back to earth. Fisting courtesy calls for the top to wipe the bottom's buttocks clean with paper towels.

PRIMARILY FOR BOTTOMS:

If you bottom, remember that the interplay between the two of you relies on communication. Establish some code words or phrases for your fisting session like "Ease up, slow, stop, continue, hold it there, pull out, time out." Make sure you and your partner agree on the response to these cues. Also set some hand gestures as sign language. A hand held up, palm toward the top means "hold it there." Both partners have the right to call an end to a session. If your top should decide that you need a break, listen to his reason for doing so.

Relax. Confidence in your partner is the name of the game. You are giving yourself rather completely and intimately to him. Don't start giving stage directions or fighting him by clamping down on his hand. These are signs that you're not really comfortable and perhaps you need to talk about some fears or concerns first. When he begins to open you, control your breathing and watch that you don't hold it or pant or hyperventilate. Breathe deep and let it out slow and concentrate on relaxing. Try to keep your hands from working overtime on your dick. While he's opening you, talk to him and let him know what you're feeling physically, emotionally and mentally. Respond to him by articulating your mood and sensations.

When you do finally take a fist, the pressure as it slides in will seem overwhelming. The widest part of the hand is near the base in a line with the thumb joint. Once this part has passed, the natural tapering of the wrist will help slide the remainder in. It will take your breath away. Many first timers find the sensations are so strong that they pop their corks almost immediately when the hand is finally in. If you do cum, you'll probably want it removed immediately. Try to hold off on your orgasm. The reward will be far more sexual ecstasy than you ever thought possible with your dick playing a hugely devalued role. Your partner will generally hold still and give you time to accustom yourself to the pressure and the sensation. You may feel as if you need to urinate. Often it's just the pressure of the hand against the bladder, a new sensation for you to sort out. Watch your breathing. Take a deep breath and concentrate on relaxing all of your body muscles. Your partner will most likely start with very small motions, increasing them as your rectum stretches and you relax. I usually let first timers play with their dicks at this point as it gives them a familiar erotic stimulation that seems to help sort out all the new ones that they're experiencing.

Advanced fisters usually will develop a taste for depth or width. Depth refers to the top snaking his hand up the colon. This ranges from the ginger probing of a single finger into the colon to the insertion of the hand to the forearm or elbow. The colon is highly elastic. It's more than just a bag. It has muscle that is capable of contracting and relaxing in waves that move food throughout your gut. Massaging the lining helps relax the tissues of the colon and as a person grows more experienced, his bowel is able to relax rather deeply and accommodate more of the top's hand and arm. Some guys get off on the sensations while others like the visual effect of something wiggling in their gut like an Alien about to burst forth.

Width refers to insertion of more than a single fist into the rectum. This ranges from a few fingers from the other hand to full double-handed fisting. Ever wonder about those rare dark red hankies? Some pious fisters can sit on the praying hands and hardly notice them.

Motion is where certain tops excel, using everything from wriggling thumb and fingers to rubbing the knuckles against the prostate. Smooth, rhythmic movements do more to send people on transports of ecstasy than rough, frenzied thrusts. Be inventive and combine different movements. You can roll your hand at the wrist while turning your arm so that the whole fist rotates in his butthole.

Sixty-nine fisting is great to do. It works best if you both have already been opened. Lie on your back so that you're head to foot. Wrap your inner leg around his so that your legs are braced against each other. Your assholes should now be exposed to each other. As much as tops get off by fisting their partners, the fact remains that the fistee gets much more out of a session than the fister. Sixty-nining restores the balance of mutual sensuality. You get back as good as you give. It's great with mirrors. You might want to tear off paper towels in advance for easier clean-up.

Toys such as dildos and more creative insertion devices are always nice. A friend uses dildos to help open people's holes. Another straps a massage vibrator to his arm. Sex shops sell different devices like tennis-sized rubber balls on a string which you push in one at a time, then gently tug out. I would recommend that you dedicate a toy to a particular person. Don't share them since some cannot be adequately cleaned to guarantee safety from viruses. If possible, roll a rubber over dildos. It will help in the clean-up.

Some folks enjoy enemas so much that it becomes a fetish in itself. There are enema clubs and various publications, gay and straight, that celebrate the joys of enemas. Consult the listings in the various leather publications.

Although I'm not opposed to someone using some chemical substance on occasion to enhance the experience or relax themselves, I am uneasy that some experienced fisters have never even tried to do without drugs. If you are not able to fist without the help of some sort of chemical, then you're using drugs as a crutch and I would suggest that you need to consider seriously the possibility of misuse or abuse. Most fisters use some sort of relaxant with the legal ones, including alcohol and prescription medications (muscle-relaxants). Many rely on inhalants such as poppers and ethyl chloride that have a pain-killing as well as relaxing effect. Many smoke either cigarettes or marijuana for the high of nicotine or THC. You will undoubtedly run across some who use hard-core, dangerous and addictive drugs. Whether or not the drug use is illicit, for your protection, you need to be on the alert for signs of drug abuse.

A COMPLETE DISASTER
S.C., London, England:

One of the worst experiences was when I went home with an RAF pilot for a fisting session. At that time, I had a good friend staying with me so I wasn't going to be at home alone with this stranger. I knew that the pilot had drunk quite a bit, but he didn't appear to be wasted. He had noticed my red hankie and had approached me. In talking with him, I got the impression he was an experienced fister and knew all about it.

Well, it was a complete disaster. After I climbed into the sling, it became clear he didn't know how to take it slow and easy while opening me up. I had to grab his arm to slow him down several times and tell him to use more grease. When he did get his hand in, he didn't know what to do. Pretty boring actually, except that every so often he would suddenly try to punch fuck me. The worst was yet to come. As I said, he didn't appear to be plastered, but I realize now that he was an alcoholic. He just keeled forward suddenly. He didn't pass out completely but collapsed on top of me in a drunken stupor with his fist still in me. It was frightening with him lying there wide-eyed and drooling while my insides were being painfully twisted. I had to scream for my flat-mate to come help. He's a small guy and it wasn't easy for him to lift the pilot off me. The worst was trying to extract his fist from me because the bastard started quarreling with my friend. It was really pretty violent to my arse.

I was really sore immediately afterwards and later developed an infection that had to be treated. He did tear my rectum but luckily only slightly. I healed up fine but was out of commission for a long time.

▼

In the US particularly, some people have become incapable of fisting without the help of crystal. They don't think that they've a problem even though the drug has become obligatory for them. They'll say that they're simply choosing to use it, but when crystal is always chosen, I'd say that they've become a slave to a habit and that's addiction. It doesn't need to be this way. I know other people who have pulled away from chemical substances entirely. They have found that drugs hinder their ability to enjoy fully a long and satisfying session. They're not reformed drug addicts or missionaries on a crusade, just quiet individuals who have made a decision to do without drugs. One has told me that, while smoking grass does indeed relax him and allows a quicker insertion of his partner's hand, he's not able to reach or sustain the same transports of pleasure as when he uses nothing. Certainly, without using chemicals, the opening process is prolonged, but he can reach and exceed the bliss levels that drugs used to give him. Although it does take time to retire the crutch of drug use, there is sex without it—and very good sex too. There is the benefit of not having to worry about drug side effects that range from headache to convulsions. With a clearer head, you'll have greater awareness and recall more of the experience.

Chapter 9: More Specialties

To sting his thigh
a light hazel whip

                          Nothing else will do

    His shoulders
    the ridges
    against
    his thistle

                 from "The Beautiful Tendons"
                        —Jeffery Beam

The activities listed in this chapter are non-invasive which means that they do not ordinarily penetrate the skin or involve insertion of anything into the body.

BONDAGE

Bondage often is experienced merely as a restraint during some other activity with a hasty release when it's finished. But a good bondage scene is meant to be savored. Don't rush into it; don't rush out of it. Make it as sensual as possible. The build up, the thrill of gradually surrendering your freedom of movement is a strong psychological descent into submission and powerlessness. Don't cheat yourself and your partner by hurrying. Whether you're weaving someone into a spider's web, manacling his limbs or constructing a rope harness, the enjoyment arises from the feelings of surrender and the gradual curtailment of movement. Bondage can be a profound mental stimulation so exciting that some folks willingly spend their entire weekend in various states of restraint. Don't just play with his body, guide his mind too.

I remember one novice who had been placed in a rope harness by his top and brought out to a leather dance bar. He normally would have been dancing his heart out, but was afraid of ruining the harness. I chided him for treating the rope as creative macramé rather than bondage. I advised him that the best way to derive pleasure from the restrictive harness was to move around, to dance quite literally against his bonds. Throughout the evening, exuberant in his sweat drenched rope, he reveled in the strictures of the harness. Struggling against good restraints should be like wrestling against a first-rate opponent. It isn't just the sight, feel and psychology of being trussed up. When you strain your limbs against an unyielding force and stretch your muscles, your whole body becomes engaged. It's a very basic struggle that heightens your awareness when your energy is held static like the Titan Prometheus whose taut bonds stretched him naked upon the rock, powerless to resist the attacking eagle of Zeus.

BONDAGE MATTERS
Kevin Drewery, Greensboro, North Carolina:
I enjoy doing a mummification where the object is immobilization. I like to leave the areas around the tits and the cock and balls exposed. It throws attention to whatever is left unwrapped. When everything else is protected, a breeze on the tits becomes a major stimulus. I also like industrial looking bondage where things clink and clank. I like the noise that's connected with movement. Leather, wood and ropes are what I like to use. I enjoy making wooden restraint items like stocks for the cock and balls. I prefer to use chains only for hoisting because of burrs and the like. I especially like rope harnesses. They restrict movement but allow easy access to the body. Nothing's more relaxing to me than a quiet afternoon at macramé.

SAFETY
Learn some basic safety rules. An essential one for submissives is: Never let someone immobilize you until you know about that person's S^3 quotient—their style, skill and sanity. Unless you have a trusted friend who can intervene if things get out of control, don't ever let a stranger tie you up. You could find yourself at the mercy of a thief, an incompetent or worse. A second rule is: communicate. Speak up if something feels wrong. If the restraints are too tight or loose, if your position is wrenching your arms out of joint, if your hands begin to tingle, you need to alert your top immediately. Don't try to be butch and bear with the uncomfortableness. It might be a warning of something seriously amiss. Let your partner know so that he can remedy it. Bondage is also a mental trip so share your desires with your partner. It does you little good if he's happily creating an intricate rope harness when you're fantasizing about being in suspensory bondage.

For tops, there are several rules. Foremost is: know what you're doing. With improper technique, you risk turning restraints into tourniquets and collars into garottes. Unless the material that you're using covers a wide enough area, it will cut into the flesh, abrade the skin or damage nerves. Too tight and you may cause ischemia which is the death of body tissues due to a lack of blood flow. Any bondage material must be at least 3/8" wide, so don't even think of using wire.

The second is: Be able to quickly free someone from bondage. Your fasteners and clamps should be of the quick release kind. Mountain climbing supply shops are a cheap source of fasteners that can be released with one hand. If you ever struggle to free a partner who passes out while in bondage, you'll wish you'd invested in a couple of these. I would discourage you from using padlocks but if you do, have a locksmith key them identically. This way, one key opens all the locks in your playroom and you won't be fumbling for the proper one during an emergency. And have lots of extra copies made and in the open so that they're right there in the event of a crisis. During every bondage scene have a pair of bandage scissors and a knife for quickly cutting through any rope bondage. If you're playing with handcuffs, you might also want to have a pair of bolt cutters and a hacksaw handy. They could prevent an embarrassing and expensive trip to the Emergency Room just to use theirs.

The third is: Never leave someone in bondage unattended. If a fire or some other catastrophe occurs, they will be unable to remove themselves from a dangerous situation. Gags must be considered as inhibiting someone's breathing. Any obstruction of his airway passages requires monitoring. If you cannot or are unwilling to check on him every couple of minutes, then don't use them.

Auto-erotic bondage is something to stay away from. It's hard enough unlocking a hood from someone else, but trying to free yourself in an emergency steals precious seconds that can literally be the margin between life and death. Every year, newspapers carry stories of deaths by strangulation when auto-erotic bondage results in accidental asphyxiation. If you want to indulge that fantasy, play safe and have a friend there to guard your well-being.

Head cages and hoods should never be suspended. I really object when SM videos show slaves standing on tiptoe because these cages are hung by a rope to the ceiling. One slip, and the bottom's neck can snap. Ruptured cervical discs, broken necks, paralysis or death by hanging are neither safe, sane nor consensual activities. The neck is a forbidden area for constriction or bondage. Even if you don't hamper breathing, you can too easily restrict the flow of blood to the brain.

Panic attacks can arise during a prolonged bondage scene, especially if a hood which restricts hearing and vision is used. Never release anyone who is panicked. They'll be in the midst of the classic flight or fight syndrome which means that they'll try either to run from you or pummel you. If you loosen their bonds, they may thrash about and hurt themselves or angrily lash out at you. Instead remove any gags, eye blinds or ear stoppers. Usually when their senses are restored, they'll feel more in control. But talk soothingly to them and calm them. Inform them that you need them to quiet down in order to safely undo their bonds. Tell them to relax and get them to speak to you in a quiet controlled voice. Have them explain their panic to you. Make them concentrate on controlling their breathing to relax. Once they gain control over their panic, they may want to continue. If they really need to terminate the scene, then keep talking to them as you remove their bonds. Stroke and hug them to help reassure them.

At the ends of any prolonged bondage or when panic has occurred, plan on at least half an hour relaxation time. Sit them down afterward and have a nice cup of tea and take time for a talk or a quiet snuggle, just don't let them leave immediately upon being freed from their restraints. Although your partner may seem fine, many people experience a good deal of delayed stress.

ROPE

Gay males have a particular fondness for rope bondage. I think it has to do with watching too many cowboy movies. Rope is made from many different materials, some of which are unsuitable for binding a person. Stay away from abrasive materials like hemp or some of the rougher nylon stuff made for boats. If you do settle on man-made materials, use only the braided kind and avoid the stranded stuff. Rubbing it across the inside of your wrist is a good way to check the abrasiveness of any rope. Avoid any rope that has a core of metal wire since this could work its way out and slice skin and muscle. If you buy cotton clothesline, you'll need to soften it by running it through the wash several times to remove the sizing and starch. Bondage rope should never be less than 3/8". Using anything less risks cutting into the skin or cutting off circulation. When you restrain the wrists or ankles, it's a good idea to wrap the rope around several times to create a cuff of rope that is less likely to bite into the skin.

Of prime importance is knowing how to tie knots. You don't want a slip knot tied to someone's wrists where it could inadvertently constrict and cut off the circulation. Get a scouting book and practice tying up your teddy bear before you attempt to truss up your friend.

Suspension bondage requires some additional special knowledge of pulleys, test strength of rope and safe anchorage of the devices. Try to learn this first hand from someone experienced. It could be a skilled sMer or someone who grew up on the farm hoisting bales of hay. For safety's sake, you don't want someone you've tied-up to crash on his head because a pulley pulled loose. Many leather shops carry special suspension harnesses but you can save yourself some money by either purchasing the safety harnesses used in window-washing or mountaineering or in parachuting. It will be worth your time. You haven't lived till you've seen someone, naked in a suspension harness, pulled by long leather thongs tethered to his tits, fly through the air like a perverted Peter Pan of pleasure.

158

VELCRO

Velcro for bondage play came from the women's community. I first learned of velcro from lesbian sмers who were returning from Michigan's Women's Music Festival. According to one, her lover had such a fondness for ripping her clothes off as part of a scene—an exciting but expensive fetish—that she had to do something to rescue their clothing budget. Rather than constantly buying new outfits, she began experimenting with tear-away clothes using velcro. To their mutual delight, velcro makes a very loud ripping noise. Her lover developed a conditioned reflex, getting excited every time she heard velcro's distinctive tearing sound. They expanded their fetish to creating a velcro board with straps. Don't underestimate the holding power of those little strips; they're capable of resisting several tons of force. Velcro has to be the quickest way to bind and unbind a person. The safety factor is really unparalleled. In an emergency, a tug is all that's needed to free your bottom. I've seen some leather restraints fitted with velcro instead of the traditional buckles and strap. It may not be as macho as rope or leather and buckles, but with blindfolds, who's going to notice? Long strips of velcro are available at sewing shops at very inexpensive prices.

BUNGIE CORDS

Bungie cords are straps either of black rubber or of woven fabric over an elastic core. They're made with metal hooks at the ends for quick but secure restraining. They're often used to fasten packs to motorcycles and this association with bikes seems to help people along on their fantasies. A simple bondage board, which allows quick fastening, can be made by setting eye hooks along the margins. Never place a bungie cord over the throat as you may inadvertently strangle him or damage his windpipe. You must also take special care not to constrict blood flow. You want a snug fit yet with a looseness that permits ample flexing and straining of the bottom against the elastic bonds. It's a very satisfying sensation for someone who enjoys struggling against restraints. One of the most erotic outdoor scenes that I've seen involved a scourging where the bottom was bungie-corded to a motorcycle in a hay storage shed.

ADVANTAGE FROM DISADVANTAGE
Charles, Atlanta, Georgia:

I tend to favor bondage that doesn't use ropes. I'm dyslexic which means that I have a hard time doing knots. My father used to punish me because I couldn't tie my own shoes when I was growing up. He somehow thought that I was refusing to learn on purpose. I'm not stupid. There's just some things that my brain isn't wired to do. I was thirty-one when I finally had a lover who was patient enough to spend the several months

159

necessary to teach me how to tie my shoes. Needless to say, I don't have that kind of time learning how to tie bondage knots.

My playroom has a singular lack of things that need knotting, yet few of my partners have ever noticed. I was at a bondage demonstration that a friend was giving. He suddenly handed me a piece of rope and announced to the audience that since I topped in bondage scenes, I was going to demonstrate the different knots as he talked about them. It was quite a shock for him to discover that I didn't know the difference between a square knot and a granny.

When you can't do things like everyone else, you make do and invent. I've learned to use boating cleats that I've tacked around a wooden frame. Using them lets me rapidly string rope in an asymmetric spider web that I can attach people to. Most spiders spin a haphazard web rather than the perfect web of the orb spider. By working with my limitation, I've solved a problem and discovered a new twist to an old standby. I've found that most people into SM are obsessed with symmetry. Securing them to an asymmetrical web disrupts their sensibilities but they're often surprised at how much they like it. A lot of them never even thought of the possibilities that a different arrangement could bring.

LEATHER AND RUBBER

Leather shops carry an amazing assortment of restraints. Padded and unpadded cuffs, restraining boots and mittens, collars and belts with restraining rings, leg spreaders, neck and back restraints and on and on. Check the various specialty shops and catalogues. Most of these come with buckles that have a little roller on them so that you can tighten them snugly but not overly tight. Others are designed to be used with padlocks. If you decide to use these, always check that you've the keys before clicking the lock shut.

A friend laments the passing of homemade or at least personally designed leather restraints. He's never bought anything from the leather shops, preferring to make it himself. While not everyone can or wants to do likewise, don't overlook the use of your belts as bondage items. Long strips of leather or rubber can also be purchased for use as rope substitute.

METAL

When using any metal item, always check for smooth welds, rounded edges and freedom from metal burrs. Make sure that chains are adequate for the weight they'll be bearing. Before using handcuffs, double check that you have keys and that they work. Over the years, I've had to help several red-faced friends free their partners because they've overlooked such a simple precaution. Most leather shops sell universal keys

160

as duplicates but these do not fit all models. When you do put handcuffs on, don't fasten them too tightly. Be sure to set the lock on them so that they don't accidentally tighten. Take extra care to avoid putting your partner in a position that might cause them to cut or bruise him.

I would discourage beginners from playing with manacles, fetters and all the various metal head cages, bridle scolds and slave collars. These may be the things which form a slave fantasy but they require a special vigilance to prevent trauma. Placing rigid rings of metal around joints increases the severity of any injury. Unlike pliable leather and cloth, the unyielding metal is more likely to damage nerve, bone, muscle and skin.

HOSPITAL GEAR

Hospitals have always relied on a wide range of restraints to secure their patients. From special carts with built-in straps to straight jackets, medicine provides a cornucopia of insidiously safe and easy to use devices designed to allow a small nurse to restrain a powerful patient. Some of these can be found at antique fairs, some at sales when hospitals move or close down and some can be gotten from friends in the medical profession. The much coveted tan leather and lamb's wool restraints have proven so popular that hospitals now keep these locked up in the head nurse's office. The cheaper but highly effective cloth restraints are still readily available. Medical supply stores offer many of these for sale, usually at cheaper prices than the leather shops.

Examination tables with their stirrups, straps and break-away sections make nice bondage tables that give you the opportunity to make any body part accessible. The tables are provided with a number of slots for adding on various attachments. These can often be modified to handle your own creations. One inventive top had reequipped his with a scaffolding that allowed the installation of a pulley with weights for ball stretching and tit torture. Realistically, few people have the room needed for one of these, although they do make excellent use of their bulky size by having an incredible amount of storage space.

DEPRIVATION

Deprivation involves deliberately blocking or removing stimulation to the senses. The object is to isolate the person so completely that his mind invents things to fill the sensory void. This is really the bottom's scene where you send him off on a trip by turning his attention inward. Plan on a good deprivation scene taking at least a couple of hours. The cutting-off of sensory information sets off curious reactions. The human brain needs the incoming signals to occupy its processing functions. Without input, it invents details to fill the void. Just like explorers of deep underground caverns who "hear" voices in the dark quiet, some folks, when left alone with only their little neuroses, just go plain bonkers. During deprivation scenes such as complete mummification, hallucinations really can set in when the senses lack any incoming information. For this reason, never leave a person unattended during deprivation scenes!

Partial deprivation has a different purpose. The object is to manipulate the person's perceptions. Through blindfolding, the top focuses the bottom's concentration on his other senses of touch and hearing and leaves the way open for the bottom to invent a mental image of what is happening. Thus, a plastic card scraped on the skin is interpreted by the blindfolded bottom as a straight razor shaving him. This deliberate directing of the senses is sometimes called sense alteration as opposed to deprivation. Mummification by itself is just a bondage scene, but when sight and hearing are blocked along with touch, it becomes sensory deprivation.

In order of sheer input to the brain, your senses are: sight, hearing, touch, smell, taste and balance. Most deprivation scenes concentrate on the first three and inadvertently on the last. Smell and taste are connected with the person's ability to breathe and therefore only the most advanced and competent of tops should ever interfere with these. For safety's sake, leave the mouth and nose alone.

For the eyes, use a light-proof blindfold but not one that puts pressure on the eye. You want to blindfold the person, not permanently blind him. Many hoods have an attachable blindfold. If the hood also has a gag, be certain that it doesn't obstruct breathing. Sometimes leather gags adhere to the mucous lining of the mouth, so take care when removing these.

Hoods only slightly reduce hearing. To really deprive someone of their hearing, you'll need special ear plugs for noise control. Most drug stores carry these. For comfort, let the submissive put them in himself. Instead of completely robbing the bottom of his hearing, many people prefer to use headphones connected to a CD or tape player. Rather than deprivation, this is controlling and directing what he listens to. He has something to focus on. For a first time mummification, this may alleviate a panic attack. Whenever you use headphones, watch the volume. Keep it high enough to mask outside noise but not enough to annoy or deafen him.

The sense of touch can be controlled by covering the skin and isolating it from sensations. Rubber gear, such as all body diving suits or fetish rubber suits, are good. There are also specialty items such as bondage bags which permit unobstructed breathing. Do not use real body bags; the air-tight plastic will cause suffocation! The most common deprivation scene is a mummification where rolls of plastic cling wrap are used

162

to wrap the limbs and body. Usually some sort of tape then is put over the plastic, further restricting movement and feeling. Ace bandages can also be used but care has to be taken to assure that they don't constrict too tightly. Strips of old sheets can even be used for that Boris Karloff look. If you do wrap the head, don't cover either the nose or the mouth. Wrap the neck extremely loosely or not at all. It's preferable to do the head separate from the body. Most people simplify things by rolling the material into a cowl or a loose turtle neck and then using a hood or a blindfold.

A variant of mummification known as encasement is for advanced, experienced tops and bottoms only! This involves materials that medical personnel use for splints and casts. Usually of plaster and less often of fibercast, these encase the entire body in a rigid, stonelike sarcophagus. It takes time to apply and to dry and harden. Special tools are also needed to cut through the cast material safely. The feelings of isolation are intense given the stonelike rigidity of the encasement. Some have described it as similar to being buried alive.

The whole effect of deprivation is destroyed when an unintended distraction slips through. Noise, especially unrelated talking, can be especially distracting, so guard against it. If the bottom experiences any breathing obstructions from bonds that are too tight around the chest or from neck wrappings, he might slip into a panic reaction. I've already advised you to leave the nose and mouth alone.

Prolonged restriction of the limbs can cause tenderness from unprotected pressure points at the ankle and knee joints. In severe cases, it creates bed sores. I place strips of foam padding between the arms and body and another piece between the knees and ankles. This not only prevents injury but helps to further isolate the body parts from one another, heightening the deprivation effect.

Limit the use of poppers and other drugs since these can give effects counter to the purpose of deprivation. Since deprivation puts people into contact with their hidden selves, the addition of mind altering drugs may only aggravate a bad situation. Of course, others offer the counter argument that deprivation's purpose is to make the person go off on their own trip. They see drugs as helping a person fly off to never-never land. In any event, use common sense and avoid drug misuse.

PHYSICAL SAFETY

Never apply adhesive tape directly to the skin since duct tape and carpet tape have a nasty habit of pulling the skin off. Make sure that you have some other material between skin and tape, otherwise you'll flay your partner. Remember too that wrapping the body blocks the normal process of cooling through evaporation. He'll still sweat but since he's wrapped in a water tight cocoon, it can't evaporate to cool him. To compensate, the body will increase sweat production in an effort to cool off. Adjust the room temperature for his comfort or he'll sweat buckets. Since he's well wrapped, you might need to have it slightly cooler than you would for naked play. Prevent dehydration by plying him with water and juices. You must have a pair of bandage scissors. These have a blunt nub on one tip so that you can safely poke it under a bandage or wrapping without stabbing the person. Don't use regular pointed scissors and never use a razor or matt knife.

Beware of contact lenses during blindfolding. Considering the length of time required for deprivation, you're better off having the bottom remove his lenses beforehand. He really won't be needing them and it eliminates the danger of corneal abrasions.

MENTAL AND EMOTIONAL SAFETY

The duration of the isolation may spark feelings of abandonment and rejection. He may panic, thinking that he's been possibly left to a slow death by starvation. His neuroses may also get the better of him. Forgotten emotional traumas tend to come clawing their nasty way out of a person's psyche when they're freed of distractions. (See Drewery's tale.) Best check him frequently for stability and offer reassurance that you're still monitoring him. Signs of a panic attack are rapid breathing and pulse rates, incoherent babbling, bizarre threats or even a reluctance to answer you. Be familiar with the person. You're more likely to calm someone if you've insight into their minds. He's also more likely to be calmed by the sound of a familiar and trusted voice.

WHIPPING

Mention whipping to someone and they will think of either the classic bull whip or a sailor's cat-o-nine. Bull whips belong to a special class called signal whips. Contrary to popular belief, they're not meant to strike the animal. The tip would split the animal's skin, opening the way for infestation by blow flies. Instead, the cracking noise, which is made by the tip of the whip as it breaks the sound barrier, guides animals from one direction to another by startling or signalling them. Australian and American "cracking" whips have three basic designs: the totally flexible signal whips which are filled with buckshot for weight; bull whips which have a short rigid handle; and the stock or target whips which have a longer rigid handle that makes them much more accurate. The weight in their handles is necessary to transfer the proper energy to the tip for both the crack and for accuracy. Cheap versions of signal whips lack the proper weight and therefore the necessary precision for safety.

Accuracy depends upon practice. While bull and target whips have a certain sex appeal, most of us have limited apartment space. A shorter signal whip of four feet is much more practical than a bullwhip of six or more. The basic strike positions are the side shot, over-hand and straight-on with the correct arm-motions being identical with pitching a baseball or casting with a rod and reel. Signal whips are true specialty items. Many haven't the skill to use them safely. My advice is to forgo these for a while. Investigate flogging with cat-o-nines instead. It will give you the experience that will make a future encounter with a whip master mean something.

Sound is an important aspect of whipping. The crack of the whip is actually a sonic boom. The tip really does break the sound barrier. That mini-sonic boom creates a compression wave of air that can be felt. For some, the thrill of whipping is not the taste of the lash. It's the dynamics of the whip's cracking and the feeling of that compression wave breaking against their body. This sound and fury phenomenon makes demonstrations of whippings a surprisingly, highly erotic experience for many who thought they'd never be interested in them.

As with bondage, there are certain musts for you if you intend on being the submissive. Treat these as four edicts for flogging.

1. Never allow anyone to whip or flog you without being *absolutely* certain of their ability, sobriety and responsibility.

2. Make sure that you are in a comfortable and protected position.

3. Communicate. Tell your partner what you want, where you want it, how hard and how quickly. Give him feedback and let him know when you've had enough.

4. Relax and relish each stroke.

Years ago, I was cautioned to be wary of playing with someone who wears a whip as advertisement. This is a person whom you are expecting to lash your shoulders without striking your face or to stripe your butt without damaging your kidneys. Find someone who can vouch for that person's skill. If not, then give a test. Place a cigarette on the edge of a table. A few inches further in from the cigarette, place a beer. If the person is capable with the whip, it's possible to strike the cigarette without spilling the beer. If not, then you must weigh the risks. The tip of that whip is moving faster than sound. An ill-aimed strike can just as easily split skin as remove an eyeball. A white cane could be the outcome that you must accept. Guy Baldwin can knock a row of cans off a fence stile one at a time. George Whaley can pick a piece of paper off a bar vest. That's accuracy you can trust. Why settle for less?

Know the terminology for various implements. Canes, rods, switches, paddles, slappers, cats, knouts, quirts, scourges (tipped or knotted), signal whips and bull whips refer to specific devices. Be certain that you are speaking of the same instrument as your potential partner! I've had people tell me that they wanted a good whipping when what they desired was a light spanking with a belt.

FLOGGERS

Cat-o-nines were designed to strike the body. Many of these look fiercer than they really are. Much of it has to do with surface area. A rigid device like a paddle has a set shape that determines the area over which the force of the blow will be spread. Given the same amount of force, a small paddle will smart more than a large one because it concentrates the energy into a smaller area. The larger one will actually hurt less because the energy is spread out over a large area.

Now, take a good look at that flogger. Instead of a fixed surface, it has a variable shape. Spread those thongs out and look at the surface area it covers. If they hit your back flat and fanned out, the energy is actually being spread over a pretty wide area. It becomes more of a blow or a smack than a strike. If, however, only the tips of the thongs hit you, it will sting, even if it delivers the same amount of energy because the surface area has decreased and the force is now concentrated to one small spot. Your delivery of the stroke then affects the blow tremendously since the way you handle your flogger affects the concentration or spread of the thongs. Control is critical.

Practice before you use it on anyone. A good sized pillow gives you the same dimensions as a person's back. Use it for target practice. You need to develop control over where those tips are going. Keep them in sight and never let the ends curl around his body. The safe areas are the fleshy buttocks and the upper back, usually around the shoulder blades (but not on the spine). You don't want to leave marks on the neck or face, nor do you want to hit the kidneys or eyes. Some tops routinely put a leather weight lifter's belt on their partner to protect the lower back and kidneys from wayward strikes.

If you're just beginning as a top, start with these two positions. The first has him upright with his back perpendicular to the floor as he stands with his backside to you. Secure him so that he doesn't move at a critical moment. The other has his back more or less parallel to the ground as he crouches on the floor, butt towards you as you stand over him. There are other positions but these afford you with direct and easy access to his backside without forcing you into strange contortions. In both positions, the path of your hand during the stroke should be roughly at right angles to his back.

Start slow. Caress his back with your hands first, perhaps giving him a massage. Gradually roughen things up. Give a few light slaps with your hands, then harder. Introduce the cat to him by dangling its thongs on his back. Tickle his skin with the tips, then pet him by dragging the braids over his shoulders. Take your time. You're working to psyche him up. Let him luxuriate in the feel of the leather touching his skin. His mind will already be racing with thoughts of the more intense feelings to come. Allow him to contrast the gentleness with what he anticipates. Stay attuned to the rhythm of his breathing and his body movements. They'll clue you to his readiness and impatience to begin the actual flogging.

With light swings, land the thongs fully, but gently on the parts he wants whipped. Gradually, increase force of swing and land less of the thongs on the back. This will increase the sting of the stroke. Keep things even. I've seen a lot of people who develop a lopsided approach as they scourge one side decently and then rather wimpishly treat the opposite side. Move around to cover the areas that he's indicated could be whipped. Your forehand ought to be as strong and accurate as your backhand. Think of varying the strokes. You could, for instance, flick the cat like a wet towel to inflict a swarm of bee stings to the backside. Get someone experienced to show you their strokes and then practice.

As mentioned before, the noise is part of the experience. Consider changing implements to vary both sound and sensation. Remember that the braids make a distinctive noise as they travel through the air. Once your aim has become good enough, you can plan strokes that almost hit his skin but which let the air fan him. The sound and the air movement, without the actual strike, tease and toy with his expectations. If your partner is bent over a set of stocks so that his back is parallel to the floor, you can skim his back by flicking the thongs like a myriad of snake tongues tasting his back.

SHOPPING

The severity of the implement depends on several factors. Materials, construction, design, weight and size of the handle. The materials and construction used make a huge difference. For those of you into pain-less fantasy whipping, look for wide cut thongs made of soft and supple leather on a relatively short handle. Deerskin is the best material for this. It's so soft and cushiony that it absorbs much of the force itself like crushed velvet. For beginners or the occasional SMer, it will deliver a sound and fury that give both top and bottom the psychological thrill of a furious flogging. The top can really let fly with some good swipes without turning the bottom black and blue. With wide supple strips, the bottom enjoys a tingling massage as the implement delivers a decently audible smack at the intensity of a light spanking. If you're looking for stimulation short of pain and discipline short of abuse, these are for you. They aren't very good if you're playing with a heavy bottom, that is, someone who really wants to feel the pain and wants the welts and bruising. These just are too gentle to stripe someone's back.

When purchasing a flogger, pick it up and hold it. It should fit in your hand comfortably and feel balanced. The handle length and weight should be enough to control the thongs. Give it a good swing as if you were throwing a baseball. The handle should feel like it's helping you throw the thongs. If you've room enough, try tracing out a figure eight that's lying on its side. It gives you a forehand and a backhand in one smooth motion. Next examine the thongs to see if they're capable of delivering the sort of stroke, bite or caress that you want. Go ahead and slap it into your hand to feel it. Pay attention too to the sound it makes. Does it thud, thwack, whistle, crack, whoosh or sound like overdone pasta?

Inspect the workmanship for quality. Look closely at the leather to be sure that it's cut cleanly and evenly. Make sure that any braiding is tight and any stud work is secure. You don't want your cat to unravel and spill its guts in the middle of a scene. If it feels fine and balanced in your hand, delivers the sort of sensations you want and is well made, you've found a useful playroom toy. Now, for some reason, fancy braiding, colored leather, enameled inserts in the handle and all sorts of artistic designs have become confused with quality. If you want to buy a cat-o-nine based on its heirloom potential, that's fine. I tend to put these things in the same category as gold-plated handcuffs and fine Wedgewood china, nice but too flamboyant for my tastes. I want a decent toy, not an art or status object. I have played with some very elaborately crafted and excellent whips and they handled quite well. If someone presented me with one, I'd happily accept. I just don't care to pay for the fancy expensive extras when a plain black leather one stripes someone's backside just as well. I'm a sensualist, not a materialist.

The thongs of traditional cats are made from cowhide. These may be thick or thin, wide or narrow, braided or plain, supple or stiff, dressed or split. Each delivers a distinctive strike. By knotting the thongs or fastening bits of material on the ends, more energy and bite can be added to the cat. A number of new materials have come into use. Plastics, acrylics, neoprene and rubber have not simply replaced the traditional thongs, but have reshaped the entire genera. Weird design hybrids now combine deceptively delicate plastic "birch" rods with cat-o-nine handles, beautifully made and wickedly wonderful. Every year, someone manages to invent something new. It's usually the smaller, less established shops—especially those owned by women.

Canes seem to be an English obsession. Traditional punishments in the schools, birch and willow are the time honored materials. These won't fly apart, as do the cheaper bamboo imitations, and have the resilience to give a proper bite. They're thin so that they sting and will give a decent stripe on the backside. They're also fairly cheap. Newer plastics have been substituted for natural woods. These vary in their composition, thickness and flexibility. Their big advantage is that they clean up in a snap. Bleaches, detergents and alcohol don't faze them.

Before playing with any whip or flogger, you should inspect it to really know how clean it is. Since these are capable of breaking skin, they could inject bits of blood from someone else into your body. Make it your business to ask when the whip was last used on someone and if blood was drawn. Be certain that the whip was properly cleaned. George Whaley of NYC recommends first cleaning a whip with a strong disinfecting detergent, preferably Simple Green, then wiping with hydrogen peroxide, which will foam if any blood or tissue still remains. Restore the suppleness to the leather by using a dressing such as Dr. Jackson's Leather Hide Rejuvenator.

CLIPS AND CLAMPS

Objects that pinch, tweak and bite are among the commonest SM toys. Alligator clamps, paper clips, bag clips with and without teeth, manuscript clamps . . . well, once you begin looking, you'll realize your house is already filled with SM supplies. Even your laundry room is full of clothespins of varying strength—plastic for beginners, wooden for the more advanced and little nasty tormentors for a vicious bite.

When playing with clamps, try tethering yourselves together. I've done this with beginners who are a little shy of tit clamps. From my nipple to his nipple, the chain lets me arch back and pull his tits with mine. Bottoms are more likely to push their limits when they know that whatever they feel, you feel too. The visual erotics of the situation usually gets their hormones raging.

If you're lucky enough to have a playroom, a pulley allows all sorts of interesting games to be played with clips and weights. If you're going to flog him, have him kneel and first hook his tit clamps to a light weight suspended by the pulley. Now whenever you strike him, every time he jumps, the weight will tug gently on his tits. Even if the weight is trite, the combination of time and motion will make sure he feels it. Avoid the temptation of starting out with a heavy weight. The small weight will sneak up on him and really give his tits a prolonged workout. Remember, "These things must be done delicately."

Old fashioned incontinent clamps look like large hair barrettes lined with foam. They were used to clamp the penis to keep urine from dribbling out. A variation is now made out of highly flexible nylon with a movable band that controls the force of the clamp. These new designs [try Gillian's Toys in NYC] will fit over both the cock and balls. Whenever you perform any cock and ball torture be careful not to cut off the blood flow for longer than ten minutes. Tissue death could result in his penis and balls turning black and falling off. If you do cock and ball bondage on someone, release the bonds just before he comes. Loosening them just prior to orgasm will usually enhance his pleasure. It's amazing how truly painful those thongs and laces become immediately after cumming.

Not everything need come from the leather shop. Egg toppers look like a pair of scissors that end in a flat ring. When the handles are squeezed, metal teeth extend from the inside of the circle. These teeth bite into the eggshell allowing the cap to be removed from soft-boiled eggs. Placed around someone's cock or balls, it changes into a dungeon device. You can also make a simple homemade maypole out of a cock-ring and several leather thongs. Tie the ends of four to six thongs to the ring, then lace or braid them along his tool and nuts. If you want to be nasty, fasten clothespins or alligator jaws to the other end of the leather and anchor them to his dickhead or stretch them up to his tits.

HEAT AND FLAME

At any scene that involves flames or heat, have first aid supplies handy for emergencies. These include a fire extinguisher, ice cold water, a clean cotton towel to sponge the water and telfa pads to dress any burn. Always stay away from the face. The dangers of facial scarring, blinding, damage to mucous membranes and psychological trauma place the face off limits for heat scenes. Keep poppers and other flammables away from the flame. It's an accident waiting to happen. If the vapors ignite as someone is sniffing from the bottle, they'll inhale a sheet of flames. There's not much that can be done to treat burned lungs.

WAX

Wax here refers to playing with candle wax made from paraffin, a petroleum product. Hot paraffin wax quickly cools and solidifies. The warmth, near pain and the sensations as it changes from a liquid to a brittle coat on your skin can be extremely erotic. I was accused of still smirking the day after one session as I idly picked bits of wax from my chest and belly hair while sunning at the Belmont rocks in Chicago.

Beeswax and beef tallow candles melt at too high a temperature and their drippings will burn the skin. So, buy the cheaper paraffin ones but avoid metallic colors since these often contain poisonous metal salts. White, red and black are the three best colors, not only for looks but for temperature. Use the color candle which will give the greatest contrast on the skin of your bottom. Black for light skinned and white for darker. Red has the reputation for having the hottest temperature of the three colors.

170

Make sure that you buy regular candles and not the dripless variety. You can control the temperature somewhat by raising and lowering the candle. Practice on yourself first to give yourself an idea of what he'll be feeling. The skin of your body varies not just in thickness but also in the number of nerve endings. The inside of your arm is more sensitive than the outside. Your genitals are not only made of thinner skin, but they are also laced with a myriad of nerves. Don't assume that if he can tolerate something on his chest that he'll be able to take an equal amount on his nuts.

Start at a reasonable height, then adjust for the best effect. You'll want to drip the wax onto him drop by drop and avoid pouring a hot puddle onto him. Take your time. Roll the candle to melt the wax evenly. Dribble it over the chest and belly. Try to hit his tits. If your aim is good enough, you might be able to encase them. Genitals tend to be a little more sensitive, so treat them gingerly until you know what he can tolerate. For the bottom, the feelings are of near scalding liquid heat which quickly cools to a rigid splotch. When these splotches are numerous and interconnected, it's a strange sensation of a thin shell which cracks and splits with movement. On the tits and genitals it forms a shield that gradually insulates as it builds up.

Some people like to shave before a wax scene so that they don't have to deal with trying to pick wax out of their hair. If that's the case, remember that a newly shaved area will perceive sensations as being greater, so go gingerly. Other people rub a little oil onto a hairy bear first and then comb his hairs before a waxing scene. It simplifies the clean up and lessens the pain of pulling the cooled wax out of his fur.

Another popular candle scene is to have the submissive lie on a table and place lines of votive candles on his body. Before you do this, check the bottoms of the candles and remove any metal tabs or foil that you see. The heat from the flame can pass through the metal and brand him. This is a wonderfully visual control scene. The submissive must have the discipline to hold still. As the candles burn, their wax will eventually spill over, but any body movement will also trigger a cascade. Make certain that you only do this to a person who has done hot wax scenes before. You should restrain a beginner and watch him closely. When a candle does spill hot wax, he might otherwise buck and upset the candles so that the flames burn his skin. Quickly remove any candle that does overturn. Have ice water, a fire blanket and telfa pads handy for first aid.

If you're lucky enough to have a candle making kit with a special water bath heater for melting paraffin, you can dip his body parts or paint the melted wax onto him. (Physical therapists do this to get deep heat into joints of arthritic patients.) There is one major caution. It's *absolutely* essential for safety that the temperature stay under 110° F. If

171

you let it get hotter than this, you will scald your partner. Test any wax on your wrist just as though you were checking the temperature of milk in a baby bottle. Painting and dipping are very sensual as the heat penetrates into your deeper tissues and wax builds up. Cracking it off is like breaking open a chrysalis. If you manage to get a coating of wax over his penis, without his becoming erect, it's great to then stimulate him to a full hard-on as his dick breaks free of its waxy case.

HOT ASH

Cigars hold a peculiar fascination for many. Beyond the look and smell, the attraction extends to the hot ash and the glowing end. With either cigarettes or cigars, you probably won't actually want to touch the skin with the embers. Pinching a tit between your fingers, you can bring the hot end nearer and nearer. It's important that the person not jump or move, otherwise his nipple might accidentally brush the glowing end. Talk to him constantly and, if necessary, bind him so that he cannot make any sudden movements. Back away when he indicates. Most people only want the sensation and sense of danger from the heat. A few actually desire that the hot tip of the cigarette or cigar be quickly touched to their skin. You should never do more than redden areas which is technically a first degree burn. Given their greater size, cigars burn much hotter than cigarettes. By merely bringing them near the skin, you can easily cause a first degree burn so keep the cigar moving. How quickly this will happen depends upon the type of cigar, when it was last puffed and how dry the bottom's skin is. If you and your partner do want to touch the glowing end to skin, I would suggest that you use a sprayer to wet down the portion of the anatomy that you'll be reddening. The moisture will help regulate the intensity. You'll need to be very careful that no glowing ash breaks off and sticks to his skin.

If your bottom has chest hair, you may want to trace out a design by singeing the hair, though this does get a bit smelly. If you flick your ash onto someone, do it from a height that gives it time to cool before landing. This will also allow you some reaction time to whisk away any burning ash that may land. As with wax and candle play, have first aid supplies handy.

A burning flame from either a match or a lighter is much hotter than a smoldering cigar. It's very hard to gauge between just warming the skin and a second degree burn. A snuffed out match head is also quite hot due to the coat of burned phosphorous. Use only one type of match and test it on yourself to see how long it takes after snuffing for it to cool sufficiently.

172

ALCOHOL

An old Chautauqua tent routine early in the twentieth century featured a dancer with a flaming baton who periodically tapped the burning ends to her body. The bunting would leave a bit of the flaming alcohol burning bright blue on her skin for a second or two to the amazement of the rural audience. The alcohol used is the same sort that's in those little glass laboratory burners. This pure alcohol flames at a fairly low temperature so that it takes a few seconds before it burns the skin.

Recently, this old gimmick has resurfaced in the sm community as a scene. If you're curious about it, learn it from someone who has mastered the trick. Done correctly, it's a good stage show and provides a thrill to the submissive who feels the heat and confronts the deep seated fear of being burnt. Done wrongly, you risk serious burns and nasty scars. Never use liquor or drinking spirits since these also contain sugars which burn at a much higher temperature than does pure alcohol. The burning sugars will also stick to the skin causing severe burns. Keep any flames well away from the face, eyes and head hair. It is extremely important that you have a fire blanket at hand to smother flames should something go amiss. Never blow on the flames to extinguish them; you'll only provide it with oxygen to burn faster. You might need to shave your partner's body hair first unless you like the odor of burnt hair.

BRANDING

An actual branding is such a heavy scene that most people never see or smell one. More common is the pseudo-branding which makes use of the fact that the body often confuses the sensations of extreme heat and cold. Instead of heating the iron, you freeze it. Much of the allure of branding is psychological with the preparations providing a great deal of the thrill. Do it right, cowboy. Freeze some water in a large coffee can. Set up an electric fireplace and perch the coffee can over the "flames." Stick the iron into the can. Then saddle him up and ride him around the playroom with a bit in his mouth. Horse-whip him with a riding crop, then truss him up. Pull the branding iron from the can and cold brand him on his tush. Afterwards, you and Trigger can snuggle up and watch an old Lash LaRue flick.

ELECTRICITY

Electrical toys fall into two categories: single and dual contact devices. Only one device resides in the first, that's the Violet wand. This is the only electrical toy which is safe to use above the waist without risking cardiac arrest. All other devices, whether powered by batteries, transformers, hand cranks or cords that plug directly into the wall, rely on an electric current passing from one pole to another. When this current crosses the chest, it can disrupt the heart's normal rhythm, leading in some cases to irregular heartbeat and sometimes to heart attack. No competent person violates the basic rule of nothing above the waist.

Quack medicine spawned a plethora of different electrical health products. Many of these relied on a pulse of electricity to stimulate muscle contractions. Others used the tingling of an attenuated electrical shock to simulate cures of illnesses that ranged from backaches to female problems. Chicago and Peoria, IL seemed to have been the centers of manufacturing for many of these early devices since Sears & Roebuck once carried a number of them in their catalogue. (The Chicago Museum of Science and Industry has several devices on display near the Queen's Fairy Dollhouse.) Most were made between 1880 and 1940 till the US government cracked down on fraudulent and dangerous medical products. A second crackdown occurred in the nineteen-sixties as the FDA sought tighter restrictions over the extraordinary claims of unscrupulous manufacturers.

Many of these still surface at antique fairs and can be acquired at very reasonable prices. A violet wand with attachments from 1920 will cost about sixty dollars at an antique fair. Compare that with a tab of near three hundred to purchase one brand new with only one attachment! I've stumbled across several rare items while antiquing. While no one has written a comprehensive guide, the Sears catalogue from the eighteen-eighties, reprinted for Sears & Roebuck's centennial, serves as a primer on the earliest devices. Check for copies at your library. Before you use any antiquated item, have someone trained in electrical work check it out thoroughly. The insulation on the wires most likely will have decayed or frayed and will need replacing.

SINGLE CONTACT

The violet wand operates along the same principle as those plasma spheres that are so popular in the yuppie catalogues. A static generator charges a tube of rarified gas which gives off a bluish-violet glow when charged. When the tube is brought near a grounded object, it discharges. The wand is built so that a spark jumps between the glass tube and your skin when they're about an eighth to a quarter of an inch apart. A lot of people mistakenly call it an "ultra-violet wand" but it produces no ultra-violet light. A wool sweater on a dry winter day produces an identical bluish static discharge. The wand has an adjustment that regulates the intensity of the spark and it can get quite strong. Never use these anywhere near the eyes. A static discharge on the eyeball could cause a burn scar that permanently clouds the vision.

Sold mainly as skin sterilizers and toners, violet wands create a feeling of tightness as they are run over the skin. The smell of ozone and the crackling static discharges add to the aura. Marketed as Violetta wands, they often came in attractive briefcases complete with a variety of rakes, cups and rods that provide different sensations. One attachment is a metal tube that the dominant can grasp as he turns the wand on. With his other hand he can then stroke, tickle and titillate the submissive as sparks fly from his fingertips to his partner's tits and cock. Because the light produced is bluish, if you use the wands under red lights, they can be pretty spectacular.

DUAL CONTACT DEVICES

Whether powered by batteries, hand cranks, transformers or household plugs, these gadgets pass an electric current through the body. That means that they should never be used above the navel for fear of seriously disrupting the heart. Leave the train transformers alone. And for safety's sake, never use wires plugged directly into a wall and keep water away!

Magnometers are hand cranked devices from telephones or old military hand generators that use magnets and copper wire to generate an electric current. How fast you turn the handle determines the strength of the electric shock. Not all are so industrial looking. I have run across some rather elaborate Victorian magnometers set in polished brass and inlaid rosewood. These beautiful but stinging antiques from the golden age of medical quackery make visually pleasing toys for genital stimulation.

Less commonly encountered are battery operated devices. Many of these were destroyed as acid from leaky batteries corroded the metal. When they do turn up in garage sales, they often puzzle the folks who find them. The Electreat looked just like a metal flashlight but with a roller instead of a light at its tip. It was meant to be held by the person so that the electricity flowed from the roller through the body to exit from the hand which held the device. This meant that the current passed over the heart which we now know can trigger heart attacks. They were, however, made with different attachments that allow them to be used safely, including an anal probe for treating bowel irregularities.

Cattle prods are also battery operated but these were designed for use on very large animals with skin so thick that they use barbed wire for scratching their backs. As humans are much smaller and have very thin skin, these have the potential of sending a person into shock or leaving a very nasty burn. Stun guns were designed for protection against muggers. They zap a would-be assailant with enough voltage to incapacitate them, allowing the victim time to get away safely. Again, this is far too strong a device and needlessly risks neuro-muscular damage.

Relaxicisors were built as a passive form of exercise. The marketing ploy was that, since electricity causes muscles to contract, it could firm-up muscles by sending pulses of electricity through them. Two pads are placed on the body and, as the electric current passed between them, any muscle tissue along the electric path duly contracts. It didn't take sMers long to figure out that the anus and the prostate, which are muscles, would also contract. Depending on its strength, the current has the additional attraction of being able to cause discomfort or pain. The government made the sale of these illegal so that technically you shouldn't be able to even purchase them from an antique dealer.

The commonest dual contact toy in use these days is the TENS unit which was developed to help people cope with chronic pain. Much smaller and more versatile than the old relaxicisors, these electronic nerve stimulators are marvels of electronic miniaturization. About the size of a cigarette pack, they deliver a pulse of electricity and control both the frequency and the strength. Attached to these pulsing units, aluminum cigar tubes become anal probes and metal scrub pads become cock-ring electrodes. The pulsing current causes the anal muscles and prostate to contract giving the sensation of being fucked electronically. Some sM suppliers carry an egg-shaped PAL [short for Polish Anal eLectrode because they're made in Poland] for an even better fit. For those of you with bucks to spend, specialty shops advertise in the leather publications and will make a special electrical-conductive acrylic butt plug. Dry skin does not readily conduct electricity. A cheap electro-conductive paste can be made by mixing a little table salt with KY jelly, but be sure to clean any metal toys afterwards. The salt will eventually corrode the metal.

Learn how to play safely with electrical toys from someone experienced. If you buy an antique, be sure to check the wiring for electrical faults and have any irregularities corrected. The danger of shock from electrocution is a real but avoidable risk.

Chapter 10: Maladies

PREVENTING DISEASE TRANSMISSION

Once upon a time, all humans thought that diseases had supernatural origins. Sickness was either a God-sent punishment or the result of a curse by someone in league with the devil. When plague spread, the official response was to find some poor unfortunate from a disenfranchised group, usually a cranky old woman, and burn her as a witch. Although this method never ended a plague, the authorities always felt much better having demonstrated their commitment to the public's welfare. Despite the efforts of the far right to return to these halcyon days of traditional medicine, public health researchers have overwhelmingly stuck to scientific inquiry. Diseases spread from one person to another by a chain of infection—not by malevolent spirits. This chain consists of three links: an infectious agent, a means of transmission and a susceptible host. The infectious agent is nothing more than a virus, bacteria or fungus that causes an illness. The means of transmission is the way it spreads among people such as sneezes, sexual intercourse or contact with a dirty telephone. The susceptible host is someone who has no protective immunity to the infectious agent. This could be because the person has no defense against that particular germ or because the immune system has been damaged but not because they missed church. Eliminate or break any of these three links and there's no infectious disease. A vaccine works by removing you as a susceptible host. Wearing a condom blocks the means of transmission for STDs. An antibiotic kills off the disease-causing bacteria or fungi and you recover.

As an example, syphilis is a bacterium to which all humans are susceptible. No one ever develops immunity to it. It's transmitted by intimate contact with an infected person usually during sex. Since everyone is susceptible, that leaves only two ways of preventing it. First is to prevent contact by either abstaining from sex or using a latex condom as a thin barrier that the germ cannot cross. The second way is to use antibiotics to stop syphilis from infecting you. That's what the shot of penicillin does. Unfortunately, all human beings are susceptible to HIV (the virus that leads to AIDS) and there's no vaccine and no drug to eliminate it. Our only way of breaking the chain of infection is to remove the means of transmission. That means you must either abstain from sex or you must take precautions such as using latex condoms. I will now discuss various older and more recent maladies.

BACTERIAL

Gonorrhea, syphilis and clamydia are all caused by microscopic organisms that spread easily through sexual contact. These three thrive in your mucous membranes which means that you can start your own little garden of microbes in your mouth, throat, rectum or urethra. Gonorrhea, also called the clap, usually causes a pussy discharge from the penis and pain on urination. In the rectum it may cause excessive farting. In the nose and throat the symptoms can be similar to a severe sinus infection with discharge and bad breath. If gonorrhea infects the eye, it causes blindness. Therefore, never piss or cum in anyone's eyes.

Syphilis has three phases. The first is a small lesion called a chancre which stings a bit and will go away after about a week. This doesn't mean that your body has gotten rid of it. The germ is only hiding. The second phase may appear a short time to several months later when a severe rash breaks out, usually across the torso. This too will eventually disappear without treatment. The third time syphilis shows up, it creates irreversible damage and can kill. It can rot away portions of the body, destroy brain cells, cripple with arthritis and ravage the nervous system to result in deafness, blindness, madness, and spasms. Penicillin can cure it even at this late stage, but the damage cannot be undone.

Clamydia will bring itself to your attention when suddenly your nuts become swollen and very tender. Your ejaculate may take on a peculiar yellow tinge as pus mixes with your semen. Untreated, it can cause sterility and might lead to a withering of the testicles. There's a fourth bacterial infection, called non-specific urethritis. It causes a discharge of pus and sometimes a tickling or painful urination similar to gonorrhea. The infection is the result of some microbe other than gonorrhea. Most respond well to treatment.

HERPES

Herpes simplex I, known as cold sores, and Herpes simplex II, called genital herpes, are not as particular as their common names would indicate. An outbreak of Herpes I cold sores on the penis is every bit as painful as Herpes II genital sores. Herpes is highly contagious. The small blister (~ 1 / 32" across) or cluster of blisters sheds viruses even before the blister bursts. Any mucous membrane or even a minute break in the skin, say a scratch on a finger, can allow the virus to enter. Once inside the body, it invades cells and replicates itself. Your body's immune system quickly makes antibodies that destroy the virus particles and the sores disappear. However, herpes viruses splice their genetic blueprint into the DNA of your own cells. Sadly, they have a preference for nerve cells which makes outbreaks very tender and painful. Episodes of blistering are usually preceded by a tingling or itch that the sufferer quickly learns to identify as the start of another bout. Luckily, most people's immune systems develop a quick and efficient response and the outbreaks become less frequent and of shorter duration. For some, medications are

178

needed to help contain the severity of outbreaks. Your health care provider can prescribe these drugs. Always take a good look before you kiss, suck, rim or screw. If you see any tiny blisters, cover it in latex. Better still, take a rain check.

While not an STD, Herpes zoster is in the same group. It's the common chicken pox virus. When you had it as a child, your body didn't eliminate it. It only went into hiding. When you get severely stressed and your immune system is depressed, it reappears as shingles. These are very painful blisters that cluster around your waist area as the virus moves out of your spinal cord. People who are HIV positive with low t-cell counts are susceptible to outbreaks. Your physician can prescribe medicine that can assist in recovering from it.

HEPATITIS

Infectious hepatitis is an inflammation of the liver caused by an organism. Your liver removes poisonous wastes from your body, provides readily available energy and helps in creating enzymes necessary for digestion of food. Five hepatitis viruses have been identified so far. SMers need to guard against two in particular. Hepatitis A Virus and Hepatitis B Virus, often abbreviated HAV and HBV. The most common and serious type among gay males is HBV.

Shortly before the AIDS epidemic burst upon the scene, Hepatitis B Virus was so rampant among gay men that it was known as the gay disease. Over 60% of gay men who had been sexually active for over a decade had been infected with Hepatitis B. Medical personnel assumed that if you contracted Hepatitis B, you were either gay or an intravenous drug user. A vaccine finally became available in the early eighties. Even with safer sex practices, Hepatitis B infection rates remain high among gay men with over half testing positive for it.

The virus is passed mostly through sexual contact with infected semen and blood, although it has been found in all body fluids. HBV is many times more infectious than HIV. You can contract it by having oral sex or even just deep kissing. It is not spread by sneezes, toilet seats or fine china. Although it is hardier than HIV, it still cannot live very long outside the body. The virus attacks the liver, disrupting its functions. Most people never develop symptoms beyond a flu-like illness with a vague fatigue or diarrhea. Others develop the classic symptoms of chronic fatigue, loss of appetite, jaundice with yellow skin and eyes, pale clay-colored craps and brown smelly urine.

As with most viruses, once you've caught the disease, there's no treatment. Bed rest and abstention from alcohol and cigarettes are about the extent of care. For those grievously ill, hospitalization may be required. Most recover from the disease and develop permanent immunity to HBV within six months. However, one out of every ten people becomes a long-term carrier, while others remain sick with HBV for years. Even if you recover and clear the virus from your body, your liver is likely to suffer some damage. Some people are unable to drink alcohol for the rest of their lives. A bout of HBV increases your risk of long-term problems such as liver cancer or cirrhosis.

A vaccine has been available for about ten years and works in 95% of cases. The immunization requires three shots over six months or three shots over three months with a booster after a year. Your health care provider will want to give you a blood test afterwards to be certain the vaccine has worked. The price, under a hundred dollars, is much cheaper than a bout of hepatitis would have cost you in sick days. Some health care plans will cover the cost. Contact your health care provider, county health department or local gay health clinic for further information. Every gay male should know what their HBV status is. If you've not been exposed to the virus, get immunized!

Hepatitis A Virus is spread through fecal material but is far less common than HBV. Again, symptoms can range from being completely absent, to a classic case of jaundice, or to permanent disability. Recently a vaccine has been developed but immunity may only last three to five years.

The Hepatitis C Virus (HCV), a fairly recent discovery, is also spread through oral/anal contact (rimming). Unlike Hepatitis A and B, HCV can be caught again. People do not seem to acquire a lasting immunity. Several cases have been documented in which individuals have been re-infected. One poor fellow has contracted it three separate times. Whether this virus becomes epidemic among gay men remains to be seen.

Hepatitis of any sort diminishes the enzyme functions of the liver and can cause severe impairment leading to disability, disfigurement or death. Get tested; get immunized! Repeated infections mean repeated damage. If you like to rim, use a barrier of latex or plastic cling-wrap. Your partner's douche doesn't flush away the virus. If anything, it increases the likelihood that hepatitis virus will be shed from the gut.

CRITTERS

Amoebas and paramecium are microscopic one-celled animals. They can cause severe recurring bouts of diarrhea. Not many physicians are attuned to these parasites. A gay physician who knows your sexual habits is more likely to spot these than a puritanical one who knows nothing of gay medicine. Amoebas can be difficult to treat. They have a neat trick of encapsulating themselves in a hard coat that protects them from medications. Whereas the antibiotic will kill off paramecium, the amoebas may lurk in the folds of your bowels safely encased in their little shells till it's safe to come out again. Anyone who happens to rim you may just ingest some of these little surprises and so it spreads.

Crabs and lice are blood sucking insects that attach their eggs (nits) to the shafts of hair. Crabs are the pubic lice which look like flat miniature crabs and prefer the forests of your pubic hairs. Body lice are more elongated and tend to roam through the forests of your body hairs. Often, the bugs are passed directly from one person to another, but they also like to hitchhike on furniture, clothes, rugs and even toilet seats. Most people become acutely aware of the infestation within seven to fourteen days of colonization. For sheer agony, try not scratching your crotch during a business meeting while these things are chewing through your pubic skin for a sip of blood.

There are several treatments. Try an over the counter product, such as Rid, that contains a natural pedulicide. It will kill some but not all of the little pests. Those that survive are often made sterile so that, if you follow the course of treatment, even these survivors will die of old age in two weeks. You will also have to wash or spray any clothing or bed linen that's been in contact with your body. Otherwise, you could re-infect yourself. If the over the counter remedy doesn't work, see your doctor about a prescription for Kwell or some other heavy duty insecticide. These work quite well but are very toxic to your liver. The other way to deal with the crabs and lice is to shave. A bear who becomes host may find that trimming back the fur deprives them of cover and lessens the amount of medicine needed to kill them. Pubic shaving isn't simply for kinky looks. The mania for crew cuts on crotches and shaven cock and balls began in the bathhouse days as a way of controlling outbreaks of crabs. No hair, no crabs.

Scabies are little burrowing mites that chew tunnels under your skin. They're just big enough to be seen with the naked eye, so they tell me. I've never been able to see them without a microscope. The first sign is a small itchy spot that seems like a spider or flea bite but which suddenly spreads into an intensely itchy and scattered rash. They prefer the crotch, the webbing between your fingers and toes, the skin behind your knees and anywhere else that may be warm and tender. They are highly contagious. I know of one person who spread them to over a dozen people in just one weekend. They love to hide in textiles. If you visit your mother while you've scabies, you may have to decontaminate her and her house too. Because they tend to stay in their burrows except to lay eggs or migrate, they're difficult to get rid of. It's a slow process waiting for them all to crawl out into the poisons you must smear over your body. Get to your health care provider for early treatment and follow the instructions to the letter.

181

TB: ENCORE FOR AN OLD ENEMY

Tuberculosis is an ancient enemy that's renewing its acquaintance with this generation. Its victims have been discovered among 5,000 year old Egyptian mummies. In dank medieval cloisters, it propelled pious monks and nuns to early sainthood. Aesthetically but effectively, it wasted away the consumptive poets of the Romantic Era. But it took the rise of modern tenements to make tuberculosis (TB) a major plague. Until 1942, there was no effective treatment. Rest cures, nostrums and surgery only gave the illusion of control over the uncontrollable. The reality was deadly simple: if you sickened from TB, you died from TB.

The bacteria that causes tuberculosis wasn't discovered until 1882. The rod-shaped bacillus is spread through tiny airborne droplets coughed or sneezed out by an infected person. When someone inhales one of these microscopic drops, the bacteria begin to reproduce in the warm, moist conditions of the lungs. In an effort to stop the infection, special cells within the body surround the growing bacteria and form nodules of inflamed tissue that show up in an X-ray. TB can also spread to other parts of the body including the brain, bones and kidneys. Luckily, among those with generally good health, most who become infected never develop symptoms. Only about one-tenth will sicken, developing the classic TB symptoms of low grade fever, persistent cough, night sweats, unintended weight loss and—in advanced cases—blood spitting.

With the discovery of the antibiotic streptomycin in 1943, it became possible to cure tuberculosis. This discovery was so important that it merited the 1952 Nobel Prize for medicine. By the mid-sixties, TB seemed to have been vanquished. American cities no longer needed the fleets of vans that patrolled the streets offering free chest X-rays. The huge sanitariums were slowly abandoned and the acreage sold. In the seventies, many hospitals stopped requiring annual chest X-rays for health care workers and made the skin test optional. The early eighties saw the lowest rates of TB in history with many physicians never having seen a case. Then, things went horridly wrong.

In the mid-eighties, NYC had under three-hundred-fifty cases of TB. In 1992, over four thousand new cases were reported. The rise in homelessness, drug-abuse and AIDS have led to a resurgence of TB. The good news is that most of these can be cured with a regimen of medicine. The bad news is that about one third of the cases are caused by a new strain of TB that is resistant to the current drugs. Despite all our technology and drugs, we find ourselves on the edge of helplessness once again. Once thought all but wiped-out, tuberculosis, like Freddy Krueger, is back among us wreaking havoc.

For those who are HIV-positive or immuno-compromised, TB poses a special risk. Because HIV weakens the immune system, those who are

HIV-positive are more susceptible to TB. Studies show that half of the PLWAs who become infected with TB sicken as opposed to one-tenth in the general population. The symptoms of TB are so similar to those of AIDS—night sweats, coughing, weight loss—that many never suspect TB.

Everyone, regardless of their HIV status, should have a yearly TB skin test. It takes less than thirty seconds to give. Two small tines prick the skin on the inside of the forearm with a substance that will cause a slight reaction if TB infection has occurred. If a bump of 5 mm ($\approx$ 1/5") or larger appears within a few days, it means that you've been exposed to TB. Consult your health care provider immediately for advice, further testing or treatment. If you do develop a low grade fever, a chronic cough, etc., don't assume that it's another bout of PCP. Ask for a TB screening. A sputum exam can check for signs of early active disease and a chest X-ray can identify the progress of any damage done. Prompt identification and treatment will help conserve your health and prevent you from infecting others.

KAPOSI SARCOMA

Kaposi Sarcoma, KS, is a cancer that affects the capillaries which are the smallest blood vessels in the body. First showing up as bruise-like purple spots usually on the arms, legs or head, the lesions can spread throughout the body both internally and externally. I've known some who have died within months of the appearance of a lesion and one friend who was diagnosed six years ago. Several treatments seem to offer promise though a cure seems elusive.

Researchers continue to gather evidence that suggests that KS among gay males is spread by an infectious agent, most likely a retro-virus, independent of HIV. Studies, which have examined the role that fecal material plays in the probable transmission, strongly implicated oral-anal contact as a likely route of infection by whatever it is that causes KS. Additional infection by HIV may weaken people enough to allow the onset of full KS. It's probable that most individuals with intact immune systems may never show signs of disease, although some cases of KS have occurred in HIV-negative individuals.

Rimming is the licking of your partner's anus, which health researchers refer to as oral-anal contact. Rimming a well-washed butt hole is a highly pleasurable activity for many but which carries several risks. Although the likelihood of catching HIV by rimming is low, other diseases, such as hepatitis, KS and STDs are quite easily passed from the ass to the mouth. Keep something between you and infection! Protect both of you by covering that hole with either a plastic film or a dental shield.

Chapter 11: AIDS

They visit him
Grown thin
No flesh
No bones
Nothing resembling a body

Love's wrapped him in an ill suit
No visible trace left
                    from "Lovesick Shirt"
                    —Jeffery Beam

HIV: AIDS

AIDS is a disease caused by the Human Immunodeficiency Virus infecting and destroying the special cells of your immune system. If you become infected, HIV splices itself into your genetic make-up so that you and the virus become inseparable. With a weakened or wrecked immune system, you have no defense against even the simplest of illness. The vast majority of HIV cases are spread by exposure to infected semen or blood. For your life's sake, assume that everyone you play with is infected with HIV. Follow these two simple rules.

1. Avoid internal exposure to semen unless you're trying to become pregnant.

Observe the adage of cumming *on* not *in* someone and avoid getting semen anywhere near the asshole. Use latex condoms along with a water based lube containing nonoxynol-9. This will greatly reduce your risk of becoming infected but, unfortunately, condoms cannot provide complete safety. They can break and they do slip off. Nothing beats the horror of realizing that the rubber you so carefully rolled on your partner's dick slid off while he screwed you—especially if it slipped off before he came. Make it a part of your sexual routine to reach down and check that the condom is still on his cock. For increased safety, have him pull out just before orgasm so that you can both see the ejaculation for a sexy and safe visual thrill. Never use oil or petroleum based lubricants such as Vaseline or baby oil. They will quickly dissolve latex condoms. Crisco, a vegetable oil, also rots latex condoms though at a slightly slower rate than petroleum-based products. FDA studies seem to indicate that natural lamb condoms can let the AIDS virus pass through.

Never let anyone talk you into anal sex without a condom by insisting that they've just had an HIV test and that they're negative. A person can become infectious with HIV today and it will still be at least six months before the test can detect signs of an infection. All the HIV test tells anyone is what their status was six months ago. So, the only way to be certain your partner is non-infectious tonight is to check his blood half a year from now. If someone tries to convince you to let him screw you without a condom because he's tested negative, don't let him. Several friends of mine were infected by self-proclaimed HIV-negative bastards. The general rule is the more someone tries to convince you that they're negative, the more cause you have to believe that the reverse is true. Always assume anyone you're with is positive for HIV. Never allow anyone to stick his dick in your ass without a latex condom on—even for just a few thrusts. The rates of infection for unprotected anal intercourse are just about the same whether or not the partner has withdrawn before ejaculation. Most men drool pre-cum before they ejaculate and many have no awareness of it. Do you really want to place your life on the line by trusting that your partner knows and can control his bodily reactions and secretions? Sex is momentary; HIV is forever.

Oral sex seems to be relatively low risk, but not completely safe. Since the mouth begins the process of breaking things down for digestion, HIV has a rough time surviving. Saliva appears to inhibit the virus. It seems that as long as you've no sores, split lips, cuts or abrasions, the risk is very low. If you've had any dental work done, even a simple cleaning, or if you're prone to biting the inside of your lips, you'd be advised to forgo sucking till things have had time to heal. Research seems to indicate that some people have caught HIV through oral sex. The folks in Public Health cannot give the all clear to any activity that may have caused even one person to become infected, nor do I. They recommend that you slip a condom over any dick you want to suck. I would urge you to talk with someone knowledgeable about current advice for safe sex. You have to decide the level of risk you want to accept. No one can decide that for you.

2. Avoid the blood of others unless you're having emergency surgery.

Needles, scalpels, razors and knives should never be used without prior cleaning and sterilization! Disposables should be used once and discarded safely. If you are an intravenous drug user, don't share needles or syringes. Use new ones if at all possible. If you must re-use or share, soak the works in a ten percent solution of bleach for a few minutes and rinse clean. Get yourself into a treatment program. IV drugs weaken your immune system, making you more susceptible to infection.

Never break the skin unless you thoroughly understand universal precautions for health safety. These are the guidelines established by hospitals for safely dealing with body fluids, especially blood. (Ask any health care provider.) The over-riding rule is that you regard everyone's bodily fluids as infected and act accordingly. Blood sports should always be learned from a knowledgeable and accomplished person.

Make a point of cleaning alligator tit clamps, especially if the metal teeth have poked through the plastic guards. The rubber pads of the Japanese clover clamps should be cleaned after every use. Because they abrade the skin, they can collect blood and other body fluids. Scrub them in a good detergent, then soak the tips in a ten percent bleach solution for a couple of minutes and let air dry.

It's not a good idea to share latex toys. The rectum has many small blood vessels which may break and allow viral transmission. Dildos develop many little fissures that can protect and hide any virus that may be shed. Even soaking in bleach and washing in a strong detergent can't absolutely guarantee that all the fissures have been cleaned of virus. Be safe and build up your own dildo collection and keep a few new, unused ones for company. If the dildos are small enough, you should be placing condoms over them anyway for easier cleanup.

If you break skin in a really heavy whipping scene, be aware that the tip of your implement, which breaks the sound barrier, can atomize blood and body fluids. These droplets can enter via the eyes and respiratory tract. There's no hard evidence that the virus is spread by aerosol but when surgery personnel use high speed saws and drills, they now gown, glove, goggle and mask themselves like moon explorers.

The virus is basically fragile when outside of the body. Soaking instruments for several minutes in a ten percent solution of bleach, cooking them for thirty minutes in a pressure cooker or steam autoclaving will kill the virus. By themselves, hydrogen peroxide, surgical scrubs and alcohol are not effective viricides. Leather goods, however, cannot be soaked in a bleach solution without destroying them. Instead, wipe clean your whips, scourges and skin abrasive toys with a strong detergent and let them air dry for several days to assure the demise of any remaining virus. Some whip masters wipe their toys with hydrogen peroxide after cleaning. The foaming of the peroxide will quickly highlight any missed bits of blood or tissue. Always recondition your leather goods after any decontamination to avoid deterioration of the material.

Dental dams and plastic cling wrap may help lower any risk during rimming. The rates of HIV transmission for these activities are low but still the subject of concern by health care professionals. The effectiveness of dental dams can be lost if you lose track of which side is which or if saliva and secretions spread from one side to the other. The risk from rimming is in the spread of some other rather nasty viruses and parasites from one person's rectum to another's gut.

There's a lot of discussion currently about the nature of HIV infection. Don't follow the debate too closely. A characteristic of any investigation is that most leads turn out to be false ones. In fact, solutions often come from unexpected quarters. Most of the people I have met and worked with in medicine and public health are honest and dedicated to discovering the secret behind HIV infection. Medical science, to them, means trying to sort the truth from a mountain of data. The problem is that AIDS is infused with so many social implications. I remember in 1983 during a seminar in Ann Arbor, MI a physician friend of mine commented that AIDS was going to be the opportunity of a lifetime with "papers to be published and reputations to be made." It has become even more complicated than that with the addition of economics, politics, religion and so on.

When reading medical journals or interpreting the results of different studies or when judging the rhetoric of politicians, activists and agitators, you need to be highly critical of any statement or claim. Information by itself says nothing. Someone must interpret it and frequently a particular bias colors that interpretation. Our own community is not immune to distorting the facts. Some gay activists seized upon the Concorde study as proof that the drug companies were conspiring to poison us with expensive drugs. I do believe that AZT is vastly over-priced and represents bald-faced profiteering, but I think that the conspiracy theory is a bit of hyperbole. No one has ever claimed that AZT was a cure. We, the gay community, are the ones who pushed to have it approved. The results were so stunning with the bed-ridden returned to improved health that we all demanded that the FDA fast-track the drug. I object to the revisionist view that we were passive dupes.

The sad fact is that little can be done against viruses. They were unknown until 1932 when the first electron microscope discovered them. Even today, no one is really certain if they should be counted as living things or not. Until recently, we had no drugs that could assist the body in controlling a viral infection. Even today, we've only a handful of effective medicines, none of which works as a cure. They simply slow down the progress of infection. Throughout the world, the humble aspirin remains the drug most often given for HIV. Frequently it's the only one affordable, but it does seem to help. Preliminary studies seem to show that a single aspirin tablet a day interferes with HIV. It's not all that surprising. Plants use chemicals to ward off infections, including viral ones and aspirin was first isolated from the bark of willow. A number of botanists are convinced that the means for controlling HIV and other viral diseases will come from plants. For now, though, we've precious little. Vitamin therapy, aspirin and prescription drugs can help slow the destructive advance of HIV. Use whatever means is at your disposal to prolong your life but be skeptical to keep the charlatans and opportunists at bay.

187

DEBATE, DENIAL AND SILENCE

By far the most chilling description of AIDS has been that it's a disease of multiple losses that affects both the HIV positive and negative. From the time that the initial diagnosis of HIV infection is known, you sense the loss of that open-endedness of life. From a possible future of fifty years, you're suddenly faced with a fraction of that. The tangible and intangible things of life are questioned. Will friends and family remain with you when word breaks? How long will your health hold out; is your job secure? . . . Doubts creep in about the surety of existence as the latest T-cell counts become infinitely more important than the Dow-Jones index.

Many still feel the social stigma and hide their illness. Still common in the SM community is the shock of discovering that an acquaintance has died of meningitis or pneumonia with no prior knowledge that he had even been HIV-positive. Periods of hospitalization are often kept hidden from friends and club members. Some fear ostracism from friends and sexual partners. Others don't know how to deal with the awkwardness of sympathy. Outright denial still exists. Obituaries of "life-long bachelors" still officially note death from a brain abscess or a suspicious "accident" without a word of HIV or AIDS. Others despair and quit playing safe, risking exposure to new strains of the virus and reinfection by active HIV. Some turn activist and become involved with education, volunteerism or political confrontations. Others, not wanting to be a bother, disappear from sight.

Men seem to have a perverted sense that disease makes them less masculine. Since HIV also carries the stigma of being sexually transmitted and that usually means having been screwed in the ass, many feel a need to conceal their illness. Society also does the inadvertent hatchet job. When I worked in medical education, the hospital would put together panels of people who had HIV infection. The IV drug addicts, who had gone through recovery programs only to discover they had contracted the virus, received great sympathy from the staff. The gay men received qualified condolences. Some of them told me afterward that they got the unspoken message quite clearly from the staff that somehow catching AIDS from a needle was a horrible twist of fate but to get it from a dick up the ass was reprehensible. It's still easier to claim that you got AIDS from a needle or a blood transfusion than from gay sex.

WORD GAMES

We rely upon word games to protect ourselves from the reality of HIV infection. In our everyday speech a barrier seems to have been erected to separate AIDS from HIV infection and HIV-positive from HIV-negative. Too many people use them as social delineations. In this HIV-status conscious society, the negative doesn't want to play with the positive and neither really wants to be reminded of the person with full blown AIDS. The truth is the virus resides in all categories. The HIV antibody test only tells you that you've formed antibodies to fight the virus. A person can test negative and still be infected with HIV if he hasn't yet developed the antibodies. HIV antibody status, T-cell counts and the symptoms of AIDS are only indications of the disease's destructive advance. Yet, they're used by many of us as grounds for discrimination. The far right makes no such fine distinctions. In their minds, if you're gay, you're infected with AIDS. The two are synonymous.

As a community, we SMers have had AIDS fundraisers and memorial plaques. But collectively, are we dealing with AIDS issues only from a safe distance? Rather than confronting HIV on the personal level, I wonder if we've inadvertently reduced the issues to an abstract state. We raise money in a bar full of healthy-looking people, turn the proceeds over to a healthy-looking member of an organization to help sick people whom we never have to see or deal with.

I've often watched my lover's parents, both in their late sixties, as they've driven to their elderly homebound friends just to chat. His mother explained it simply.

"We need to look out for one another. What with everybody's family so far away, it just gets so darn lonely, especially when most of them can't drive anymore."

Like most senior citizens, they've learned not to hide from the unpleasantness of the big decline. In fighting isolation, they confront sickness and death. They know that looking-out for one another unites them into a caring community.

A friend, now dead, who was in the wasting syndrome, mused on the changes that his manifesting full-blown AIDS had wrought. One is that trite but true lesson of fair weather friends. While he was simply HIV-positive, his playroom was a popular spot for visiting SMers to Chicago. Once he developed some of the classic illnesses of AIDS, many of his SM friends proved feckless. Without visits, letters or phone-calls, they proved themselves to have been just superficial friends on the sexual level. His AIDS symptoms scared them off.

"Do they think that I'm any less infectious when I was without symptoms? It's clear they're more afraid of the visible signs of this disease than they are of the unseen infection. Some are damn hypocrites. I know for a fact that they're positive too. Have you noticed that several of them have lost weight over the last year, how their butt cheeks and their upper arms have that old man sagginess to them? They're afraid to come here now and face their own future."

The word games extend beyond the gay SM community. I've had angry talks with straight friends who work in medical fields. They say that although HIV is incurable it's becoming "manageable." My response is that this glosses over the truth. Treatment or not, HIV eventually leads to AIDS and that to death. Therapy, while it has improved, has not reached the point yet of letting people live a near normal life span as with diabetes. We need hope but not at the price of self-delusion. They also say that HIV really shouldn't affect the way we live life. Any of us could be run over by a truck, shot by a vigilante or choke on fried chicken. But HIV does change your life. Knowledge of HIV infection alters your perspective. Whether it's you or your companion who becomes positive, suddenly, you're aware of a before and after. You're drawn to this inescapable event and everything forever after is done with an eye to the clock.

Counseling, therapy and support groups can assist in adjusting to the new state of things. HIV is easier to endure when you can speak about it with friends and relations. Just a few score years ago, cancer patients had to keep their disease a secret for fear of being run out of town by frightened neighbors who believed they could catch it from a sneeze. When my grandpa was wasting away from cancer in the nineteen-fifties, my parents cautioned us not to mention it to the neighbors. They kept him hidden in the back bedroom. The similar conspiracy of silence that ignorance and hatred enforce remains the worst aspect of HIV whether or not you're infected. By avoiding candid discussion, we erect barriers between each other at the very moment when we need to be closest to one another. While many SM clubs do a good job getting the word out on safe sex, many fail to really educate their members on taking care of their own. We really need to teach each other to care.

A CELEBRATION OF LIFE
Robert Bremner, London, England:
I had a partner who had told me he was negative but I insisted that we have safe sex and I even put the condom on him. I strongly suspect that he deliberately pushed it off whilst he fucked me. When we had finished, I discovered that the condom was up my bum and he had cum inside me. It was then that he calmly told me he had AIDS. I had had rheumatoid arthritis as a child so I already had an impaired immune system. My doctor had warned me that if I ever became positive for HIV, I would probably develop full blown AIDS immediately. Within a couple of weeks of the incident, I had an attack of rheumatism with sore joints and blood in my urine. My physician said that was a sign that I had indeed caught AIDS. He said that he thought I would be lucky to live out the year. A blood test later confirmed that I had become positive.

Once I knew I'd been infected, I lost interest in having sex. Being posi-

190

tive was always on my mind. I could only think about the unfairness of it all. And of course I was absolutely furious at the fellow who gave it to me. But you can sustain that intensity for only so long. Eventually, you have to just get on with it. I had taken care of a number of ill friends and I thought that I knew what it was like. But, you really can't know until you're on this side of the disease. The experience of becoming positive for AIDS means that you've suddenly become a member of a community set apart from the rest of humanity like people who have been hostages or concentration camp prisoners. You're living something totally removed from the lives of others. They listen to our stories and say they understand or they know, but they just can't, not really. The reality of this only comes from the experience.

Meeting Dennis helped me move beyond self-pity. He embraced life and lived it more intensely the sicker he became. When his doctor told him that he only had a few more months to live, he said he needed to take piano lessons immediately if he was going to learn to play it. And when it was clear that he would die within the month, he complained that he'd not made his pot yet. Making pottery was one thing he'd always wanted to do, so he signed up for a pottery course. He only lived long enough to make it to the first class, but there he was, blind, emaciated and half-paralyzed, happily sculpting this misshapen clay thing. But he'd made his little pot and it pleased him no end.

As I said, I had backed away from sex. I couldn't help see it as the thing that gave me death. Dennis wouldn't have any of that. Even though I had mixed feelings about sexual play, he convinced me to make the effort to resume my sex life—safely. For him, sex was a celebration of life, a universal gift to give us all a taste of heaven. Like all gifts, it's just simply there for us to accept or refuse as we choose. Dennis was more than enthusiastic to accept. I fisted him just an hour before he died. I'm sure he would have liked to have died that way, but he knew I couldn't have handled it. The doctor had left an overdose of morphine for him to take but I could never have given him the injection.

It's been a year since he's gone, over two since I was told I had just months to live. I've had different health crises but I take care of myself. Even though I have a low T-cell count, I'm still here. There are too many things that I want to do yet. I've a house boat to redo. I'm taking a navigation course and also studying Chinese. I don't have sex as often as I used to, but I no longer avoid it. Dennis was right about it being a celebration of existence. Life and sex go on.

THE ROLE OF ACTIVISM

Something was wrong that October morning in 1956. I looked out the window at the school across the street. No one milled about the playground; classes had begun. My mother had not wakened me. Cuddling my blanket, I toddled into the kitchen. She sat quietly, her eyes red and moist. On her lap was a book, one finger marking the page.

"What's wrong?" I asked.

"Grandpa's gone away."

"Oh," I said and stared out the kitchen window at the bright sky. The brisk autumnal wind stretched the school flag so taut that I thought all forty-eight stars would pop off. Sun-bleached clouds raced from west to east. The maple in front of the house had begun to turn. My mother sobbed softly, the book on her lap open. "Death Be Not Proud," the page counseled, "by John Donne." I knew something profound had happened. I wondered what it meant.

While no one wished him dead, no one was surprised when grandpa sickened and died. He had lived a good life and raised a family. At his funeral, the priest read Donne's poem. Prayers were said for his soul. A simple headstone marked his grave.

Thirty-two Octobers later, when I learned of my friend's death from AIDS, I felt rage instead of resignation. Parents were supposed to die before their children. Friends, younger than I, should live to the fullness of old age. It's a terrible thing, this loss of the order of things.

My friend had had no funeral at which to say farewell, no grave at which to visit. From the Ellipse in Washington, D.C., I watched fifty stars whip against a blue autumnal sky. I stood lost on acres of quilts looking for lost friends. The wind blew echoes of names from a distant podium that stood dark against the White House. Behind me, a woman sobbed for her son. Her throat cleared. She began, "Do not go gentle into that good night." I turned to look at her. As she spoke, her hands lightly caressed her son's quilt as a mother would a sleeping child.

I tried to understand this woman as she recited the defiant lines. Was she lamenting his insufficient struggle or lauding his valiant fight? I didn't ask, but I knew why she stroked the fabric of his quilt. Around us were thousands of portraits, mementos, messages and personal possessions sewn into fabric. Each panel held a bit of somebody who had been swept back into the chaos of the dark night. With nothing else to perpetuate their memory, this was their shrine. Remembrance keeps part of them alive. But remembrance is not enough.

Throughout this epidemic, the rage in me has built. Warnings, pleas, lamentations for the dead have left those in power as unmoved as were the people of occupied Europe by the deaths of millions of Jews, gays and other undesirable minorities. Society's inaction has been on par with the collusion of the occupied European countries when the Nazi smokestacks belched. Theirs was a sin of omission that found them content to let the Nazis rid them of a long standing social problem.

As gays, we've tended to collect in our own ghettos that are islands of security against the hate of society. John Rechy, in his 1979 novel *Rushes*, posed the question of who had really created the gay leather ghetto culture, the straights or the gays? Outrageous and grandiose behavior created a sense of control from the despair, hostility and resentment felt by gay men. The naked truth is that power confers legitimacy. If you've no power, you've no right to be respected. Absolute power corrupts, but so does absolute weakness.

The gay ghettos allowed us limited control over our lives. But they also hid us. A fact of ghetto life is that the outside world takes great pains to blind itself to conditions within them even as those within are painfully aware of attitudes outside. AIDS has visited the lessons of the Holocaust on us. Friends of mine in NYC speak of having had sixteen deaths among their acquaintances in one week. My relatives and straight friends think I've exaggerated the number of my companions who have died. No one could have hundreds die within a few years. Our retreat into the ghetto has allowed authorities to act as if nothing unusual has happened. Like the villagers around death camps, they pretend not to see the smokestacks of the crematoriums. And we, as did the doomed of those camps, have marched placidly to our collective deaths.

Thousands of gay men died out of sight in a government-media collusive secret. No coverage meant no general outrage. The gentle protest of the AIDS Quilt was too discreet to rupture the status quo. ACT-UP and other activists shake them out of their stupor and drag them into the death camp. Yet still, many with power avert their eyes from the carnage. They avoid the moral issues by focusing on decorum and courtesy. —We might be inclined to listen to you if only you would follow correct procedure. We agree in principle but we must oppose the manner of your protest. The goals are laudable but we find tactics of blocking entrances and shouting slogans too discourteous.—

Their insistence on polite dissent focuses attention exclusively on the unreasonableness of the protesters instead of on their own convenient oversight of thousands of deaths. What they really want is to continue their formal ignorance of AIDS till the smokestacks have finished belching the rest of us into the sky. Somehow they think that they can control AIDS, that with us gone, the Holocaust will burn itself out. In England, 85% of the cases are among gay men, yet they receive only 5% of AIDS funds. In spring of 1993, the health minister slashed AIDS funding to the gay community by two thirds because it's clear that "the epidemic isn't spreading among the general population." AIDS educators and researchers argued in vain that the low numbers indicate a successful prevention campaign. The authorities still have not learned that AIDS respects no closet whether it's that of a gay, an IVDA or a young teen experimenting with sex.

As the plague continues to spread in the US, more families must grapple with their emotional, spiritual and social beliefs to make sense of a personal ordeal with AIDS. Suddenly the abstract "biblical" punishment of sinners becomes their own Golgotha. When faced with a threat such as AIDS, societies react in two very different ways. The one is to jettison the unworkable explanation and seek new remedies that expand the boundary lines of society. The other solution is to dig a deeper trench and become even more "moral," more American, more family-value oriented. When their teenagers begin to die, they will pummel us with the epistles of Paul and blame their toleration of us as reason for God visiting this affliction on them. They will blame us for killing their children. We have another battle looming before us where we, the victims of their indifference, will be pilloried for the consequences of their inaction.

I am out to my parents, my nine siblings, their spouses and their children. Consequently, whether I'm HIV negative or positive directly affects the forty immediate members of my own family. Beyond that are the other blood relatives and further yet are the relatives of my lover's family. Every homophobic remark confronts them with the issues. They sense the injustice and I hope that, should my time come, they will rebel at the shame that society will try to make them feel. Reflecting on the losses endured by mothers during the Spanish Civil war, Delores Ibarruri Gomez, La Passionaria, wrote, "It is difficult to measure the amount of grief a mother's heart can contain: It is equally difficult to measure the capacity for resistance that such hearts can acquire."

In the SM community, we too grieve and mourn and pray, but every loss must also increase our courage and resolve to end the intolerance, complacency and the hatred that has allowed so many deaths. Each should reinforce our identity and reduce our own willingness to compromise or settle for less than full rights. Do not go gently into that dark night, little faggot. No one gives a shit for the acquiescent dead.

PARTINGS

For the survivors who watch friends leave singly or in twos and threes, to be left alone out of so many is incomprehensible. You become like the survivors of the calamities in the Book of Job who say, "I alone have been spared to tell you of this." You may grapple with the reason for being left behind, feel guilt for survival and cope with the isolation when friends have died. Yet, of all the uncertainties and anxieties of AIDS, none seems as difficult as parting after a sojourn among friends.

During the Middle Ages, a sojourn was a stopover during a wearisome pilgrimage for rest and hospitality from others along the route. Sojourns are measured out by the day. Of indeterminate length, they

194

may be the briefest of halts or one that settles comfortably into a stay of years. Life itself may be seen as a series of sojourns on our travels from cradle to tomb, since it too is a sharing of time and place with fellow pilgrims. Our trek through life is full of comings and goings, of meetings and leavings. These partings, whether temporary or permanent, divide into three kinds: those due to relocations, those to death and those to a gradual drifting away with never a definite good-bye.

With a frantic spinning of wheels on the road, modern life has become a ceaseless migration of peoples. Ours is the automobile culture, allowing few to remain in one spot more than several years. Relocations forced by schools, jobs, love and family obligations uproot friendships and compel farewells. Even if you yourself stay put, the ebb and flow of people jostles your settled existence. You may feel as if you live in a way station, forever welcoming those to whom you'll soon say good-bye. Modern life has given us little choice but to cherish and enjoy companionship, and, when the time comes, to say farewell and look forward with hope to meeting again.

AIDS, especially in the SM community, has made another kind of parting familiar. We all know someone who is never coming back again, someone whom we have known and loved and lost. Many of us have ceased to tally memorial services, count the obits or delete the names from address books. I've club directories and listings that date back to 1984 that I can't bear to toss out or erase, knowing that these are my last tangible links with friends. Yet, for all its pain, death gives a certainty to parting. Death provides a point of closure, a permanent good-bye.

But AIDS has also added uncertainty to life's journey. Many friends, especially in the leather community, have become the Vanished. Those whose lives once intersected ours have simply disappeared. Unlike relocation and death, the gradual loss of contact with acquaintances has no clean point of separation, no definitive parting of ways. Ten years ago, any of us would have merely thought that we'd lost track of each other and that perhaps someday our paths would again cross. Now the anxiety of AIDS haunts those losses of contact. Sometimes word drifts back, and we cannot help thinking with relief, "Good, they're still alive," but often there is only the silence of the void, without murmur, without closure.

So as sojourners, we stay for a time and then take our leave. In these partings, we experience a sense of sadness but also a detachment, a letting-go. The importance of things changes—some increase, others decrease. In a world where the chances are that many of us will never meet again, our memories must serve as our links to one another. What then will we remember of these times? Both bright and dark details, the

195

productive as well as the destructive times. And we do share difficult times, full of conflict, uncertainty and death. Yet, most importantly, these are also times of great friendship, reconciliation, purposefulness and an exuberant lust for life that always seems capable of overwhelming the darker and ambiguous meanings of the surrounding chaos, violence and fear. In a time of loss, we live not with fear but with the fullest measure of life. What should we recall of our fellow sojourners? A certain amount of failed potential to be sure. Friendships that might have flourished; deeds that might have been, had not our human frailties intervened. But such remembrances should not be filled with a sense of deprivation, or loss or a yearning for a past that never was. What we feel and experience is real, human and true. Never doubt it. Although the scope of our vision may vary, we all strive, as the Book of Judges says, to do "that which seemed right to himself." This coming to terms with the world to the best of our abilities is at the heart of Masoch. It is the spirit of masochism. There really is no finer thing than this.

Readers should consult and follow the AIDS Risk Reduction Guidelines for Healthier Sex provided on page 255 of this book.

PART II

Chapter 12: Myths and Metaphors

WHY A GOOD TOP BOTTOMS OUT

Some in SM look askance at those who slip back and forth across the line that separates the S from the M. Mainly espoused by exclusive tops who nervously safeguard their own southern approaches, this tired view still flusters the top who occasionally bottoms. To counter their embarrassment, some justify being the submissive by claiming that it's the only way to gauge just how hard to lash that whip, or know which clothespins give the best stimulation. Thus armed with such first-hand knowledge, a person can be a better top, as though improving technique were all that mattered. It's a bit like saying, "I'm not really enjoying this. I'm only trying to pick up a few helpful hints." I haven't heard anyone seriously suggest that exclusive bottoms ought to top so that they gain insight into being better bottoms. Truth be told, as liberating as SM sex is purported to be, many are still shackled by the idea that roles have either an exclusive masculine or feminine character. As my mostly deaf mother loudly phrased it in a crowded restaurant to my lover and me, "I know what you two do. All I want to know is, which of you takes the woman's part?"

Our culture has done a terrific job in imparting a psychological dread of appearing less than macho. Men have a penis that thrusts and delivers while women have a vagina that yields and receives. Therefore any role that controls and renders action is masculine while any role that involves submissively receiving is feminine. It's a close call to say which terrifies macho men more, receiving a bouquet of flowers at work or getting a dick up the butt. Openly admitting that they enjoy the bottom's role, even in vanilla sex, is quite threatening to their masculinity. They avoid any activity that appears feminine for fear that others might think that they secretly dress in gold lamé lycra, wear purple pumps and dust their dungeons as they trill along to Doris Day recordings.

In the SM world, there's an added layer of anxiety. We're still saddled with the left-over images of fiction writers: the all-knowing, ever-hard, hyper-masculine Dominant and the naive, utterly pliant, ever-in-training young smooth submissive. In this imagery, a top can never admit to any lack of experience, skill or ability. His pleasure is paramount. The bottom is a submissive pig who will enjoy anything, even when forced, so long as it comes from a masterful top. Never communicating his per-

197

sonal desires or needs, the bottom must aspire solely to be an object that maybe might, perhaps, someday merit elevation to Tophood. Few stories that present this imagery ever mention who had anointed *his* top as a top—an SM Church hierarchy, perhaps. The top, however, can never strive to be a bottom. Somehow that is a step down from the altar of masculine deification.

These images date from the published fiction of the pre-eighties before the notions of safe, sane and consensual or the concept of sensuality and mutuality were publicly preached. To a modest extent, writers and publishers are bound by the reality of their reader, but the world created in porn is at best a distorted reflection of real-life. You'd best recognize it as fiction and treat the images as fantasies. Jack-off literature is meant for masturbation and not for setting real-life standards. Take from porn whatever erotic desires intrigue you and explore the possibilities presented, but don't be tyrannized by it or by those who mistake wet dreams as realities. There are indeed exclusive tops as well as exclusive bottoms. But those who switch are the majority. In a study done for the *Journal of Homosexuality* in 1986 on SM pornography, the SMers interviewed indicated a preference for either top or bottom, yet, under the blanket of anonymity, all of them conceded that the actual role they assumed depended upon the situation, their frame of mind or their partner's preference. Obviously something more than perfecting technique as a top is at work here.

Greek ideas can help expand the notion of why tops should feel free to bottom. In Greek mythology, Hercules was not simply the epitome of masculinity, but beyond both belief and emulation. Strangely, Hercules often takes leave from his hyper-virility. The Greeks seemed to delight in humbling him. Pottery paintings abound in which he is depicted lolling in women's clothing—complete with pearls. One famous myth relates how Omphale, Queen of the Amazons, enslaved him. He cooks, spins and grovels at her feet. He not only works as her female slave but he dresses the part down to the wearing of perfume.

Why would the Greeks do this to their mightiest and manliest warrior? An obvious answer is simply to lampoon an unrealistic role model, similar to bottoms who fantasize about humiliating macho tops. But the stories serve a deeper purpose. In humbling Hercules, they curiously made him more sympathetic as a character, more human. It's as if, to counter an overdose of masculinity, he needed an equivalent dose of femininity to restore balance. Unquestionably, as the hyper-virile hero, he's over-bearing, incredibly stupid and his adventures are unbelievable, more of a Marvel comic book creation than a mythic figure. In being overly masculine, he loses his humanity and his rapport with others. Yet, his compulsive feminine role rapidly deflates and restores him to human proportions. Each time he finally snaps out of his excessively feminine state, Hercules is humbled and equally regrets having acted overly masculine as well as feminine. Once a sense of balance between the two aspects is restored, people are more inclined to like him.

The Greeks also held yearly religious ceremonies during which men and women reversed roles. In Athens, adult men and women paraded in drag at a festival to the god Dionysus. This wasn't to promote frivolity nor to teach the sexes what behaviors to avoid nor to highlight some aspect of masculinity and femininity. This was a socially required self-exploration relating to knowledge, freedom, power and self-sufficiency. The exchanging of the purely masculine or feminine roles is an examination of power relationships. For the men who have assumed the feminine role for the day, the one who commands becomes the one who is commanded. The one who would inflict pain experiences that pain himself. Here are the roots of SM's power exchanges. From active to passive, from mastery to surrender, it also connects you to the world through an increased awareness of reality and illusion. After experiencing the traditional submission of the feminine, a man must question all his previous perceptions of the world.

Whenever a male finds himself in a situation of weakness, he becomes acutely aware that he has a body. Through voluntary subordination, helplessness and submission, he becomes utterly powerless physically, mentally and emotionally. To be submissive is to know how vulnerable the body is. In western culture, men do not lay hands upon another unless to humble that person or instill a sense of hierarchy. Something as simple as placing my hand on your shoulder during a conversation signals that I'm superior to you and that I'm patronizing you just as an adult would a child. To touch, strike or whip is to breach that guarded cultural space between us. This is the threat and thrill of sadomasochism.

SM's role-playing calls into question what we know and how we think we know it by confronting the assumptions of rational thought with a psychological tidal wave. Role-playing may only be an act of impersonation, of assuming the aspects of power and powerlessness. But it can result in reaping keener understanding from those exchanges. A "new" program for juveniles accused of murderous assault involves a scenario where the crime is re-enacted with the offender having to assume the role of his victim. This role-playing dramatically alters aggressive behavior and has lowered repeat offenses by sixty percent. Its effectiveness really shouldn't surprise anyone experienced with SM role-playing. The recognition of the unknown or hidden-self is the most significant event in Dionysian theater where failure to reconcile one's contrived life with the revealed psyche results in disaster. For the ancients, encountering the god Dionysus meant facing the consequences of having settled for a partial or one-sided view of the world and themselves—usually an especially arrogant view of their own self-importance. The god relentlessly revealed the boundaries of their limited vision as self-erected barriers from which they had to break free or be destroyed. The real icon in SM should not rest with simple images of top and bottom but of an individual growing in his identity, assuming a fuller persona that understands the value of both.

In *Urban Aboriginals*, Geoff Mains correctly identifies leather as incorporating Dionysian tradition. The popular understanding is that Dionysus represents the wildly irrational, uncontrolled aspects of human nature and Apollo that of logic and emotional constraint, the one being an unbridled frenzied presence at the margins of humanity while the other a paradigm of control at the center. This split is not a Greek belief of the fourth century B.C. but rather the interpretation of the nineteenth century German philosopher Nietzsche. As usual, truth is less tidy than Teutonic thinkers would like.

Dionysus is a thoroughly strange Greek deity. He is always the Other, the lone outsider in mythology. A male god dressed in women's clothing who, unlike the other male gods, was never depicted with an erection, he's always arriving from someplace on his way to elsewhere. He is a god strictly for adults because only they could participate in his rites which were often celebrated at night with intoxication, mania, and bizarre behavior. He is god of wine and revels, but also god of disorder. His gift seems to be a healing chaos that grants relief from over regulation. Puck in Shakespeare's *Midsummer Night's Dream* is a variant of Dionysus. The play is a good example of confusion and disorder making things right when logic and law were leading to disaster.

By his appearance, Dionysus throws society's accepted concepts of masculine and feminine, and therefore the moral order, into confusion. As the disrupter of normal society, he saves civilization from the dangers of excessive moral control. His presence argues for a more complex definition of life and sexuality than the male dominated world allows. His stressing of both aspects in one person creates a dynamic process that is balanced and symmetrical. Rather than being merely the irrational half of human nature as Nietzsche claimed, Dionysus actually combines the rational with the irrational. He is the god of ordered chaos, allowing growth and change. This Dionysian view charts a path that travels between ignorance and knowledge, from deception to revelation, and out of misunderstanding towards comprehension.

There's another Greek myth that accounts for people's differences. Aristophanes presents the tale of a race of spherical people who offended the gods. They were punished by being split into masculine and feminine fragments that looked like everyday men and women. Zeus then dispersed these incomplete beings as further punishment. These disjointed entities spent their lives searching for reunion with their other halves. Whether these other halves were of the same or opposite sex depended on the original composition of each being. Thus two male halves can as easily make for a well-rounded being as two female halves or a male and a female. If you re-state the myth with dominant and submissive parts for the masculine and feminine, you end up with top/top, top/bottom and bottom/bottom.

Most smers these days top as well as bottom. Some may enjoy the top role exclusively in certain activities, but crave the bottom's role in others. An exclusive top in bondage may be an exclusive bottom in whipping scenes. The moral is that you must be true to your whole self and not just to parts sanctioned by others. Explore both roles to purge these false notions of the masculine and feminine from yourself. Take back what has tyrannically been removed from your life and discover your own true nature.

SM LANGUAGE

During a scene, sm communication relies on imagery and symbolism with speech playing an important but devalued role. One reason for this is that the euphemisms, evasions and lies of the modern world have bled words of their meaning and turned language into calcified thought. Another is that language, as a rational device, often hinders communication when it attempts to explain the irrational elements that arise in sm encounters. Rationally explaining a compulsion is somewhat contradictory. Finding words that will convey your sm experiences to others poses a problem. What language can possibly re-create for them what they've not seen, heard or felt, especially when learned experts have taught them to fear and loath the dangerous places you've been? Other smers will comprehend what you're attempting to communicate but few others will. So, you fall back on analogies and metaphors. You try and liken your experience to something in their life, just as Mick did in his coming-out story where he likened the pain/pleasure of a whipping to a friend's indulgence in spicy curry. If you've traveled to Central America and eaten an iguana for dinner, how do you describe it to a Mid-Western farmer? You rely on a metaphor within his experience. "It tastes like chicken."

People often talk of setting limits within a scene or of pushing boundaries further by acting out a particular fantasy. What are they trying to say? During one sm education meeting, someone made the pronouncement that no one could define what was meant by limits or boundaries. That's not true. These terms are merely metaphors which help you communicate your experience. sm language relies on several different analogies, one of maps, one of play, and another of theater. We've just been using them so long and often that we've forgotten their meanings.

LIMITS AND BOUNDARIES

Comparing the human body to a map is one of the more beautiful metaphors. Certainly it's one of the richest. We equate our bodies with features charted by maps without really being aware of how often it's done. Nerves form pathways. Blood courses beneath the surface. Faces can be craggy. Tits constitute mountains. Assholes or cunts become caverns. Waves of orgasms leave behind streams, puddles or little lakes. The metaphor is sometimes turned around. The Grand Tetons always amuse French-speakers since the name means Big Boobs.

Maps and explorations are not ideologically neutral. They inevitably alter the meaning and authority of others. English surveyors of the early seventeenth century needed the Crown's permission to map the realm. Spanish maps in the sixteenth and seventeenth centuries were state secrets. To learn the lay of the land was to gain independent mastery, something that Church and State feared. Looking at the attempts of governments to regulate our bodies and sexual information about it, you'd think the Spaniard was still operating.

We explore our bodies as well as the land. The natural world has well marked boundaries, recognizable limits with points of departure and return. The unchartered world, whether surrounding us or within us, is unprobed and unknown. Largely overwhelming and threatening, it frightens us until we acquaint ourselves with it through small explorations. It becomes familiar and enjoyable to us only when its limits and boundaries are made by us. Without such explorations there would be no idiosyncrasies, no personal interpretation, no style—only the insipid monotony of penned cattle. We often refer to these learned restrictions on our sexuality as the closet from which most of us have made the escape.

Your SM borders may be defined by society, by your own limitations or by those of your partner. Similarly, the early colonial maps of North America showed some borders defined by the presence of their neighbors, others by natural objects such as rivers or lakes. A few were open-ended, fading into Terra Incognita, the unexplored territory. This unknown country stretches out before us, no matter how long we've been into SM. I was conducting an interview with former *Drummer* publisher Tony DeBlase when a smiling Vance Reeger wandered over to show off his new cutting of an eagle. (A cutting is an incision of skin to create a scar that forms a design.) Tony rose and examined it keenly and said, "I never heard of a cutting in the gay male community until we got exposure to women who were doing it routinely. You see, even after

202

so many years, there's still many wonderful and beautiful things to explore."

Not everything that you explore will be claimed nor held in perpetuity. The Vikings explored but never claimed America. Just because you investigate or practice an activity for a time, doesn't obligate you to it forever. Circumstances in our lives change and we move on or are forced to abandon our previous haunts.

SM exploration demands more than simple cataloguing or a static listing of wants. It should be a continual journey of discovery that actively maps your limits and boundaries. It's a deliberate attempt to chart the unknown, to extract clarity from chaos in a very personal exploration. No map can be plotted without physical exploration. There is no other way to distinguish hear-say from fact or reality from fantasy. But it also calls for you to interpret and make sense of it as you constantly sort out sensations, accustom yourself to pain/pleasure intensities and learn the self-control and mental discipline to persevere when fear and reflex would force a retreat. SM should be an adventure summoning you to self-discovery and luring you from comfortable paths. You can't experience SM like a tourist on an air-conditioned holiday coach tour that takes you to the same tired places that everyone else visits. Packaged tourism demands nothing except to be herded by your handlers. I once overheard two undergraduates talking of where they had spent their spring holidays. One had been to Aruba. When her companion asked where it was, she replied, "How the hell should I know? My parents flew me there." SM is likewise full of people who have no idea where they've been or even where they are. Endeavor to break away from the herd and really challenge yourself.

Most boundaries are defined, maintained through learned fear and self-control. Society not only fences-off a safe area but often electrifies it to make sure that you stay put. Stepping out of that known realm is both an act of courage and curiosity. Beasties and dragons prowl that Terra Incognita as our minds fill it with bogey men. Most of us have had to confront and overcome the learned fear that SM meant someone nonconsensually beating the shit out of us. Exploring is really about mastering yourself. The map metaphor helps explain this as you struggle to describe your observations and experiences.

When you dare go where society has decreed dangerous, it will regard you with degrees of resentment, closed-mindedness and even indifference, dealing with you just like parents who punish a child that escapes from the security of the designated play area. When you truly step outside of your culture and upbringing, it forever alters your idea of the world. The concepts nurtured by society become too restrictive for you like a chrysalis which splits to let loose the changed being within. It frightens society threatening its control when your new viewpoint creates a desire for new explanations and a need for a fresh relationship between yourself and your community. The ensuing interplay leads either to new terms or to attempts to reimpose the old order—by brute force if necessary.

Realizing that fragments in life often pass for the whole, you join the company of many explorers who have wandered the land like Dionysus. They also had to confront others with the displeasing knowledge that theirs was not the only world. Small-mindedness erects barriers that create the illusion of unrelated worlds. To SMers repudiated by society and not sharing in its codes, the institutions of civilization are understood quite differently than by those embedded within its framework. SMers develop their own view of societal structures and see the coercive apparatus much clearer. Repudiating a world which has repudiated him, the SMer can easily see that those in positions of power are driving for domination and use the symbolism of the state to buttress the mystique of their position and secure domination. Ritual surrounds the courts, church, army and even the process of arrest. The uncertainty in society of people's motives means that one can never truly plumb the full depths behind actions. SM disturbs those in power so deeply because it lays bare the nature of power exchanges. Because your explorations threaten these systems, your experiences will be trivialized and attacked.

Be open about your explorations, if you can. Not everyone will listen or comprehend. Nor will everyone achieve the same level of understanding nor be as slow or fast as you, nor journey by the same road, nor encounter identical obstacles. Since everyone is different, their explorations will be different. People can arrive at different parts of the same country from different places via different routes. Don't fall into the trap of becoming a false messiah in the belief that your SM experience alone is the way, the truth and the light and that no one else's holds truth. That's absolute arrogance.

TOYS AND PLAYROOMS

SM fun takes place in playrooms among playmates who share their favorite playthings from their toy boxes. Sometimes you teach people new games and other times you learn new tricks. References to various play activities, such as role-playing and water-sports, butt-play and mind-games, abound in SM language.

Insects are the only group of animals that don't engage in play as an activity. One scientist remarked to me that insects are best understood as pre-programmed biologic machines which lack the necessary capability and flexibility for play. The greater the capacity for play, the greater the intelligence of a species. Even some mollusks (octopi and squid) manage a level of play. All mammals play and clearly enjoy it. Play allows for imaginative experimentation, an activity that gives you confidence and freedom within your environment. It gives you a chance to catch a sense of meaning and recognition for situations that you may not fully understand, such as power relationships. Practice allows you to become familiar in the handling of something and thereby lets you gain ability and control. It's a feeling-out of your independence.

Mutual and community play also serves to bind groups together. While this is often portrayed in nature documentaries as wolf cubs frisking about, our closest relatives, the pygmy chimps, use sexual play. You won't see groups of these chimps at public zoos. They're too indiscreet for the moral police. It's as if God created a species to refute the moral teachings of every fundamentalist preacher. An infant is likely to awaken an adult male with a blow job and female chimps say hello by performing cunnilingus on one another. Whereas the species of chimps of the National Geographic films wage war on one another, these pygmy chimpanzees have learned to use sexual play to ease social tension. They're also our closest relatives.

Among humans, play teaches values and allows us to say, "This is the way I want my life to be." Life is an unbounded course extending ahead to an uncertain unclear destination. Unlike pre-programmed insects with their set ways, you operate on principles that help you determine your direction in life and give shape to your existence. This formation of values eventually becomes your ethic, the public set of principles by which you govern your dealings with life. Ethics give you a sense of direction, like a compass. Without them your solutions to life's problems would be piecemeal and based solely on contingency without any consistency.

Ethics arise from a play of values by which you learn how life is affected by the balance of choices that you make. Play creates profound moments of discovery as well as profound mistakes, both of which lead to the shaping and reshaping of values. You learn that revaluation of principles takes place with every step you take. There's no unique and final solution to life's problems. Play teaches a way of seeking out alternatives and gives rise to the skills necessary for traversing those potential routes. You become aware of the richness, nuances, texture and structures only of those things in which you fully participate. And such participation often demands your involvement again and again.

We are alike in one fact, that we are all different. We all share basic human characteristics, yet everyone is unique because each of us contains a special arrangement of those human elements. Every personality is an ever changing kaleidoscope. The facets of human nature shift from Mother Teresa to Freddy Krueger. Play permits you to try out these different personas and roles without being overwhelmed by them.

The ability to see within yourself the elements of both the saint and the psychopath allows you an incredible flexibility. As your life rolls on, that ratio changes. Not only are you different from others, but you're different from the person you were just hours ago.

Play leads to human individuality rather than uniformity. You recreate discovery during play whereas learning by rote means competency in the routine but unimaginative in the execution. Technique offers a general guide for a scene. Technique enriches you but is always less than you are. By itself, it's only a simulacrum of the real and never identical with it. Style is your reinterpretation which gives activities meaning and value for you. Perfect technique is mechanical mastery; style makes it your own. No other animal has imaginative ability, objectives or the understanding to create self-sufficient excellence. If you slavishly imitate others, you deny the very capacities of inventiveness that mark you as being human. An artist is his own material. Instead of copying, invent ways to generate something beautiful and individual. Life offers enormous amounts of material and when you add to it the richness of imagination, the results can be overwhelming. Style is not a thing that one can learn. It is an expression of the individual, of his freedom to act with initiative, spontaneity, exuberance and control in order to shape an unformed future. Humans find pleasure in retracing the creative steps, in catching and matching the imaginative content. The lives and works of others become unfinished statements to which you add. Innovators open new dimensions with creative energy and imagination. Style demands expression in new ways which reorganize the creator and remake him. The doing of an action becomes beautiful only when you have interest and pleasure in your choice of action.

THEATER

"It may be a good thing to copy reality,
but to invent reality is much, much better."
—G. Verdi

The metaphor of theater is beyond doubt the most pervasive in SM. To list all the references in SM which allude to it would probably require a small pamphlet. Of all the metaphors used to describe SM, it is probably the one experience that every human has shared.

From Stone Age ritual to Broadway production, humans have sought to represent reality. Even when stripped of words, sets, lights and costumes, the theater of the mind creates representations of life's existence and meaning. Theater links human beings with the effect of communion. As Aristotle said, the purpose of theater is to cause a change for the better in the viewer. The Athenian theater of Dionysus taught culture, morality and imbued a sense of identity that was not just the wild Bacchanal orgy so often depicted. Designed to promote contemplation on moral obligations, it conveyed a social message that was not intended as mindless entertainment. The stodgy chorus stood for the conservative element of the community that judged the individual's actions. Characters are frequently undone by those very forces that they had rigidly refused to recognize and master in themselves. Their downfall hinged on the incompleteness of their character. Typically, a loss of balance rather than forces of the irrational destroys them. Dionysian theater was neither emotional or irrational. In fact, Herodotus, the father of history, tells of a playwright being fined for moving his audience to tears. Dionysian theater was serious business which stripped away layers of rationalizations and forced the participants, including the audience, to face truth and confront their nature and their destinies.

ROLE-PLAYING
Kevin Drewery, Greensboro, North Carolina:
SM is Stimulus and Manipulation. I like the concept of the box in the Hellraiser movies which sends little things out to explore a person's body so thoroughly that they die in orgasmic SM delight. The main character's dialogue is to me poetically erotic. When I plan a scene, I try to script at least some dialogue that emulates that. I can concentrate on what I'm going to say because I demand specific and limited language from my partner once the safe words are established. The only things I want to hear from his mouth are: "SIR!," "yes" or "no." "Sir" must even precede his giving me safety statements. Whether he calls me Sir, Dungeon Master or whatever depends on the scene but I want him to address me with respectful language. Not everything within a scene is artificial or acting. I had a trainee who did not like to be spanked. He and I agreed to use this as a very real negative reinforcement during his training period. Whenever he spoke without permission or responded inappropriately (failing to say "Sir"), this real punishment was administered.

I don't like to use gags. First because I'm not a mind-reader and second, because I feel that that's relinquishing too much control. When you're gagged, you really become dependent on someone being able to interpret your gestures. Body language is hard enough to figure out without being both bound and gagged.

I'm used to institutional and authoritarian systems. They offer me reassuring and familiar frameworks. No surprise since I went to rigid schools and spent time in the military. The clear rules of authoritarian control help keep things focused during an SM scene: the roles, the rules, the progression of events. If there is a problem, then something that had been agreed on earlier is said or done that calls attention unambiguously to the fact that something's wrong. We'll try to resolve it within our established roles, with me attempting to re-establish his confidence level. Most times, I will call an intermission, a break in the role-playing that allows me to offer that compassion or support that the role I've assumed will not allow. It's really not so strange to think of it in these formal terms. Role-playing of any sort develops its own momentum. If a group of actors are rehearsing a fight scene and someone has an accident like a broken nose, it does take a few moments for everyone on the set to calm down and put aside their assumed roles in order to respond to the genuine mishap. Likewise, if I'm done up in military garb with camouflage paint on my face, calling my trainee "dog breath," I need to call a formal break to differentiate my persona as the Drill Instructor from that of the compassionate partner. I'm then able to give the support my partner needs and help resolve his problem. We can then restart some of the activities, rebuild the intensity, regain the momentum and re-enter the scene.

▼

The theater of SM is not generally a public spectacle staged for the benefit of others. As private theater, an SM scene between two people is more like a rehearsal that is performed solely for the benefit of the performers and not an audience. Theater doors are most often locked to assure privacy. A rehearsal provides a period during which alternatives can be staged, unfamiliar roles tried out and the range of one's power to convince, persuade or control can be tested without public scrutiny. A mouse can assume the part of the lion or the dragon that of a lamb. The plasticity of power relationships and structure becomes apparent with SM theater so that a department manager who wields authority in the workplace can relinquish that role and become the submissive wearer of a dog collar.

A rehearsal provides complete freedom of invention but it requires an adroitness to create believable images and situations that follow an inherent logic and consistency. While in some sense an SM scene is a performance, it is without the demands of final form and perfection. A scene that delivers less than perfection bothers some people, but flawlessness isn't the goal, integrity is. A teacher of mine counseled that wisdom is knowing the difference between perfect and good enough. As a human being, you can never achieve perfection; you can only aspire to it, doing your best in the time allotted. Besides, SM is supposed to achieve an end through a conquest of obstacles. It's those very imperfections that create emptiness, shadows, breaks and holes that in turn accentuate the crises, turns and peaks. Without these negatives, there could only be perfect monotony. An SM scene has its own logic and time which cannot be fully dictated without turning it into a mechanical rendering. The participants give it sensuous embodiment and alter the flow as well as the theme of the action.

Everything from the imagination expresses a psychological reality. The private theater of SM strives to tell the truth through an honest exploration of your inner self. This inner vision is nearer to the core of experience than any description of a purely physical object. SM scenes represent a personal expression of your obsessions, neuroses, nightmares and anxieties. That is the shock of recognition, to see a presentation of your repressions, to recognize a concealed portion of yourself that is normally beyond the pale. SM theater makes no real contradictions between objective and subjective reality. Both are equally realistic but concerned with different aspects. SM is not the traditional scripted play so much as a sequence of images, allegoric phantoms and sensations. It creates a rupture between things and words, between objects and their representations, expressing what language itself cannot seem to put into words.

Viewed by themselves, the actions and dialogue of SM may seem purposeless and nonsensical, yet the power of conviction imbues them with meaning. The scene's power flows from the participants' intents and their feelings of release rather than from their acting-out a scripted scene. This is disorienting to anyone used to standards, predetermined expectations and frames of reference. An SM scene acquires the strange ritualistic incantory quality of a dark splendorous religious act. It's a world turned upside-down in which the pursuit of the abject and rejected can be carried out with a saint's devoted obsession. Sainthood, after all, is achieved by pursuing humility beyond mere self-renunciation and towards the annihilation of self-pride before the absolute. Many of our activities follow the regimen practiced by holy mystics to resolve the anxieties of their age. SM also seeks to master our anxieties, but by transmuting our nightmares via erotic fantasies. These are endowed with their own peculiar rhythms, infused with our culture and shaped by our private desires.

Combine the elements of fantasy and reality in the correct proportions. Manipulate time and create a setting sufficiently real to carry conviction. Separate the play area from the normal world, just as a stage is in public theater, so that you can represent life within the confines of your SM scene.

RHETORIC

Sometimes, communication degenerates into empty rhetoric. Words, phrases and sentences often appear to have meaning but are really devoid of thought and clarity. George Orwell, author of *1984*, warned in a brilliant essay back in the nineteen-thirties of the dangers of ready-made phrases and euphemisms. Pre-fabricated phrases run rampant in many SM and Leather speeches. Mostly these deal in superlatives: the

209

most exciting, the greatest, the hottest, most memorable, etc. Others appeal to some fuzzy notion of commonality. How often have you heard a speaker affirm his commitment to his SM/leather fraternity-brotherhood-solidarity-community-group-fellowship-lifestyle-heritage-roots-traditions? These are prepackaged thoughts and cliches that allow even a clueless speaker of very little brain to string together apparent pearls of wisdom. Attend several runs, seminars or contests and you'll be amazed at the scarcity of original thought. Imprisoned within a matrix of cemented sameness, thought eventually becomes fossilized and creative life dies out. Clones not only look alike, they speak alike.

Euphemisms, however, are ideas made deliberately vague so as to hide the reality of a situation. Their function is to conceal reality rather than reveal it. *Ethnic cleansing* is this decade's most horrific euphemism. The notorious rally cry of the far right for *a return to traditional family values* is a statement that appears to have meaning and strikes a chord in many people but which actually signifies nothing. Since everyone is free to put his interpretation on what the phrase means, many back it thinking that everyone else interprets it identically. Thus a false consensus based on ambiguity arises. Power-hucksters can then use this as a screen for their own vain-glorious aspirations. Sad to say, SM and Leather now have their versions of unscrupulous politicians, inept "experts" and public relations manipulators. As with their straight counterparts, the difference between the public image and the private reality, the apparent honesty and the concealed deceit can be huge. Cloaked in the jargon and euphemisms of SM Solidarity and Leather Brotherhood, some pretty shady and narrow-minded characters manage to worm their way to the forefront on both the local as well as national levels.

Luckily, you will find that most serious SMers still prefer the quiet of their own private playrooms. Relatively few crave publicity, political power or adulation. Many are patient teachers and good leaders in their own quiet way. Still, you need a good dose of healthy skepticism. Don't be over-awed by rhetoric. By being attuned to the warning signs within language, you stand a better chance of spotting SM charlatans. You, as an individual, don't need them as partners and we, collectively, don't need them as our representatives. Trust in SM depends upon honesty, something that rhetorical hype and hypocrisy undermine.

Chapter 13: Threats to SM

SM and leather are under attack from within and without. The one enemy, the ultra-right, is blatantly hostile, but the other, the shaman of sales, is an ingrained part of SM. It's easier to see the direct threats against our sexuality by the fundamentalists than to recognize the sexual models thrown before our eyes by merchandising. Our self-image is manipulated, aborting its identity by transforming it into a marketing neotribalism. Yet these two powers of America are shaping SM more than SM practitioners realize.

THE ULTRA-RIGHT
DEMANDING THE RIGHT NOT TO BE OFFENDED

Don't stereotype or under-estimate the average bible-thumper. They grasp issues and relate them to other matters. Though often portrayed as slow, inept and stupid, many are intelligent, recognize problems and try to solve them. Many read frequently, although they limit themselves to material that reinforces their existing opinions. Full of a vengeful, punishing God, their literature recommends force as necessary in the coming Armageddon. Pat Robertson and his ilk depict this view in broad apocalyptic strokes where Christians find themselves in a war which pits a born-again Christian God and His commandments against the Devil. It's a war that they believe that they may yet lose and suffer God's punishment for having tolerated the homosexuals and sinners among them. They may be cranks but they are also powerful ministers whose daily words and deeds encourage the beating, ambushing and killing of human beings. Vicious behavior is rationalized until murder is justified as righteous self-defense, and hatred becomes evidence of moral courage.

Their venom builds on a twisted reading of scripture, a smattering of pseudo-science and a lot of inane gibberish—all of which feed upon deep fears and anxieties. If the infidel won't convert, they'll legislate their beliefs and coerce compliance. Espousing a biblical patriotism, they long to create a Christian America that most of us pray will never exist. But their vision gathers them into a fellowship of stunning proportions.

You can watch the televangelists and call them crazy, but what of the millions who support them and dwell upon their poisoned words as God's revealed own? Can they all be insane? They work, have families and friends, belong to groups and organizations, run for political office and are functioning in society. They are not insane or retarded or psychotic in any standard sense of the word. They've committed no crimes as society sees it and are quite law abiding. Yet they are also extremely xenophobic, intolerant, racist, sexist and quite willing to use religion as a higher justification to step outside the law to enforce their beliefs. Paranoid perhaps, but far from alone. Their beliefs may be delusional, but they are highly organized and their thinking flows smoothly in orderly and logical steps that rely on assumptions shared, and therefore affirmed, by thousands of others. They vote; they run for local office and they'll seize control in the absence of our dissent and participation.

THE DUTCH SOLUTION
Josh, St. Petersburg, Florida:
The first time I went to Amsterdam, I was bowled over by how open things were. Seeing the prostitutes, male and female, waiting in their storefront windows for customers, was something a boy from Florida never expected to see. I couldn't get over the attitude of the Dutch towards many things. I mean, could you imagine hash bars in the States or the government compassionately treating drug addicts like victims rather than as criminals? And then I went to the leather bars. I couldn't believe what went on there and nobody had to worry about vice-cops suddenly raiding the place. I thought that here was a society that really accepts differences.

Gradually, I began to see that the Dutch are really quite puritanical. Most don't approve of the red light district, nor what goes on in the leather bars. In fact, they would really rather not know what goes on. I realized that I'd mistaken acceptance for toleration. Most don't support drug use or SM or promiscuity. They don't agree with a lot of behaviors, but they're not willing to jail or persecute someone for those differences. So what else can you do but tolerate your fellow human beings and do what you can to keep them from danger. That's why they have a needle exchange program, and regulate prostitution, and provide rather explicit AIDS information and give out condoms. As a nation, they suffered too much persecution and murder themselves to do the same to their own people.

At first, I was disappointed but then I said to myself, "That's not all bad." I mean, I don't accept the fundamentalists, but I've never attacked one with a baseball bat or burned one of their churches or tried to legislate against them. Isn't that toleration? If only they would give me the same consideration, we'd have a much better situation here.

▼

Certainly some people are learning more of sexual truth—about gays and lesbians in general, about SM and fetishes in specifics. But many others do not want to learn. For them, the truth is already known. These are people who never question authority and who mistake ignorance and intolerance for faith. They seek only confirmation of their beliefs. In self-fulfilling prophecies, they set-up or allow situations that assure punishment for activities that they hold as sinful. Have sex outside of marriage

212

and God will punish you by making you pregnant, or giving you VD or striking you dead with AIDS. Contradict their narrow point of view by actions or just by your existence and they will brand you a trouble maker and try to turn you into a moral lesson. They are not searching for the truth. They espouse a moralistic policy that declares, "If you do not abstain from sex, you must suffer for it." They would rather their own children die of AIDS than give them life-saving information about condoms. They would rather their teenage daughters have babies that abort their hopes and aspirations than talk to them about contraception. You can present no facts, no reasonable arguments that make any difference. Sex itself is intrinsically evil to them.

Earlier in this century when chemist Paul Ehrlich of Germany discovered a cure for syphilis, the factory producing the drug had to be put under armed guard to protect it from the moralists who believed that a remedy obstructed divine punishment. The British militant suffragette Christine Pankhurst argued to outlaw the medication because "[God] had willed that there be no way of escape from this scourge except one and that one way is the way of purity." So much for Christian compassion.

Nothing you do or say will sway them. What they're really demanding is the impossible right never to be offended. What that translates to is total intoleration. Disproving their beliefs will only disclose that their hatred is real. Instead, prevent them from achieving their agenda. The glimpses of their planned future for us is not rosy. Vote. Get involved. Come-out to as many of your family and friends as possible. Work to educate the majority on just how the ultra-right's agenda will affect them. Quite frankly, highlighting the fundamentalists' outrageous suggestions, such as their effort to ban *The Wizard of Oz* (because it portrays the witches of the North and South as being good while the Bible clearly condemns witchcraft), will make more of an impression than a carefully reasoned argument of civil rights. Humor remains our most effective weapon—especially when they provide so much outlandish material.

OPERATION SPANNER
North of London, England, an informal, word-of-mouth group of SM practitioners took photos and videos of each other and shared them among themselves. Sometime in 1987, the police received one of these videos, probably from a disgruntled participant. As the tape contained beatings, an abrasion scene and blood sports, the police thought that they had acquired a "snuff" film and began an investigation, code named: Spanner (the English term for monkey-wrench).

They interviewed all the participants and discovered to their chagrin that not only had no one been killed but that all the activities were consensual, that no one had required medical treatment and that no one had suffered permanent body damage. The nearly forty men connected with the videotape spoke openly with the police, giving sworn statements—without consulting an attorney. They were absolutely certain that they had done nothing illegal.

Unfortunately, the police, having spent a rumored £1.5 million (~ $2.25 million), had egg on their face. Needing something to show for their money and time, they proceeded to trial on various counts of assault. The defense argued that since the activities were consensual, legally no assault could have taken place.

During the trial, the prosecution bordered on sensationalism in its portrayal of SM. A light abrasion of the nut-sac with emery paper was depicted as sandpapering the skin off. A butt merely reddened by spanking with a leather belt was described as left like raw meat. A scalpel scratching the top skin layer of a penis was misrepresented as the splitting of the urethra from top to base.

The elderly conservative judges declared that one cannot consent to sexual assault the way one consents to surgery or tattooing. One judge stated that any slackening of the law would encourage homosexual sadomasochism, while another held that SM was nothing more than a fantasy specifically designed to conceal the cult of violence. In their ruling, they disregarded the use of safe words, dismissed written or verbal consent and ignored the fact the tops were sometimes bottoms. One defendant, described as a sadist "willing to carry out [his] desires with anyone who would cooperate," was himself the masochist in a scene presented as evidence of his sadism!

Further, they kicked open the bedroom door to judicial scrutiny by rendering new interpretations of what was defined as permissible consenting sex. They ruled that any sexual activity that inflicts any mark, pain or injury, of a greater nature than momentary or "trifling" constitutes assault. Thus, the highest court in England designated SM as grievous bodily harm.

Not surprisingly, the rulings clarified nothing. Even Freud himself admitted failure in trying to define SM. The judges could not explain what either "more than trifling" or "momentary" meant in legal terms. The ambiguities are stunning. At how many pounds per square inch does a "lover's pinch which hurts yet is desired" become assault and is Shakespeare now guilty of conspiracy to incite SM assault? How many milliseconds in a moment? Can the size or placement of a hickey, which is a bruise by mouth suction, render it a technical grievous bodily assault?

The judges did not grasp the difference between assault and consensual SM. In a play from the nineteen-sixties, *Marat/de Sade*, the mad

Marquis has a woman inmate of the insane asylum flog him with her long tresses as he writhes in ecstatic agony. Where was the pain? Clinically, none could exist, yet here was a staged SM act for the man, whose name means sadism, in the role of the masochist. What a wonderful conundrum for the classifiers and cataloguers where the intent not intensity and the actuality not the activity fulfill the SM fantasy.

After the trial, everyone had thought that the police would back off. About a month later, however, several dozen men dressed for a leather and rubber fetish party were arrested in a police raid. The authorities explained that the wearing of leather and rubber indicates the contemplation of SM activity, and, since condoms were found on some of the men, they must have anticipated sexual activity and therefore they must be guilty of conspiracy to commit grievous bodily harm. They went on to raid the homes of the attenders. In one case, they confiscated SM videos that a teacher had made of himself and showed them to his employer who promptly fired him. The teacher was never charged with anything. As the Queen of Hearts said in *Alice's Adventures in Wonderland*, "Sentence first—verdict afterwards."

IMPLICATIONS FOR U.S. SM-ERS

Our judicial systems differ enough that these rulings will not have direct implications for SM in the States. However, since the late nineteen-seventies, the ultra-right in the US has forged strong links to the reactionary think-tanks of Great Britain. Divisive tactics and politics that have shown success in Britain have often been imported, adapted and exploited for the political gain of conservatives here. Control and power are the issues; division and fear the means. As the drive for gay/lesbian civil rights recovers from the AIDS set-back, some way of frightening Americans and of convincing them of homosexuality's innate depravity is needed. The bogey-man of SMers engaged in lurid, non-consensual assault is ready-made for them. The current high profile of SM will assure that do-good legislators will attempt to define and regulate SM behavior.

Preventing a domestic version of Operation Spanner depends on our education efforts including self-education. SMers must know enough law to avoid playing into the enemies' hands, particularly when moralistic authorities rely on intimidation rather than courtroom success to exert control. For example, although an indecency case against Boston's Dreizehn Club eventually failed, one participant was driven to suicide. The actions of the authorities succeeded in cowing many SM/leather groups, effectively ending sponsored play parties for many.

Studying and mastering the lessons learned by those who have suffered police harassment is vital in overcoming these tactics. Advanced preparation will avert future grief. Routine orientation for club members might include legal guidelines. sm practitioners ought to learn how to behave during a police detention, perhaps even by undergoing a mock-arrest and police interrogation. (Hmm, a scene with socially redeeming value!) To protect members, clubs and organizations should prepare a response to police harassment as well as a list of sm-friendly lawyers. Like it or not, smers need political awareness and participation. We must network with other lesbian/gay groups and convince everyone that we sink or swim together. Given the ultra-right's disposition, prudence demands that we ponder the consequences of an Operation Spanner here.

DEALING WITH THE POLICE

To enter private premises, the police must have either a search warrant or a reasonable belief that someone's life is in immediate danger. Ask to see the warrant. If you let them in without a warrant, the courts will assume that you waived your rights. Never attend play parties or demonstrations where someone collects money at the door. The police can arrest everyone present for frequenting a place of prostitution.

Never allow yourself to be photographed or videotaped unless you are one hundred percent certain that these will never fall into the wrong hands. The very real danger is that these can be leaked by the police to employers, family members or the media. Keeping your face out of the picture helps somewhat. A hood or mask works well. But remember that identification can be ascertained from piercings, tattoos, moles, scars and other body markings.

If you're confronted by the police, don't panic. You never want to do anything that gives the nice officer an excuse to "pacify" you. Act natural; say nothing. Kiss ass if you must, but hold onto your constitutional right to silence. You also have a right to an attorney. Smile nervously. Pee in your pants. But keep your damn mouth shut until a lawyer can advise you. Intimidation is the name of the game. If you thought you've played power and control games, just wait till you're fingerprinted and photographed at the station. Unnerving is an understatement. And that's just the start of the psychological games.

Don't be taken in by the good cop/bad cop routine. The bad cop will make implied threats designed to frighten you, including hints that your employer may learn of your activities. After all, he might have to verify your employment to satisfy himself that you're not a vagrant. More importantly, don't fall for the friendly cop who "saves" you from his buddy, the bad cop. He'll tell you that he can help you out of this difficulty if you just give him some information. Don't be a sucker. If you don't volunteer information, they probably won't have a case against you.

216

MARKETING

LEATHER BIMBO

John, Cleveland, Ohio:

The evening was winding down at the bar fundraiser. Dressed in a body harness, jeans and chaps, I was working my way through the crowd toward the restrooms when someone pinched my ass so hard that it raised a welt. I'll allow a playful grope, but this was anonymous, non-consensual damage. I turned quickly, but couldn't catch anyone's eye. However, furtive side glances from several people identified the perpetrator—moussed-up, big-haired and thoroughly drunk. When confronted, he was indignant that I was angry. In his view, I had invited his action. "It's your own fault for being a tease. You shouldn't dress like that unless you really want it." Had I missed something? When did leather cease being a source of power and start transforming the wearer into a bimbo sex object? I never expected leather to allow me to share in the quintessential female experience of sexual harassment.

While mulling over this bar incident, I couldn't help but compare it to four years previous in Chicago when a friend and I strolled in full leathers through a rough neighborhood. While I'm six foot, my friend is only five-five, causing us to be dubbed Mutt and Jeff in leather. Still, because of black leather's intrinsic meaning, the locals parted like the Red Sea around the Israelites. Over the last few years, something important has occurred that's redefined leather, something fundamental's shifted the emphasis from internal to external qualities.

▼

During the last decade, the leather community has under-gone rampant commercialization. Contests were once fun, low-key fundraisers held for the benefit of the community. Now they're serious business affairs staged with the self-importance of the Miss America Pageant. This commercialization has subtly changed a celebration of leather sexuality into a marketing campaign along the lines of teen-age ninja turtles.

The *big* contests are great fun as long as you treat them as you would Mardi Gras. More people pour into the host cities for a week-end of debauchery than for the contests. It's carnival time and nothing said or done that week-end is meant to be taken seriously. The outrageous placing of a gay SM facade on a heterosexual beauty contest established the grass-roots popularity of the first leather contests. Let's not delude ourselves; the snide term "sash queen" is a gentle reminder of reality. I sat with a lesbian friend during one contest. She saw it as the best spoof of a bathing beauty contest that she'd ever seen—right down to the swimsuit/jockstrap competition. Yet this sense of fun is slipping away. One contest promoter, who had just returned from Germany where he had sponsored competitions to guarantee an international flavor for his event, complained that the Germans just did not understand the seriousness of the title. Since they viewed the proceedings as a dance show competition rather than an SM event, he had difficulty finding someone butch enough. Imagine the shame and horror of a Mr. Germany whose hands would forever be on his hips! Actually, I think the Germans had it right. They were at least attuned to the frivolous potential. Nowadays, many competitions unintentionally become hilarious precisely because so many treat them with undue seriousness.

Contests are a mixed bag. A title's better enticements are its bequeathing of legitimacy and providing an instant platform. An amazing access to newsletters and magazines, unknown to the behind-the-scenes SM activist, can be had. In recent years, some very capable people have taken advantage of this immediate fame and promoted some very worthy causes. But I'd be a fool to contend that my academic and activist background counted more than my tanned buns in winning. Yes, I confess; I'm a former sash queen. While I can appreciate the irony that wiggling my butt at a contest made more of an impression than a dozen years' involvement as a gay activist, I feel on the balance that I gave in to Christ's second temptation. The recognition comes too readily. Although some have used contests to achieve terrific goals, many more have been exploited even as they sought to exploit the fleeting recognition.

In one major contest, a porn star with the proper appeal and looks slipped into a set of borrowed leathers and won by properly presenting the correct image and attitude that the promoters felt represented the new generation of leather. No amateur playing dress-up could waltz into Inferno, pick up implements and perform a convincing demonstration of SM skill. Although the worlds of contests and SM are not mutually exclusive, they tend to attract people of different philosophies. It's hard to imagine someone winning a future Mr. Inferno title, but then again . . .

Contests also have their politically correct phraseology. These are not pageants (and heaven forbid that you call them beauty contests) but rather "competitions," and the proper term for a winner is title-holder, not sash-queen. As a title-holder, I was advised to have business cards printed with my name, title, address and phone number. Somehow, I think these had less to do with business opportunities than with private fertility consultations. I was also told to have a photographer do a hot leather portrait and provide eight by ten glossy photos. I thought this was a joke but I've since seen other title-holders scrawling endearing inscriptions to their tricks the morning after. (Are movie stars this tacky?) Some SM bars and clubs now display autographed pictures of leather celebrities the way Italian restaurants plaster the wall with portraits of movie stars who have eaten there. The intended message is that the restaurant must be serving authentic Italian food since real Italian stars had patronized the establishment. Does SM legitimacy really flow from celebrity status?

Two thousand years ago, the Roman historian Lucretius described the ancient festival of the fertility goddess Cybele during which a competition was held to pick a virgin beauty to embody her in mortal guise.

"Bedecked with crown and banners, she is paraded in dazzling state. Tight-skinned tambourines and clanging cymbals resound to the beat of clapping hands, pan pipes stir the air. Riding in procession through great cities, she silently blesses mortals with her presence. They sprinkle brass and silver coins all along her path, scatter a snow-shower of rose petals and present her with lavish offerings."

Attend any of the big Mr. SM Cowhide Contests and you will notice something similar. Spotlights sweep the stage like lights from heaven passing over the aspirants judged worthy of the honor. Electronic devices record and magnify every word, facial twitch and gesture. From the audio system, regal trumpets blare, then fall silent. After a hushed moment of staged suspense, the emcee, with muted drum roll, announces the new titleholder. A man with exemplary qualities parades with banner and gleaming trophy to the winner's dais as the crowds thunder their applause for the newest idol in the cult of leather.

The multiplying titles are more than simply an over-publicized gimmick foisted on us by marketing interests. Like the cult of Cybele, they contain a residue of ancient celebration and ritual designed to allay our insecurities. On his ascension to the title, he assumes the identity of One beyond both himself and the masses, just as Christ represented the God-man or the Virgin the perfect mother goddess. The titles may vary, but the icon is always readily recognized.

The titleholder provides a seemingly solid image that exalts a particular ethic to those needing guidance to suppress their insecurities. Its ultimate values are sexual success and prowess linked with an unencumbered, twenty-four hour a day SM/leather lifestyle of fantasy made flesh. But like all promises of idols fashioned by our hands, it proves false, leading to constant craving, consumption and cynicism. Even after we clothe ourselves in black leather, adorn our piercings or subscribe to endless magazines, our insecurities will still beleaguer and bother us. The marketed leather image is a merciless god who entangles us more and more into the net of neurotic dogmatic obeisance. Those engaged in contests might be SM cardboard cut-outs or saints in black leather but their qualities are equally hidden behind an image that is king of commodities. And its promised fulfillment remains forever beyond our fingertips.

Propaganda is anything that claims, "This is what greatness looks like. If you really want to be stellar, you must look this way, do these things in this precise manner, own this piece of equipment," and so on. Whether the subjects are third world dictators or sexual role-models, the emphasis is always on the exterior. Glossy leather magazines will often picture title-holders of major contests with more adoring sex-kittens draped over them than GM products at a Detroit car show. Marketing techniques eclipse the quality of both men and machines with the same subliminal message, "Own this look and you'll be sexually irresistible." Appearances and acquisitions count more than substance. It expounds a fantasy doctrine of rigid perfection. To be a real leatherman, you must conform to code, speaking, dressing and playing from an approved canon. Words and images present a simulacrum—a shadow that's only the semblance of something genuine. When linked with merchandising, dogma becomes a commercialization that not only defines what the perfect look is, but conveniently offers to provide the means to achieve it. Providing a needed service to the leather community is different from exploitive and manipulative marketing.

Marketing always asserts that its message is one of liberation from the puritans. Yet, it too is a tyrant as it pronounces judgment on what is acceptable and what is not. Aspirants to the SM world become anxious slaves paralyzed by fear that they may transgress canonical rules. Within the confusing deluge of media signals and peer pressure, the insecure are presented with a comprehensive and authoritative guide to a forbidding world just entered. The popularity of marketed images arises from a need for a total manageable concept that not only shows you who to be but tells you how to be it. Unambiguously clear, it offers reassuring hints if you feel deep-down that you've not achieved the ideal. As the marketing tyrants mediate the Word of the most high, it becomes a world of bondage and imprisonment as liberation is destroyed by the anxiety to do only what is proper. Although sex is a basic component of all human relationships, we suffer from an identity crisis born of a combination of fear and fascination with sex. In this lies its terrible power and terror. Marketing tries to contain sexual fear by reducing it to a packaged consumable item—one devoid of power and passion.

The current SM world was created in large part by gays and lesbians. With the discovery of SM eroticism by rock stars and the invasion by big media, SM is being transformed wholesale into a marketplace travesty of itself. The exploitation of its scandalous reputation merely insures their merchandising success. The increasing availability of this sorry SM caricature demands nothing from the observer but a masturbatory fantasy. The inward quality of SM is turned inside-out like a Saturday morning cartoon character whose real purpose is neither pleasure nor education but sales. Those who buy the marketed image never seem at ease. Their consternation is that someone else is better or more knowledgeable or more proficient. Deep down inside, they feel like frauds and fear that someone may discover it. They instinctively know that reality never truly takes second place to image.

The loss of critical judgment and the commercialization of leather leave us open to a manipulation already so ingrained that we aren't even aware of it. A reversal of the current drift depends upon an increased exercise of common sense and a valuing of substance over packaging. The source and center of SM values ought to come from within. Plainly, SM and leather sex are evolving. There's no going back to what was, but will it continue to bring joy and delight, or will it become just another marketing tool? The current drift is in the direction that will soon see leather celebrities endorsing lines of designer SM wear.

The man who brought me out to leather has himself withdrawn from it. His leathers lie in storage. During one visit, I asked him if he missed it. "I've considered it, but what's the point? The rebels are gone and leather is just fashion now."

I can't divine what form or fetish that radical leather sexuality will assume in the next millennium although I hope I can influence its development. To that end, I've thought of a new seditious fetish attire but my fellow SMers have threatened to disown me if I actually sew club colors on a purple polyester leisure suit. Does anybody know where to buy white patent leather shoes with matching belt?

Chapter 14: The Name Givers

Leather has a way of bringing out the worst in non-SMers. A bottle is thrown from a passing car at a motorcyclist in black leather. A gay dance bar refuses to admit a couple in full leathers. A panicky first-time visitor to a leather bar blurts out his fear of being tortured. Irrational fear, hate and discrimination dog everyone's steps in the SM community. And these beasties occasionally come from within ourselves. Most of us hesitated to explore our SM leanings because of the popular images available to us. SM fascinated me for years before I felt safe and strong enough to act upon my desires. What had stopped me was fear as well as a learned shame. I lusted after the leather life but without role-models or clubs in the city where I lived, I had had only the disparaging comments of both gays and straights that simply reinforced the psychotic stereotypes. The SM publications that I encountered offered little reassurance and never effectively countered society's misconceptions. I remember that they consisted mainly of fantasies that dwelt on the non-consensual loss of control. Great for one-handed reading but not for instilling confidence and trust. Oh, sure, there was the occasional advice column, but it constituted a tiny percent of the magazine space. The predominant message was neither safe, sane nor consensual and for a kid struggling with identity, it just reinforced the belief that SM was victimization. Small wonder then that so many, in both the straight and gay/lesbian communities, stress the psychotic side and react so negatively to sadomasochism.

The basis for SM-phobia can be traced to the period about a hundred years ago when sadism and masochism were formulated as psychiatric terms. The works of three seminal figures in the genesis of modern SM intersected at the turn of the last century, one well-known, one forgotten, one influential—and all misunderstood. Their works today are little read except by scholars and researchers but have profoundly shaped modern attitudes in a curious combination of cultural memory and amnesia. Only one, the Marquis de Sade, is familiar. Much less known are the writer, Leopold von Sacher-Masoch, and the psychiatrist, Richard von Krafft-Ebing (who once lived within walking distance of each other).

While much has been said and written about discovering "our leather rooms," actually very little beyond personal reminiscences stretches the history further than the nineteen-forties. The given impression is that modern SM sprang forth fully formed like an Athena in leather. Western Europe has a unique intellectual legacy and these are the big three thinkers. Their writings deeply affected the development of western SM thought and practice as well as influencing modern social, medical and legal responses to it. A few pages cannot capture their lifeworks: a modest introduction is the most I can hope for. Nor is my reading the way, the truth and the light. Each reader interprets authors according to his own times, culture and memories. You must read their books to gain your own insights.

This chapter is the most difficult since it represents the distillation of massive amounts of information. I recognize that the SM community embraces a wide range of talents and abilities and not everyone will find this easy reading. I've rewritten this chapter several times, shortening, simplifying and removing academic jargon. SM is a complex philosophy that can be simplified only so far before it sinks into absurdity.

MARQUIS DE SADE

As a rule, people fear sadists but ridicule masochists. Our society jokes about the submissive man, but the apprehension and loathing felt toward a sadist approaches the phobia shown toward spiders and snakes. What is it within de Sade's world that frightens people so? Ask anyone—straight, lesbian, gay, SM or fetishist—about de Sade's philosophy and you'll receive plenty of opinions of what they think he said. But has anyone actually read de Sade?

De Sade would probably have been known to history as just another petty noble who lost his head during the French Revolution. Destiny intervened when he was accused of attempting to drug, assault and rape a woman. Being an aristocrat would normally have meant that the lawsuit would be quietly swept under the Royal carpet. But, the prosecution occurred at a time when King Louis XVI and his Queen Marie Antoinette faced a rebellious population who demanded accountability for the licentious excesses of the nobles. He found that monarchy needed to make an example of him. He was duly convicted in a scandalous and well publicized trial and sent to the Bastille. There he began to vent his anger at the politicizing of his sexual escapades by writing satiric pornographic novels that merged sex and revolutionary thought to fanatical extremes.

As the French Revolution progressed, he tried to portray himself as a victim of monarchical injustice. No one really believed it, and his imprisonment by the king probably saved him from the guillotine. He was removed from the Bastille just before its storming and destruction by revolutionary forces and then re-imprisoned under Napoleon in 1803 in an insane asylum where he stayed until his death. It's interesting to reflect that while Napoleon's drive for dominance directly caused the deaths of millions, society chose to use de Sade, whose crimes were imaginary, as the epitome of cruelty and lust.

The Marquis' surviving writings run fifteen volumes in the Complete Works in French (*Oeuvres Completes de Marquis de Sade*, ed. A. Le Brun, Paris 1986). Many of his writings were lost due to censorship and partially to his own denial of authorship. The surviving works are not only voluminous but written in the flowery, ponderous and rambling aristocratic style of the 18th century. Reading them is as tiring as running through jello. Most English translations worsen the problem with unimaginative and boring phrasing. Consequently, few sᴍers have ever slogged through more than a couple of chapters. As one leather woman told me, "When I finished a lengthy passage where de Sade belabored the how and why of having sewn someone's butt-cheeks together, I decided that this wasn't worth my time." Even so, his reputation is such that some of his works have only been published within the last sixty years. Censorship continues both overtly and covertly. (The descendants of the Marquis were banned in 1991 by the U.S. government from importing wine from their estates. The family name and coat of arms on the label were deemed offensive. They were obliged to relabel the wine. What's in a name?) Many community libraries are not allowed to purchase his books because of "community standards." Even when not banned, de Sade's writings are often either abridged or are available only in French.

Mark Twain defined a classic as "a book which everybody quotes but nobody reads." De Sade certainly fits in this category. His works are primarily philosophical discussions, not torrid tales. His stories are so talk ridden that discussion of past or future activities often causes more orgasms for the characters than their actual commission. In fact, *Eugenie de Farval* lacks any explicit acts. Its violence and debauchery exist in plans, dialogue and recollections—all talk, no action. In de Sade's stories, everything is discussed, described, committed, but nothing is ever resolved and no one ever has the last word. Talk is the essential element because, as he says in *Julliette*, "Philosophy must discuss everything." For de Sade, sex itself becomes a device for social criticism. Without relating story lines, I will outline a view of de Sade's philosophy. Considering the sheer volume of his surviving works, this can only touch upon his philosophy.

De Sade combined two old French traditions of sexual writing. The first presented sex basically as the pursuit of pleasure in titillating scandal booklets circulated for court gossip. Best viewed as the Midnight-Sun-Enquirer tabloids of the period, they were simply revelations (or speculations) of who was screwing whom in court. These expanded into pornographic stories in which the heroine suffered numerous travails and sexual indignations, but whose sufferings always ended happily. Voltaire's *Candide* satirized this particular genre. The second tradition arose in the early 1600s which saw an increasing awareness of the political use of sexuality. Politics began to be seen as any public or private interchange or exchange between people. This view changed the significance

224

of sex from private sensations to public representation (that meant that what went on in the bedroom might now have a separate public meaning). Sex became an important political tool as agitators worked to discredit their rivals. Pamphlets, sermons and plays helped move sexuality from individual bedrooms to the political arena. Revelations of private sexual encounters provoked public outrage for the revealer's political gain. Sex had become an effective weapon. Suddenly, the real or rumored excesses of the aristocracy, their debaucheries and their sexual liaisons became politically explosive issues. American presidential politics carries on this fine tradition.

De Sade's writings are very political. (For those familiar with Rousseau, de Sade serves up a stinging satire of his philosophy of a benevolent Nature.) [Camille Paglia, *Sexual Personae*, chapter eight, Return of the Great Mother: Rousseau vs. Sade, p. 230–247.] He attacks absolutism while simultaneously extending the individual rights preached by the French Revolution to their logical extreme. If each person has sovereign rights, then no society has the power to limit your mastery over another person. And since each person can claim sovereign rights over every other person, then relationships can only be based on the asserting of your ability over another's inability. And if you can never define precisely where your power begins and another's ends, what yours, or anyone's or any group's privileges or rights to dominance are cannot be agreed upon by any two persons let alone by society at large. The whirlwind of political confusion goes on.

De Sade realized that when philosophers cite nature as a basis for behavior, they really mean culture. Nature is unchanging while cultural beliefs are adjustable. To prove his point, de Sade inevitably uses extreme examples. Cannibalism, for instance, is included in several stories. While languishing in the Bastille, de Sade read much on the voyages of discovery, including Captain Cooke's explorations of Africa. A discussion of cannibalism, differing in its setting but not argument, appears in both *Julliette* and *Aline et Valcour*. "Revulsion is merely a weakness, a minor defect of our make-up which we neglected to cure when we were young." "Nature created us; custom shapes us"—Sarmiento in *A&V*, Sauville's tale. De Sade argues that if African natives practice cannibalism, the revulsion towards eating human flesh must be a learned response that can be unlearned. Since their culture relishes cannibalism while Europe's condemns it, a consensus on cannibalism must have been reached in both worlds (that is both societies have decided what the proper or "natural" response to cannibalism is for them). Africans decided to savor cannibalism while Europeans chose to abhor it. Of course, once any character accepts the specific argument that an individual's response to cannibalism is learned, de Sade exploits the opening. The character is further forced to acknowledge that his response to any lesser act of cruelty must also stem from cultural opinion. By dividing and sub-dividing the definitions of acceptable behavior, de Sade effectively destroys the notion of consensus.

It's not just political and social distinctions that are obliterated. Even sexual roles suffer a breakdown. Characters shift sexuality and at times seem to switch sex. Women with enormous clitorises sodomize men; male genitals are cut off and vaginas created. By eliminating all distinctions—except each individual's right to dominate all others—he leaves no way of defining positions. In the ensuing free-for-all, no group can ever hope to agree upon anything except the need for further discussion. De Sade destroys the definitions that separate normal from perverse, private from public, social obligation from individual self-assertion. De Sade's philosophy unravels certainty and explodes our cultural notions of normal.

He bases his politics upon an inequality present in the physical expression of sex. De Sade reduces all social relations to sexual ones. For de Sade, the sex act initiates a violent inequality. One penetrates; the other is penetrated. Sex doesn't just express violence; sex creates it. Sex gives you privilege over others independent of their consent. Sadean sex is at the root of our modern legal definition of sexual harassment whereby a superior takes advantage of authority to force another into sexual relations. De Sade also makes a distinction between two very different types of violent domination. The first he condemns as an inferior, unthinking sort where the perpetrator acts from unbridled emotion, such as an abusive husband who vents his frustration and anger by beating his family. To de Sade this is utterly contemptible behavior. For him, a sadist must rationally, coolly and logically plan out his assault, commit it with a studied apathy, then philosophically critique it and, if necessary, recommit the crime in order to clarify or define the assault better. A sadist continually refines his offense whereas the lowly sort mindlessly repeats his without variation.

The idea of a "pleasure contract" of mutual fulfillment is alien to de Sade. Only the pleasure of the superior matters. Notions of safe, sane or consensual are rejected out of hand. No relationship can be based on either mutuality or concern. Sex and violence fuse so completely that not only is sex murderous but murder becomes akin to sex. Inferiors are victims, not partners. With all rights denied for one's inferiors, this becomes a world of extreme violence, unbounded sex and absolute inequality. The superior's right to satisfaction of his needs—without the obligation to anticipate or plan for those needs—converts people into objects. For the sadist, objects only have meaning when they are employed for use. One story details a dining table made of naked living bodies upon which sizzling plates of human flesh are served, the victims being used as both food and furniture. They exist merely to serve their superior's whim. He has no obligation whatsoever to them. ["As long as the act of coition lasts, I may, to be sure, continue in need of that object, but once it is over and I am satisfied, what . . . will attach me? (de Sade, *Philosophy*)" "Objects have no value for us save that which our imagination imparts to them," (*Justine*.)] A sadist strives to possess "objects" until his immediate need is satiated. Discardment often equals destruction for things no longer needed. Thus, one character matter-of-factly shoves her companion into a volcano, without regret, simply because she'd become bored with that person. This complete lack of empathy with the suffering caused to others reveals the psychotic nature of a true sadist.

The cultural memory of de Sade's ethics frightens those unfamiliar with leather sex. Many believe that the leather community is composed of psychotics who routinely victimize individuals for one-sided sexual thrills. Although de Sade is a part of our heritage, it is a very uneasy legacy. We have become comfortable with modern SM philosophy which espouses an idea of mutuality that treats the participants as equals and that embraces sensuality. We've forgotten that this is actually the opposite of Sadean thought. Sensuality and mutuality are a cultural consensus, an agreed-upon understanding of what constitutes acceptable behavior within the leather community today. They are achieved through a negotiation governed by the guide-lines of safe, sane and consensual. A lack of any of these elements can be seen as a retreat into the psychotic world of Sadean sexual politics. Unfortunately, those outside of the leather community know only of de Sade. Their knowledge comes not from reading his works but from a kind of oral tradition which remembers only his lurid examples with no understanding of his philosophy. Communicating our notion of mutuality in SM relationships to others in the gay/lesbian community and to those in the straight world is absolutely essential. Otherwise our world of safe, sane and consensual SM will be continually haunted by fear, hate and discrimination.

SACHER-MASOCH

Imagine that a hundred years from now, Gertrude Stein has become unknown. Her creation of a new style of literature is ignored. Her influence on other artists and writers, such as Hemingway, is forgotten. Most of her books held by major libraries are in a foreign language. The sole title published in English is a heavily abridged *Autobiography of Alice B. Toklas*, and most editions have been printed "for private distribution only." Suppressed as an artist, Stein is remembered in this future world only for a sexual psychosis. Her humanity and contributions to the arts have been suppressed to a single fixation upon a perceived

227

perversion involving lipstick-lesbians known clinically as *steinism*. Ludicrous as this scenario seems, this has been the fate of Leopold von Sacher-Masoch. From one of the most well known and respected writers of the nineteenth century, today he is commemorated only in the psychiatric term *masochism*.

This century has visited every form of censorship upon Sacher-Masoch. The eradication of his writing has been nearly total. He's been forgotten by German, Austrian, Ukrainian, Jewish, Polish and Czech critics, none of whom care to claim him as part of their cultural heritage, though all could. His writings were burned by Nazis as "perverted," though the true reasons were his pro-Jewish stance and his condemnation of the mindless glorification of Germany. Though devoid of explicit sex, his novels have been denounced and banned as depraved by censors in both England and the United States. Except for limited editions of *Venus in Furs* and some old editions of *Jewish Stories*, his works remain unavailable in English. English-speaking critics this century have contended that his works aren't worth translating. Yet many then praise his innovative style and its influence on modern writers. The following is from a 1977 private printing of *Venus in Furs*. I quote it at length to show the schizophrenic stance adopted by critics. It begins by asserting that Masoch's works are meritless, but after spouting this "truism," the critic continues,

". . . once these criticisms have been made, one is at a loss. The book is still there, as sharp and compelling as ever, still able to cast its spell through the sheer power and persistence of the hero-author's fascination with the beauty of female domination, . . . yielding to the force of a dream rendered with almost insane fervor. Its secret . . . is that it is not a work of fiction but of mythology, the fruit of an obsession that refuses to accept the limitations of art, life or common sense and demands that the reader do so as well. It is the triumph of the subjective, autoerotic, intuitional vision of a man who knew he was telling the truth about himself in a way that no one had ever done before. This and not its eroticism is the quality by which it has survived."

This need to preface any praise of Masoch's writing with a seemingly pre-packaged belittlement is at last being challenged. There are now several French translations including a three volume edition but a reputable biography of Sacher-Masoch has yet to be published in English. The serious inquiries into his life have almost all been published within the last decade by French and German writers.[1] Outside of *Ve-*

---

[1] The only seriously researched biography is in French, *Sacher-Masoch 1838–1895*, by Bernard Michel (Editions Robert Laffont, Paris, 1989). Sacher-Masoch's diary was lost after WW II.

nus in Furs, few SMers have had access to him or his works. For that reason, I will spend more time covering Masoch in this and the following section.

Sacher-Masoch was born and raised in Galicia, a southern province of present day Poland noted for its mix of different ethnic groups and religions. His mother distanced herself from him, consigning his upbringing to a robust Ukrainian woman who, though illiterate herself, immersed and educated him with the traditions and life of Slavic culture. She became the basis for his ideal sexual woman, earthy, strong-willed with a dominating demeanor. Although an Austrian aristocrat, he did not learn German until his tenth year. He witnessed first hand the brutal uprisings in central Europe in 1848 and this deepened his concern for the region's people. He attended the University of Graz, in the modern Czech state, where he received his degree in history and accepted a position as lecturer at the university. At first, he wrote history books but later turned to fiction, becoming the most popular author in Central Europe as well as the first German author since Goethe to win French acclaim. They awarded him the French Legion of Honor. His twenty-fifth anniversary as a writer was celebrated at universities in Europe at which time he received praise from Victor Hugo *(Les Miserables)*, Alexander Dumas *(Three Musketeers)*, the Scandinavian playwright Ibsen, the scientist Louis Pasteur and many others. By the time of his death in 1895, he had published not less than 120 titles.

He carried on a number of scandalous affairs with women, among whom were a married woman and a famous actress. In his writings, he claims his aunt established his fetish for whipping, furs and dominitrixes at a very early age, but the tale is so similar to the one told by French philosopher Rousseau that plagiarism has to be suspected. He was pursued and seduced into marriage by Aurora von Remuax who assumed the name and identity of his most famous character, the dominitrix Wanda. Despite her rewriting the facts in two autobiographies, this began as a consensual arrangement that led to marriage but ended in a bitter divorce. In his last marriage to Hulga, his children's governess, Masoch seems to have abandoned his fetishes.[2]

Often embracing unpopular causes, he fought for social justice, striving to improve the lot of the peasants at a time when the aristocracy treated them as animals. He challenged his fellow writers to oppose the pan-Germanic movement begun under Bismarck that absurdly exalted

---

[2] A description exists from a traveler who met with a mysterious aristocrat, long thought to be Masoch, who arranged for a young woman visitor to beat him, but the details of this incident do not conform to Masoch's pattern. Michel has postulated that the particular individual here is a Russian Baron. *Sacher-Masoch*, Op. cit.

Germans and their culture as the pinnacle of human development and civilization. Left unchecked, this belief in German superiority led directly to the Franco-Prussian War, WW I and WW II. He took an unpopular pro-Judaic stance. Almost alone of Europe's literary figures, he spoke out against anti-semitism. Though not so much anti-religious as indifferent, he was strongly anti-clerical, arguing against the prejudiced views promulgated by religious leaders. He also proposed a European economic, social and political union.

In his writings, he envisioned a grand scheme of inter-related novels called *The Legacy of Cain*. This cycle of stories would examine six things that condemn humanity, as the offspring of Cain, to wander the earth: love, property, government, war, work and death. The series would have presented contradictions that confront humans and demand resolution. *Venus in Furs*, one of six novels in the section on love, is considered the height of his writing by English critics. Among other shockers, the highly autobiographical *Venus* provided the first published voluntary time-limited slave contract. He later abandoned the *Cain* project as his financial difficulties grew too great, writing a number of very trashy novelettes to raise cash quickly.

His writing is heavily influenced by the steppes, the broad treeless plains of Eastern Europe. Stretching in all directions, the flat landscape seems without boundaries, a place where land and sky appear to merge. Individuals are minute players within the immensity of an uncaring environment where nature would as soon destroy as create. (Minuteness does not mean insignificance since even a small figure upright against an endless horizon still draws attention to itself.) His characters seek to come to terms with their world, rather than its domination. Reaching an accommodation with it permits them the prospect of happiness, but there are no guarantees. His best stories chronicle attempts at this coming to terms, extending from mundane village life to complex relations between the sexes.

Sacher-Masoch enriched European literature not just at the margins of the bizarre and erotic but by opening the way for a psychological analysis of the unknown and unexplored self. He pioneered a new form of literature, probing the mystery of sexuality and the subconscious. He conceived a writing style that used short sentences (at a time when Victor Hugo wrote a sentence that was two and a half pages long) and experimented with using thoughts and dialogue, rather than long-winded descriptive passages, to develop his stories. In place of a unity of self, Sacher-Masoch proposed an identity composed of a many-layered personality that changed over time. Thus, in *Venus in Furs*, Wanda can be at once the pitiless Dominitrix and the lover incapable of playing such a cruel role. She rules and yet desires to be ruled. His stories of role-reversals between the sexes and his real-life indulgence with anonymous correspondents reveal a fascination with the ambiguities and contradictions of personalities that await discovery. He concentrates on his characters' states of mind as they confront the world's cruelty and isolation within the surety of rigid philosophy or the dogma of religion. For Masoch, life is arbitrary because it is based on delusion and self-deception. Forced to improvise resolutions based on their intuitions and emotional responses, characters often act irrationally, struggling to make sense of an absurd world where perfect answers are only illusionary. To guide themselves on this imperfect earth, they fashion a personal order from their desires. If they fail, it's because the world itself is degenerate and flawed.

Life may be cruel and rich in drama, but it's also ludicrously funny. From the time of ancient Greeks, comedy has had a cruel edge, relying on one person's pain and discomfort to amuse others. Masoch exploits this tradition. The hero of *Venus in Furs* is left tied to the bedpost in a fancy hotel as Wanda and her Greek lover drive off. To the character, it's cruel humiliation but the idea of an aristocrat dressed as a peasant butler tied to a four-poster with whip marks on his back to be discovered by the hotel staff is pretty funny. An episode of TV's *Cheers* reprised the situation when Rebecca left Sam—clad only in his underwear—tied inside the elevator of a posh hotel.

A word needs to be said about the infamous slave contracts. I refer to the one that Masoch wrote with Fanny von Pistor since this was a real contract as opposed to the fantasy version presented in *Venus* [see Appendix of the present book]. Enslavement is not an accurate description in this case since true slavery, by definition, must entail permanent, unconditional, involuntary domination. Masoch's bondage was contractual with both mistress and slave authoring and agreeing to set conditions. It was time limited in two ways, a six months total duration—with a renewal option—and a daily "free period" during which he could conduct his affairs. (Imagine de Sade giving his victims the afternoon off for personal business or being told not to snoop in personal correspondence.) It was also action-limited in that he could refuse to do anything dishonorable. What constitutes dishonorable is left to the interpretation of the "slave" who can negate the entire contract by invoking this open clause. The enslavement then is only fiction, conforming to the dictates of safe, sane and consensual.

His eroticism may be bland for twentieth century tastes and his style that of the Wagnerian era, but his attention to the role of desire in life and his sense of theater directly influenced other writers. Kafka's *Metamorphosis* includes a character, Gregor Samsa, whose first name is Masoch's submissive alter-ego and whose last name is an anagram of

SAcher-MASoch arranged to rhyme with Kafka. Gregor is also dominated by women and has an undue attachment for a painting that depicts a woman in furs. James Joyce's character in *Ulysses*, Leopold Bloom, not only incorporates Sacher-Masoch's first name but is himself a masochist. Other writers such as Henry James and the playwrights of the Theater of the Absurd have direct roots to his works. Yet, despite this debt to him by modern writers, he's not even mentioned in literature courses.

His influence forgotten, Masoch, once celebrated by the erudite of Europe, has become scorned, even by the few critics who mention him, as a mere pornographer which strains the definition of offensiveness beyond even Utah's standard. Certainly, changing tastes in literature cause some loss of popularity, but what accounts for a complete eclipse? This amnesia began nearly a hundred years ago when the Viennese psychiatrist, Krafft-Ebing, published his *Psychopathia Sexualis*. This pre-Freudian work was the first attempt to categorize sexual behaviors using case studies. In linking Masoch's name with de Sade, he ironically guaranteed world-wide immortality for Sacher-Masoch's name but banished his life's work to oblivion.

KRAFFT-EBING

Ever wonder why when public discussion of homosexuality arises, whether in news coverage, politics, religion or letters to the editor, a number of other topics are inevitably dragged in? Fem men, bull-dykes, child molesters, public masturbators, sadists, masochists, "recruitment" of innocents, mental illness, necrophilia, murder, mayhem, sheepshaggers and the fall-of-civilization-as-we-know-it always become connected. How did all these things become jumbled together in the public's mind? Blame it on a book, first published back in 1890, that became a secret best-seller. The odds are that your grandparents or parents have a copy hidden on the top shelf of their bookcase. (Try looking behind the *Complete Works of Shakespeare*.) Last published in the 1960s, it was the first book to classify sexual perversions. The book was based on several discredited theories but science is too taxing for most people. Simplistic assumptions that reinforce existing beliefs win more supporters than complex explanations.

PSEUDO-SCIENTIFIC ASSUMPTIONS

A little over a hundred years ago, the human egg was discovered. Medicine noted that the fertilized egg progresses from single-celled to multi-celled to a fish-like stage with gills and tail and eventually to a fully evolved human infant ready to be born. Krafft-Ebing was among those who believed in the Lombrosian Theory which held that every human fetus retraced evolution resulting in some people being born less evolved than others. These individuals were throw-backs to primitive forms, similar to the belief that a wolf-cub could be born to a domesticated dog. It claimed to be able to pinpoint every person's evolutionary status, with racism playing a major role in the hierarchy. Negroes were reversions to humans from millions of years ago, rated slightly higher than the apes. Many illustrations of the time pictured negroes and gorillas on the same page. Indeed, Africans were held to be especially dangerous because, being so primitive, they were totally incapable of governing their sexual behavior. But by no means was race the only determining factor. Homosexuality was incomprehensible unless seen as a throw-back to the days of ancient Rome or Greece when homosexuality was the standard. As less evolved beings, both blacks (by millions of years) and homosexuals (by two thousand years) were regarded as genetic criminals who were prone to violent acts. ". . . [B]orn for evil, against whom all social cures break as against a rock—a fact which compels us to eliminate them completely, even by death."[3]

In 1890, the Viennese psychiatrist, Richard von Krafft-Ebing revised and expanded his *Psychopathia Sexualis* in which he adapted this Lombrosian Theory to classify sexual behavior. This book was not an obscure document but a work that became the definitive text on sexual behavior until Kinsey's research sixty years later. Unlike Kinsey's research, Krafft-Ebing's study and recommendations immediately affected the legal and penal systems around the world. It remains on the shelf in medical and legal libraries and forms the basis for many oppressive laws regulating sexual expression. This antiquated medical work is still used as "proof" of homosexuality's disease status.

For Krafft-Ebing "normal" did not mean "typical." He never envisioned a range of acceptable human sexual behavior.[4] Instead of aver-

---

[3]Lombroso, *Criminal Man*, 1911 p. 369. Published shortly before his death, this was the first time that Lombroso collected the papers and speeches of his career.

[4]Normal sexuality for men was expressed in a stronger sex drive than women, being drawn towards the opposite sex with that attraction based on her physical qualities, being pleasure-oriented, and being by nature aggressive and impetuous. Natural instinct and social position are "frequent causes of disloyalty in man," a politic way of saying that it's normal for men to commit adultery. On the other hand, "the unfaithfulness of the wife, as compared with the husband, is morally of much wider bearing, and should always meet with severer punishment." The love of a married woman for another man is described as "a phenomena in the realm of Psychopathia Sexualis which sadly stands in need of scientific explanation." *Psychopathia Sexualis*, 1947 Pioneer Publications, Inc., p. 78.

233

age, he meant an idealized "evolutionarily-advanced" sexuality. What a surprise to discover an upperclass Teutonic heterosexual male at the pinnacle of God's ordained world! His personal version of male sexuality became the only "normal" one for men and his personal concept of female sexuality that for "normal" women. All others he declared abnormal and indicative of inherited weaknesses. Such people were thought to be evolutionary reversals, a degeneration into genetically inferior human beings and therefore criminals. Commenting on homosexuals, he stated,

"the welfare and the interests of society are best served by his confinement in an insane asylum, where abstinence from alcohol is enforced and proper treatment (if necessary, hypnotic suggestion), offers promises of a final cure. . . . Scientific investigation shows that a man mentally and sexually degenerate *ab origine* [from birth], and therefore not responsible, must be removed from society for life, but not as a punishment."

One came under scrutiny, not for acts committed, but for merely being suspected of having been born different. Acts alone no longer constituted the sole reason for medical, legal or moral intervention. One's mere being or innate desires were raised to a more significant level than the actual commission of an act. An act merits punishment, but genetically-initiated desire is a loaded gun that threatens civilization and demands the quarantine of the affected individual to protect society. The legal and moral authorities of the US listened. From these arguments arose the legal codes that prohibited the serving of alcohol to known homosexuals (still on the books in many states), kept gays and black men from interacting with children or serving in the military and allowed the involuntary commitment of lesbians to mental institutions.

ACADEMIC STUPIDITY

In this book, Krafft-Ebing announced that sadism had an exactly equal opposite. For this phenomenon of pleasure through suffering he invented a new word, masochism. Krafft-Ebing defended his naming of this disorder after Masoch by citing the example of John Dalton who had discovered and described the phenomena of color-blindness, known as Daltonism, which he had recognized in himself. Krafft-Ebing's implication is that Masoch discovered masochism within himself and published his "discovery" within his novels. His argument contradicts accepted practice. The medical tradition calls for the first person who observes and describes a particular phenomenon in a *published scientific paper* to name it by either resorting to the Greco-Latin lexicon or by endowing it with one's own name.

The phenomenon of deriving pleasure from pain was known to antiquity as algolagnia, a term already in use that was available to Krafft-Ebing and one that Freud would later use in his own works. Additionally, Krafft-Ebing's claim that Masoch was the first writer to describe the sensation is erroneous. Rousseau in his *Confessions* had explicitly depicted his algolagniac experience as a child as well as his escapades with Madame de Warens. Since he was not only the first modern to describe the perversion fully but a contemporary of de Sade and one of those whom the Marquis satirizes in his work, the syndrome might have better been called Rousseauism. But as the discovering physician almost always uses his own name and not that of the patient, the proper name should have been Ebingism. Why then did Krafft-Ebing fly in the face of three established alternatives?

Nothing reinforces orthodox beliefs like a catchy phrase, motto or word. The term sadism had crept into use around 1840. Not only would a parallel name appeal to Krafft-Ebing but he would want something that would be instantly recognizable. Masoch's name was well known and the association would be easily understood. Hence Masochism rather than algolagnia or Rousseauism or Ebingism. There is another, more subjective reason. Krafft-Ebing had lived near him during Masoch's persecution for his pro-Jewish and anti-pan-Germanic beliefs. Elements of the smear campaign conducted against Masoch by the German language papers seem to have influenced the pro-Germanic Krafft-Ebing. One is the allegation of homosexuality. Although Masoch had numerous affairs with women and wrote over a hundred stories with heterosexual characters, the one story that he wrote which featured a gay character has been used as "proof" of his deviant and latent homosexual tendencies. Indeed, this is still being cited by modern psychiatrists as proof positive of latent homosexuality.

In his last revision of the *Psychopathia*, he wrote a lame excuse claiming that others had verified Masoch's behavior. Krafft-Ebing basically admitted to relying on gossip. Nor was he above playing loose with the facts. He stated that he had seen a letter written by Masoch at the top of which was his trademark rubber stamp of a Slavic dominatrix. Krafft-Ebing deliberately misleads the reader:

"One of these letters dated 1888 shows as a heading the picture of a luxuriant woman with imperial bearing only half covered with furs and holding a riding whip as if ready to strike."

The description implies that the woman is naked except for the furs. Beneath them, she is actually clothed from bejeweled-head to booted-toe in a traditional over-dressed ethnic costume. Little matters like this raise doubts about the reliability of other "proofs." After reading the book, a furious Sacher-Masoch nonetheless saw no point in arguing publicly with what he called "academic stupidity." The effect though was devastating to Masoch's work.

Within the *Psychopathia Sexualis* masochism is defined and connected with the most grotesque and distasteful impulses including necrophilia, pedophilia, sadistic mutilation and psychotic murder. Krafft-Ebing made Masoch's name synonymous with incredibly repulsive and obscene acts, none of which were part of any of Masoch's own writings or behavior. Readers of Masoch felt compromised. Since a reader tacitly admits to enjoying the author's own likes and dislikes, many found themselves uncomfortably linked to this newly named perversion. As the term masochism gained in popular usage, few cared to be connected with the name's acquired reputation. Since repudiation was the only publicly acceptable course of action, within a few years, Central Europe's most celebrated author was no longer read.

Krafft-Ebing also denies both the pre-existence and cultural significance of "perversions" which he claims began with Sacher-Masoch. Although Masoch wrote in German, his outlook and the location for many of his stories are Slavic. Krafft-Ebing expresses total contempt for this crucial fact. Fur, for example, has long been a symbol of authority throughout Europe. (Napoleon and the Austrian Emperor Franz Joseph were invested as monarchs with imperial fur capes. In England, Queen Elizabeth still wears ermine on certain occasions of state.) Slavic culture heavily emphasized this aspect with the inclusion of fur in the motifs of secular and religious ceremonial dress. The wearing of fur must be interpreted as heightening Wanda's authority in ways similar to the wearing of a policeman's uniform by a top. At one point in *Venus*, she demands "Quick, quick give them back to me or I will lose all my feeling of authority." Fur's ability to symbolize absolute power yet simultaneously represent the ultimate in sensual softness presents a potent psychological image whose importance Krafft-Ebing reduces to mere deviant behavior. (Incidentally, Masoch also introduced a new word into the German vocabulary—*negligée*.)

Masoch used metaphors to make associations that he himself may not have been fully aware of. How does one comprehend connections that have been made intuitively? Psychoanalysis attempts to assign specific meaning to both deliberate and inadvertent ambiguities. To grasp the many-layered meaning of Masoch's favored whip requires a knowledge of the man and his cultural history. As illustrated in Masoch's stamp, the whip held by the woman is a traditional and versatile Slavic instrument of punishment called a knout. The Eastern European knout consisted of several parts used for increasing degrees of severity. The leather thongs held by a ring form one unit that was often used by mothers to discipline children. It looked fierce and made a loud slap, but the flat broad straps presented a large surface area that smacked more like a paddle. The straps could be slit into thongs, then braided and the tips knotted. With the ring attached to a handle, it fashioned a flogger which was used in the military for discipline. (A famous photograph shows Masoch reclining at the feet of Fanny von Pistor who holds a braided knout in her lap.) Finally, iron tips could be added, making it a feared means of legal punishment with four or five strokes being sufficient to break a man. In Russia, this form of the knout was also a method of capital punishment. This rather disturbing connection of matriarchal discipline to an imperial death sentence was dismissed by Krafft-Ebing as "unsatisfactory and far-fetched."

Krafft-Ebing undergoes some amazing contortions when explaining sadism and masochism. He claims that his data demonstrate that pathological female masochists are rare. Rather than question his research methods, he reasons that, since women are hereditarily disposed towards masochism, spotting a "true" female masochist would be impossible. He insists that female sadists are extremely rare because women are not genetically disposed towards dominance. However, he then claims that pathological sadism is a common observable trait among men, since the male's tendency is towards aggression—completely failing to state how aggressiveness among males could make sadism so apparent when passivity among females hid masochism. But he really lets his pre-Freudian-slip show when he admits that among males, whose natural tendency he had just asserted was sadistic domination, masochism is very common. Those rare female sadists must have been terribly busy in this heterosexual *wunderland.*

Although Krafft-Ebing states that he is merely recording observations and categorizing them, he is engaged in more than dispassionate observation. His use of detailed case studies provides a smoke screen that obscures the line between scientific facts and personal judgments and prejudices. The accuracy of those individual cases is not the issue; their relation to sexuality is. Sex is a matter of biology which normally is decisive. With few exceptions, humans are born male or female. Sexuality however is defined by discussions during which people talk to people about sex and its meaning. Without it there could be no definition of what it is to be female or male or straight, or gay or lesbian or asexual or even an SMer. Sexuality is a way of informing, defining and controlling. This discourse of sexuality results in both power and knowledge and it is this that Krafft-Ebing commandeers. On the basis of his medical authority, he claims incontestable expertise and exerts control over his readers who accept his information as fact and extend his control over themselves. As with de Sade, he has more to contribute about representations of power than about sexual desire.[5]

Despite the flawed nature of his work, Krafft-Ebing must be judged in the light of his times. Twentieth century notions of liberal, conservative and reactionary have no meaning in the world of 1890. Positions once espoused by liberals have become the platform of the ultra-right and vice versa. Meanings of words have changed and once accepted social conditions have become incomprehensible to us. Given his time, Krafft-Ebing did an immense amount of good by publishing the first major treatise proposing a systematic order for cataloguing atypical sexual expression. He proposed science as a means to unify sexual regulation under a single system that helped remove many religious and superstitious notions from medicine and law. Although obstinate, he did try to free himself from the confines of his era, never an easy task when all of one's culture seems to affirm the naturalness of your prejudices. Although Krafft-Ebing never apologized for slandering Masoch, he eventually perceived the universality of homosexuality across age, sex and cultures. In 1901, he presented a paper in which he reversed himself, risking his reputation to declare openly that,

". . . the heterosexual are apt to be more depraved than the homosexual. That contrary sexual sensation [i.e.: homosexuality] cannot be necessarily regarded as physical degeneration, or even as a manifestation of disease, is shown by various considerations, one . . . of which is that these variations of the sexual life may actually be associated with mental superiority. The proof of this is the existence of men of all nations whose contrary sexuality is an established fact, and who, nonetheless, are the pride of their nation as authors, poets, artists, leaders of armies, and statesmen. A further proof of the fact that contrary sexual sensation is not necessarily disease, nor necessarily a vicious self-surrender to the immoral, is . . . the fact that all the noble activities of the heart which can be associated with heterosexual love can equally be associated with homosexual love and also the passions and all the defects of love."[6]

Krafft-Ebing went beyond recanting, stopping just short of declaring

---

[5]On medicine's expropriation of sexuality: "Lombrosianism, therefore, represented one episode of this 'seizure of power' by the medical establishment. The new School of Criminality, after all, was based on the theory and research of a physician, i.e. someone whom fellow doctors could respect; his pronouncements on crime were assumed to carry the same authority as his medical diagnosis. . . . The concept of the criminal as a biological freak was simple and easy to grasp." p. xviii, preface to *Criminal Man*, Op. cit.

[6]Krafft-Ebing, Richard von, *New Studies in the Domain of Homosexuality*, in the *Annual for Sexual Intermediate Stages*, ed. Hirschfeld, Magnus; Leipzig, 1901. Quoted in the preface to the 1947 Pioneer Publications, Inc. edition of *Psychopathia Sexualis*.

homosexuality a virtue. Unfortunately, he died a few months later without amending the *Psychopathia Sexualis* to reflect this new position. The publisher who finished the last revision did not include this late change. The American Psychiatric Association took over seventy years to act on Krafft-Ebing's last paper.

MODERN MASOCHISTS

If you adhere to the code of safe, sane and consensual, you may be a top or a bottom, but you can only be a masochist, never a sadist. To those accustomed to equating "top" with "sadist" and "bottom" with "masochist," this sounds silly. Definitions, however, must reflect the intentions of their originators. What de Sade and Sacher-Masoch spelled out in their work is quite different from the misunderstanding that we inherited from Krafft-Ebing.

In his fictional, ferociously sexualized world, de Sade depends upon relentless logic, non-consensual dominance and constant tumult. Sadean sex begins as an intellectual activity that leaves nothing to chance or emotionalism. Motives must be fully developed and defined; sexual activity exists only as an impersonal demonstration of intellectual speculation. Within his stories, a father may violate a daughter, but the commission is neither illogical nor spur of the moment. Every act, no matter how outrageous, is a well thought-out violation endowed with logical philosophical justification. Emotion, passion and the subconscious play no part. The sadist's obsession with clarity demands endless experiments and continual refinements of definitions. De Sade's philosophy whirls with a perpetual motion of things that the sadist must discuss, do and classify into categories that need further subdividing into finer divisions for additional investigation. In espousing a belief that humans can and must comprehend every detail, de Sade assumes that the sadist shares God's attribute of omniscience. Curiously, instead of a God-like comprehension and command of the vast (sexual) universe, de Sade's characters become mired in the infinitesimal, the infinitely small. Constant division of the sadist's world into finer and finer points serves only to shrink his sphere of influence. As everything must be examined ever more closely, sadism spirals inward to an infinitely smaller point—a philosophic and sexual black hole. It ultimately isolates the sadist from the universe he sought to dominate.

Masoch concerns himself with an alternate vision. As finite creatures, humans are born into an infinite universe beyond their comprehension or control. Their task is merely to come to terms with the world around them as best they can. Masochistic philosophy attempts to reconcile the individual with existence. As such, it is a form of negotiation that carries a dual connotation. The first implies that individuals have met in order to reach an agreement, as in negotiating a contract. The second implies successfully finding one's way through difficult passage, as in negotiating a treacherous coast. As a way of confronting the world, masochism entails both these meanings but does so on the intuitive level, operating on insight and gut feelings instead of logic. Masochism also engages a superb sensual absurdity whereby the participants experience a "punishment," normally reserved for the commission of a crime or infraction of rules, in order to commit an offense new to society—the enjoyment of what was intended as a deterrent to pleasure.

In place of logic, Masoch relies upon metaphors, filling his works with an intuitive jumping-about that insinuates connections between dissimilar things. These loose associations present obscure and ambiguous meanings. Even as author, he may not have been aware of all the implications. Nonetheless, their powerful images can shake our souls even if their secret eludes us. Consider his vision of the Blessed Mother herself placing Christ upon the cross to initiate the supreme masochistic act in the physical absence of both His heavenly and earthly fathers. Does this fusing of the Virgin Mary with a dominitrix represent blasphemy, kink or revelation? Whether or not you can decipher his meaning, the image remains unsettling.

Although de Sade is always obscene in his sexual description, Masoch never is. The sadist relies on a precise demonstration of forced sex, but the masochist's arousal emerges from the suspension of explicit sex. The postponement of sexual gratification, the act of waiting itself, becomes the essential and critical element. When the flow of time can be experienced acutely and purely, you are able to explore situations that spring from the deepest strata of the mind. Suspension of time allows for scrutiny of the darkest pools of anxiety. Masoch understood that sometimes it is more important to feel than to know. He defined a masochist as a supersensual being who acts from intuition, not intellectual thought. Curiously, his characters are often intellectuals. Masochists are usually at a loss to explain their compulsions. A sadist never shuts up.

When the nineteenth century psychiatrist Krafft-Ebing equated sadism with masochism, he thoroughly muddied the waters. The two may bear some superficial similarities, but they are not, as he claimed, two sides of the same coin. They are different currencies altogether. Most importantly, whereas the sadist possesses without consent, the masochist, top or bottom, must negotiate for a willing partner. Beyond locating one, the masochist must spend additional time educating and emotionally supporting that potential partner. In turn, the partner tries to live up to the expectations. Both foster a relationship built on trust, respect and concern for one another. What they create is a contract of mutual dependency, shared expectations and limited duration. Sadistic domination is the opposite. Another's body is no more than a piece of paper upon which the sadist writes. A proper sadist would have nothing to do with a masochist. De Sade has a monk tell Justine, "They would send away any girl who would come here voluntarily." Since masochism is a negotiated and contractual relationship, one cannot really be a sadist within a masochistic fantasy.

In the 1980 tirade, *Against SM: A Radical Feminist Analysis*, the claim is made that the terms "top" and "bottom" are only euphemisms to obscure the horrid reality of SM violence. The objections focus on de Sade's philosophy of violent domination that implies the unwilling subjugation of a person to the status of a possessed object, in short, slavery. The book argues that "consensual" is not the same as "self-determination" since consent might be given reluctantly under pressure and might change over time to a de facto enslavement such as a housewife totally dependent upon her husband. A masochistic partnership can indeed turn into a psychotically sadistic relationship—as can marriage, employment or any other association. That does not automatically put every human relationship on par with sadistic enslavement. Sadism is neither safe, sane nor consensual but masochism is. In modern SM practice, the bottom is not only a freely consenting partner but is ultimately the one in control—hardly the definition of a powerless victim.

I see the preference for the terms "top" and "bottom" as an instinctive clarification of both the roles and the philosophies. A caring, attentive and competent top better fits the profile of Sacher-Masoch's partner than of de Sade's victimizer. Instead of being two sides of the same coin as Krafft-Ebing claimed, sadism and masochism are two separate currencies. Top and bottom are the two sides of masochism; perpetrator and victim those of sadism. As adherents of safe, sane and consensual behavior, we are just modern masochists.

Enlargement of Sacher-Masoch's trademark Slavic dominatrix whose imprint he stamped on his correspondence. The original is about two inches. She holds a knout with iron tips which was used for capital punishment in Czarist Russia.

APPENDIX

THE THREE SLAVE CONTRACTS OF SACHER-MASOCH

During his life, Masoch was involved in three slave contracts. These are arranged in chronological order. Two of them were actual documents. The other appeared in the semi-autobiographical, but fictitious, Venus in Furs. *In this first version, Masoch has included some very broad protections, including free time and an escape clause that invokes his honor. Since personal honor covers quite a broad area, finding an excuse to cancel the contract wouldn't have been difficult. While dressed as his alter ego Gregor, the peasant servant (Gregor was the generic name for butlers in Central and Eastern Europe), Masoch was actually confronted in the marketplace by an acquaintance. It so embarrassed him that he cut short the fantasy holiday and returned home.*

Fanny von Pistor was a successful actress who courted notoriety with a string of lovers. Unlike most women of her era, she was financially independent which freed her from men's control. She guarded that freedom carefully. Her insistence on adding opt-out clauses for herself showed that she was wary of any longterm entanglements with Masoch.

Contract between Fanny von Pistor and Leopold Sacher-Masoch
On his word of honor, Mr. Leopold von Sacher-Masoch undertakes to be the slave of Miss Fanny von Pistor and to carry out her wishes and orders absolutely during these six months.

For her part, Miss Fanny von Pistor will demand nothing dishonorable of him (that would cause him to forfeit his honor as a gentleman or citizen). Moreover, she must spare him six hours per day for his work and never look at his letters and writings. At each infraction or oversight or any transgression of personal affront, the Mistress is to punish her slave according to her whim. In short, the subject will obey his czarina with abject submission. He will welcome her scraps of favor as delightful gifts. He will make no claim of any worthiness to love nor any right to his mistress. In exchange, Fanny von Pistor pledges to wear furs as often as possible, and especially when she will be cruel.

The following was added by Fanny von Pistor presumably in case she grew bored with Masoch.
At the end of the six months, this term of servitude will be considered as void by the two parties and there are to be no unpleasant incriminations. Everything that would have happened is to be forgotten, with a

return to the former romantic relationship.

The six months need not be consecutive. They may be subject to profound interruptions, finishing and beginning at the whim of the Czarina.

The signatures of the participants confirm this contract.

This is how Masoch retold it as a fantasy in Venus in Furs. *Fiction can be so much more interesting than dull reality. The contract becomes a collective fantasy involving Masoch and the readers. Notice that the fictitious Wanda, unlike Fanny, expresses no reservations about the duration of the enslavement. In fact, she ups the ante by including a suicide note. Masoch also indulges in the fiction of being a full-time slave, something that as a writer, he couldn't really afford to do. The clause about personal honor is conspicuously absent.*

Contract between Miss Wanda von Dunajew and Mr. Severin Von Kusiemski

Mister Severin Von K ceases as of this day to be the fiancé of Miss Wanda von Dunajew and renounces all the privileges that he had acquired as her lover. In return, he pledges on his honor as a gentleman, to be from now on, the slave of this woman, for however long that she herself chooses not to return his freedom.

While the slave of Mistress von Dunajew, he shall bear the name of Gregor and completely satisfy all the wishes of this mistress, obey every order and submit to his mistress, regarding the smallest hint of her kindness as an extraordinary indulgence.

Not only is Mistress von Dunajew allowed, according to her pleasure, to punish her slave for the slightest laxness or the least trangression, but she even has the right to kill him should it please her. In short, he becomes her complete property.

If Mistress von Dunajew ever returns freedom to her slave, Mr. Severin von Kusiemski will forget all that he has experienced or suffered during his enslavement and never contemplate, under any pretext or in any way, vengeance or reprisals.

In exchange, Mistress von Dunajew promises as his dominator to wear furs often, particularly when she is cruel towards her slave.

————

The day's date was listed at the bottom of the contract. A second document consisted of just a few words:

"Worn out by these years of life and the deception that it brings, I willingly put an end to my useless life."

. . . "It is of course necessary that you recopy this, Severin," said Wanda.

. . . I quickly rewrote those few lines which could label me a suicide and gave them to Wanda.

This is the version that Aurora von Remuax, his future wife, wrote when she adopted the persona of Masoch's fictitious Wanda von Dunajew while ensnaring him in marriage. Aurora came from an impoverished and dysfunctional family and saw the successful Masoch as someone who could rescue her from desperate circumstances.[1]

Written by Aurora/Wanda, this contract lacks the brevity of those by Masoch, being quite repetitious and a bit over-blown. Although it does mention the possibility of death, it is highly unlikely that she would actually kill someone she hoped to marry or that either she or Masoch really believed his life would ever be forfeit.[2] *The reality of the Roman Catholic Austrian legal system rendered to nothing this fantasy contract and would never have upheld her "rights" over her slave, especially that of torture to the death. If Masoch ever chose, he could have simply walked out, which indeed he did a decade later. Curiously, the part written at the bottom has the appearance of being Masoch's rephrasing of the contract. The case could be made that he is actually agreeing to his own wording and not to Wanda/Aurora's, which would allow him the right of interpretation. As far as appearing to fulfill his fantasy, she certainly did her homework and knew which buttons to push.*

Contract between Masoch and Wanda (Aurora von Remuax)
My slave,

The conditions under which I accept you to suffer as slave by my side are as follows:

Utter, absolute renunciation of yourself to me.

Beyond my will, you have none.

You are an unquestioning instrument between my hands that accomplishes all my orders without question. If you forget that you are my slave or you do not obey me in all things absolutely, I shall have the right to punish and correct you according to my pleasure.

Anything that I happen to grant you that is gratifying or pleasing will be but mercy on my part.

---

[1]ReSearch Publications has published a translation of one of her two accounts of life under the name of Wanda von Sacher-Masoch. Unfortunately, the editors have narrowly interpreted her story as a woman's struggle for autonomy and ignore the contradictions in her version. Nor do they mention that she penned two different variations. She claimed in her first book that Masoch forced her into assuming the role of Wanda. Masoch's biographer, Schlichtegroll, pointed out her deliberate and calculated stalking of Masoch and included this copy of the contract. As with most marriage breakdowns, the truth is hard to discern.

[2]The consternation caused in Austrian society when Rudolph, the heir to the throne, committed suicide illustrates the disgrace that it brought upon both victim and family.

You shall be neither son, nor brother nor friend. You are to be nothing but my slave prostrate in the dust.

As does your body, so also your soul belongs to me. Even if you reach a point where you suffer greatly, you shall relinquish your feelings and opinions to my authority.

The greatest acts of cruelty are allowed me and, should I mutilate you, it is required that you bear it without complaint. You shall work for me as a slave and, if I immerse myself in opulence leaving you in deprivation and trampling you underfoot, you must, without protest, kiss the foot that trampled you.

I shall be able to discharge you at anytime, but you will not have the right to quit against my will and if you attempt to flee, recognize that you have given me the means and the right to torture you as far as death by all imaginable torments.

Beyond me, you have nothing. For you, I am everything—your life, your destiny, your happiness, your adversity, your torment and your joy.

You shall comply with all that I shall command, be it good or evil, and should I demand a crime of you, you must become a criminal in order to obey my will.

Your honor belongs to me as do your blood, your spirit and your ability to work. I am your czarina, the mistress of your life and of your death.

If it happens that you can no longer endure my domination, and that your chains have become too heavy, it may be necessary for you to kill yourself: I will never return your freedom.

«I am obliged by my word of honor, to be the slave of Miss Wanda von Dunajew, to do all that she demands of me and to subject myself without resistance to all that she would inflict on me.»—Dr. Leopold von Sacher-Masoch

246

THE WANDERER
Leopold von Sacher-Masoch

Masoch wrote this short story as the prologue to what he had conceived to be his life's work, an examination of humankind's fate which he referred to as The Legacy of Cain. *Our destinies, he believed, were determined by war, love, the State, possessions, death and work. Of these, only work promised us any control over fate and therefore it alone offered hope of happiness. He had planned a series of six books, which he called a cycle, each dedicated to a single topic which would be explored in six short novels. The first two books were completed and went through several printings and translations in his lifetime. Of the planned thirty-six stories of this project, nineteen were completed. Only one,* Venus in Furs, *has ever been translated into English and that distorts and diminishes Masoch's vision. He never intended these stories to be read in isolation from one another since each looks at the topic from a different viewpoint and offers a solution.* Plato's Love, *which is part of the same cycle on love as* Venus, *explores the relationship of a gay man and a straight woman.* Moonlight Sonata *chronicles a woman's tragic love-life as she searches for happiness. Similarly, the other three examine love as the six stories work together to expound the theme. Masoch's use of the word "cycle" to describe these books gives a warning: to read any story by itself is like taking a single spoke from a wheel. It's not going to take you where the author had intended.*

The situation described within The Wanderer *is quite real. During Masoch's time, a religious fervor percolated through Central Europe that made the current fundamentalists look docile. Self-proclaimed prophets wandered through the region emulating John the Baptist and preaching an apocalyptic vision. Messianic groups and bizarre sects arose among both the Christian and Jewish faiths. Occasionally, they attracted the attention of the State which would suppress the offending movement. Some of these, especially the Jewish groups, migrated to America where a number of their fanatical sects survive.*

This translation is not intended for critical academic use. My purpose is to make Masoch's work more accessible for the average English reader. To that end, my goal has been a smooth translation that preserves the nineteenth century tone. Masoch had an incredible eye for detail. To do him justice, I've given preference to image and mood over a slavish and often incomprehensibly dull word for word translation.

Rifles shouldered, we stepped cautiously, the old gamekeeper and I, through the primeval forest that flowed its dark mass against the base of the Carpathian Mountains [A mountain system in east central Europe straddling the border between Poland and Czechoslovakia.—Tr.] Night shadows were beginning to darken that shoreless ocean of thickly crowded pines. Nothing broke the silence—neither cry of animal nor rustle of tree. Nothing but the sporadic play of light, thrown like a dull golden scrap of hairnet over the moss and foliage by the setting sun. Occasionally, between the crowns of the motionless pines, the cloudless, pale blue sky appeared. The odor of decaying vegetation hung heavily in the interwoven branches. Nothing crunched beneath our feet; we trod as if on a felt carpet. We were grateful for the sporadic rocks, rough and mossy, that lay strewn over the slopes of the Carpathians, throughout the forest and scattered as far as the plains where they knifed through the golden wheat—silent monuments to a forgotten epoch when ocean waves had scoured the jagged flanks of our mountains. It seemed a distant echo of creation's changeless days when suddenly, a powerful wind arose, howling and rolling invisible waves through the towering tree tops, quaking the pine needles and bending the taller vegetation in the direction of its passing.

The old keeper stopped, brushed his white hair which the north wind had disheveled and frowned. Below us, in the ethereal blue, an eagle soared. Scowling deeply, the keeper shaded his eyes with one hand and watched the bird. Then, in a grumbling voice,

"Does sir wish to shoot?"

"At this distance? No thanks."

"The gale drives it toward us," muttered the old forester, remaining motionless.

He was not mistaken. The winged black dot grew larger with each passing second and I could already see the brilliant plumage. We had reached a clearing that was fenced in by dark pines against which a few white birches stood like skeletons.

The eagle circled overhead.

"There, shoot now, sir."

"This one's yours, old timer."

The keeper briefly squeezed his eyes shut, their lids fluttering, raised his rusty rifle and cocked it.

"Is sir positive?"

"Without a doubt. I would only miss it."

"God willing, then."

He shouldered the gun with a deliberate air. The shot flamed out; the forest reverberated the report. The eagle flapped its wings. One instant, it began an upward, overhead spiral, the next, it plunged like a heavy rock.

We careened towards the spot where it had fallen.

"Cain! Cain!" from the thicket roared a deep and implacable voice like that of God rebuking the first of our kind in Eden or later cursing him who had slain his brother.

The branches parted. Before us we beheld a fantastic apparition, a super human.

Of enormous stature, an old man stood in the undergrowth, long white locks floating around his bald head. A grey beard descended past his chest and, beneath his great bushy brows, his eyes were fixed on us like a judge, a merciless judge. His homespun clothes were tattered and patched and he carried a gourd slung with a strap over his shoulder. Leaning on his staff, he shook his head gravely. At last, he stepped out, lifting the dead eagle whose blood he silently studied as it ran through his fingers.

The keeper made the sign of the cross.

"It's the old man of the wood!" he murmured in a tone of terror, "the wandering mystic!"

Without another word, he grabbed his rifle strap, slung it over his shoulder and vanished among the centuries old trees.

Against my better judgment, my feet seemed to take root and my eyes locked with the ominous old man's. I had heard some talk of a strange cult that many people held in excessive awe. I could now satisfy my curiosity.

"You've traveled far, Cain!" said the drifter after several minutes of facing me. "Is your thirst for death unquenched by the blood of your brother?"

"But, is an eagle now forbidden?" I retorted. "Is hunting at present banned?"

"Ah, yes, he is a murderer," sighed the old one. "He spills the blood of every living creature. Are we compelled to do this? Me? Not I, but you. . . . Yes, yes, you are one also. You are a descendant of Cain. You carry the sign."

I felt a growing unease.

"And you," I said at last, "who are you, then?"

"I am a drifter."

"A drifter?"

"One who flees life."

He laid the bird carcass on the ground and regarded me, his eyes now filled with endless sorrow.

"Repent," he spoke again in that penetrating voice. "Repudiate the legacy of Cain. Search for truth. Learn to renounce and scorn life. Treasure death."

"Where is the truth? Can you point the way?"

"I am no saint," he replied. "I don't even possess enlightenment. But I will tell you what I know."

He set his things against a tree trunk which had fallen in the clearing and sat on it. I positioned myself across from him on a boulder, hands on knees, ready to listen. As though meditating, he stared straight ahead for some moments with his head in hands.

"I, too," he finally began, "am a son of Cain, the grandson of those who ate from the Tree of Life. To atone, I am condemned to roam, to drift until the day I am freed from life's grip. I too have lived; I have enjoyed a frivolous life. I have possessed all that could sate man's insatiable appetite, and found that it meant nothing. I have loved and been made a fool, been trampled underfoot when I surrendered myself utterly to love, yet I was revered when I mocked the good-fortune of others— revered as a God. I have met souls whom I held as kin to mine and bodies that my love thought pure; I have seen both sold like common commodities. I have found my wife, the mother of my children, in the arms of a stranger. I have been enslaved by women and I have been their master. I have been as Solomon the king in loving plenitude. I grew up in the lap of luxury, without the vexations of human misery; then one night, the edifice of our fortune collapsed, and bankruptcy buried my father—not even enough to pay for his coffin. In the ensuing years, I struggled; I knew adversity and black despair, starvation and sleepless nights, bone-weary agony and sickness. I strove against my worldly brothers, countering trickery with trickery, violence with violence. I killed and I lost two of my own to death—all done in passion or for the sheer hell of it. I have also loved the State of which I was a citizen and the people whose tongue I spoke. I had high position and titles and I swore allegiance and trooped zealously to war under the colors. I also hated, slaughtering those who spoke another language, and for that received only disgrace and scorn. . . .

"As children of Cain, I had neither concerned myself with the sweat of my brothers, nor bothered to reward those of their kind for my pleasures. Then I, in my turn, was yoked and bent beneath the lash, toiling for others. Unremittingly, exhaustedly, I labored to increase my lot. Happy or miserable, rich or poor, I feared but one thing: Death. I trembled at the thought of quitting this life. I cursed the day that I was born, thinking only of the end that awaits us all. But an insight made me wise. I saw the strife of the living, I saw each days' existence . . . "

He nodded his head, absorbed in his reflections.

After a time, I inquired, "And what is this knowledge that you possess?"

"The first point is that all of you—you miserable fools—you presume that God made the world as perfect as possible and instituted a moral order. What catastrophic folly! The world is defective; life is an affliction, an unhappy pilgrimage and all who live, live for death and deceit."

"And so for you, man is but a brutal beast?" I asked.

"Without doubt the craftiest, the bloodiest, the cruelest of the ravenous beasts. What other is so inventive in the maltreatment of its own kind? Everywhere, I see only wrangling and rivalry, only murder, pillage, chicanery, subservience. . . . All the suffering, all the effort for no other reason than to live at any cost and pass that miserable life on to other generations!

"The second truth," the old one continued somberly, "is that satisfying one's carnal desires serves no real purpose; for what is gratification but the end of a craving that consumes us? And so it is that after a brief and futile illusion, everything fails to fulfill the yearnings of life. But hear me, it is not deprivation that makes us miserable, it's this continual pursuit of happiness that never ends and never can. What is this happiness that always seems within our reach but never within our grasp, that dangles before us from cradle to tomb? Can you tell me?"

I shook my head without speaking.

"What is happiness?" continued the old man, "I have looked for it wherever there's a breath of life. Happiness—could it be peace that we so futilely pursue here on earth? Could it be death? Death which prompts so much terror? Happiness! Who does not first look to love for it and, in the end, is left sneering cynically at the memory of imagined ecstasy. What shame to admit that nature can so enflame us with a consuming fire that we carry out her dark designs. She harries us well. To woman, she dispenses countless charms that allow her to reduce us to her yoke and command us 'Toil for me and my offspring!' Love is but a war of the sex organs. Relentless rivals, woman and man forget their natural hostility in a brief moment of giddiness while under the illusion that they can start anew and put strife aside forever. Pathetic idiots are they who think that they can arrange an everlasting truce between these two enemies. You might as easily change the laws of nature and order a plant, 'Blossom, but never fade and beware of going to seed!' "

He smirked with neither bitterness nor malice; his eyes radiated the serene calm of sublime wisdom.

"And I sense the same curse upon possessions. Gained by force and fraud, they provoke reprisals and spawn discord and countless crimes. Hellish greed impels the offspring of Cain to grasp at everything within their reach, and if they can't monopolize what would be sufficient for thousands, they continually scheme to snatch whatever they covet. And so, they squabble over whatever might be possessed, one trying to gain and another to maintain."

251

He stretched out his arms as if to brush away a terrible vision.

"But the one cannot fight against the many, so they form alliances which they call communities, nations and states. And laws issue forth that sanction total usurpation. Our sweat and blood become the currency bankrolling the whims of those who love pomp, sex and the crack of arms. Justice is a sham. Those who arise by the will of the people are either corrupted or eliminated and those who would have benefited are cheated. Eventually, the swindled revolt, and once again bestiality stands triumphant over the blood soaked ruins!

"Nations are but amplified individuals, neither less predacious nor less blood-thirsty. Indeed, nature gives us destruction as a way of life; everywhere, the strong have powers of life and death over the weak. Every crime that the law punishes in private life is committed by unrestrained nations against each other. One cheats, one pillages, betraying, slaughtering on a grand scale . . . all under the cloak of patriotism or for reasons of State!"

The old man fell silent for some time.

"The mystery of life," he intoned solemnly, "do you wish to know it?"

"Tell me."

"The secret of life is that everyone seeks to live by crime and assault, and one must live with that suffering. Work alone can free us from original sin. As long as everyone struggles to live at his neighbor's expense, peace is impossible. Work is the penalty we pay for life. Work if you wish to enjoy life. For in that labor is a measure of our happiness. He who pursues nothing but idleness becomes captive to his own selfishness: a constant apathy, a loathing of life and a dread of death march in lockstep with him . . .

"Death! That terrible specter that arises at the threshold of our existence; Death, accompanied by its acolytes, Fear and Doubt. No one wants to contemplate the eternity that preceded one's birth nor the eternity that will follow one's extinction. Why then this attitude that we have always been and will always be? All along, death encircles us, lies in wait for us. It's pathetic to watch everyone run from it or beg for one more hour. If only they understood that it brings us freedom and peace.

"It is much better, it is true, never to have been born, but once born, dream that oft misread dream of the end, without being dazzled by falsehoods and splendid visions, when one is reimmersed forever afterwards in the bosom of nature."

The old man covered his brown, furrowed and wrinkled face with his gaunt hands and appeared to lose himself in some cryptic vision.

"You started to tell me," I began again, "what life could teach me. Can you finish?"

"I have glimpsed the truth," declared the oldster, "I comprehend that

252

true happiness lies in learning and that it's best to renounce the pursuit of pleasure. Wherefore I have declared: I no longer wish to shed the blood of my brothers nor to rob them; I have left my home and my wife to wander the roads. Satan is master of the world, and thus, sin taints both Church and State, and therefore, marriage too is a mortal sin. . . . Six things make up Cain's heritage: sex, possessions, the State, war, work, death—the legacy of Cain, the accursed, who was condemned to be a wanderer and fugitive over the earth. Justice has no jurisdiction over this inheritance. Without country or shelter, he shuns the world and people. He must drift, drift, drift. And when death should come to find him, he should go with calmness, under the sky, through the fields or in the forest because the drifter ought to die as he has lived, as a fugitive. Tonight, I thought I had sensed death's approach, but it has passed me by, and now, I must set out and track it down."

He arose, grasping his staff.

"To renounce life is paramount," he said as a look of gentle piety illuminated his features. "To desire death and to seek it are ancillary."

He left me and quickly disappeared into the brush.

I remained alone, pensive. The night fell around me. The rotting log began to emit a phosphorescent glow, revealing a world of parasitic plants and laboring insects. I dreamt. Images of the day's events swirled before me like bubbles forming and popping on the surface of a stream. I contemplated them with neither dismay nor delight. I could see the machinery of creation. I saw life and death intermingling and transforming each into the other, with death less dreadful than life. As I abandoned myself to such thoughts, all that surrounded me came to life, spoke to me and reached out to me. "You want to run away, poor fool. You cannot; you are as we are. You are fated, as are we, to be born, to flourish and to vanish as does a ray of sunlight. Don't resist; it serves no purpose."

A low rustling ran through the leaves. Above my head, eternal candelabras burned with celestial calm. Then, I thought I saw before me a goddess, somber and aloof, who embodied the continual and all-encompassing creation. She spoke to me in these words:

"You fancy yourself as a being separate and distinct from me, arrogant fool! You are a ripple on the surface of the water lit up by a momentary flash of moonlight, destined to fade away in the opposing current. Learn how to be patient and modest and humble yourself. If your life is to you what a single day is to a mayfly, then for me, one who has neither beginning nor end, it is not even an instant. As the offspring of Cain, you must live; you must die. Grasp that you are my chattel and your defiance is futile conceit. And banish that childish dread of death. I am eternal and changeless while you are mortal and fleeting. I am all life and neither your sufferings nor existence matters to me. You are as everything else that comes from me and eventually returns to me. Observe how living things prepare in autumn to await spring; some change into different beings within cocoons, others seek sheltered places for their eggs, then die in peace. Do you also not perish nightly to be born anew each morning? And yet, you fear that final sleep."

"I watch with equal indifference the fall of leaves, the wars, the diseases that carry-off children precisely because I am immortal amidst death and indestructible amidst destruction. Comprehend me and you will cease to fear and denounce me. After a brief travail, you shall escape from life by returning to my bosom."

So spoke the stately voice. Then, the silence returned. Nature resumed her morose indifference, leaving me to my thoughts.

A vague terror crept over me. I had to get away. I roused myself and fled the forest. Soon, I reached the plain which stretched peacefully beneath a clear sky that swarmed with stars. In the distance, I could already make out my village and the glowing windows of my home. A profound peace suffused me and a fervor for knowledge and truth sparked within my soul. As I ran down the well-worn path that threaded through the neighboring fields, I spied one sparkling star among the myriad in the sky and it appeared to precede me like the star of the magi who had searched for the Light of the World.

AIDS RISK REDUCTION GUIDELINES
FOR HEALTHIER SEX

As given by Bay Area Physicians for Human Rights

NO RISK: *Most of these activities involve only skin-to-skin contact, thereby avoiding exposure to blood, semen, and vaginal secretions. This assumes there are no breaks in the skin.* 1) Social kissing (dry). 2) Body massage, hugging. 3) Body to body rubbing (frottage). 4) Light S&M (without bruising or bleeding). 5) Using one's own sex toys. 6) Mutual masturbation (male or external female). Care should be taken to avoid exposing the partners to ejaculate or vaginal secretions. Seminal, vaginal and salivary fluids should not be used as lubricants.

LOW RISK: *In these activities small amounts of certain body fluids might be exchanged, or the protective barrier might break causing some risk.* 1) Anal or vaginal intercourse with condom. Studies have shown that HIV does not penetrate the condom in simulated intercourse. Risk is incurred if the condom breaks or if semen spills into the rectum or vagina. The risk is further reduced if one withdraws before climax. 2) Fellatio interruptus (sucking, stopping before climax). Pre-ejaculate fluid may contain HIV. Saliva or other natural protective barriers in the mouth may inactivate virus in pre-ejaculate fluid. Saliva may contain HIV in low concentration. The insertive partner should warn the receptive partner before climax to prevent exposure to a large volume of semen. If mouth or genital sores are present, risk is increased. Likewise, action which causes mouth or genital injury will increase risk. 3) Fellatio with condom (sucking with condom) Since HIV cannot penetrate an intact condom, risk in this practice is very low unless breakage occurs. 4) Mouth-to-mouth kissing (French kissing, wet kissing) Studies have shown that HIV is present in saliva in such low concentration that salivary exchange is unlikely to transmit the virus. Risk is increased if sores in the mouth or bleeding gums are present. 5) Oral-vaginal or oral-anal contact with protective barrier. e.g. a latex dam, obtainable through a local dental supply house, may be used. Do not reuse latex barrier, because sides of the barrier may be reversed inadvertently. 6) Manual anal contact with glove (manual anal (fisting) or manual vaginal (internal) contact with glove). If the glove does not break, virus transmission should not occur. However, significant trauma can still be inflicted on the rectal tissues leading to other medical problems, such as hemorrhage or bowel perforation. 7) Manual vaginal contact with glove (internal). See above.

MODERATE RISK: *These activities involve tissue trauma and/or exchange of body fluids which may transmit HIV or other sexually transmitted disease.* 1) Fellatio (sucking to climax). Semen may contain high concentrations of HIV and if absorbed through open sores in the mouth or digestive tract could pose risk. 2) Oral-anal contact (rimming). HIV may be contained in blood-contaminated feces or in the anal rectal lining. This practice also poses high risk of transmission of parasites and other gastrointestinal infections. 3) Cunnilingus (oral-vaginal contact). Vaginal secretions and menstrual blood have been shown to harbor HIV, thereby causing risk to the oral partner if open lesions are present in the mouth or digestive tract. 4) Manual rectal contact (fisting). Studies have indicated a direct association between fisting and HIV infection for both partners. This association may be due to concurrent use of recreational drugs, bleeding, pre-fisting semen exposure, or anal intercourse with ejaculation. 5) Sharing sex toys. 6) Ingestion of urine. HIV has not been shown to be transmitted via urine; however, other immunosuppressive agents or infections may be transmitted in this manner.

HIGH RISK: *These activities have been shown to transmit HIV.* 1) Receptive anal intercourse without condom. All studies imply that this activity carries the highest risk of transmitting HIV. The rectal lining is thinner than that of the vagina or the mouth thereby permitting ready absorption of the virus from semen or pre-ejaculate fluid to the blood stream. One laboratory study suggests that the virus may enter by direct contact with rectal lining cells without any bleeding. 2) Insertive anal intercourse without condom. Studies suggest that men who participate only in this activity are at less risk of being infected than their partners who are rectally receptive; however, the risk is still significant. It carries high risk of infection by other sexually transmitted diseases. 3) Vaginal intercourse without condom.

BOOKS FROM LEYLAND PUBLICATIONS / G.S PRESS